38 Lessons for Counselors and Therapists

38 Lessons for Counselors and Therapists

How Personal Experiences Shape Professional Growth

JEFFREY A. KOTTLER, PH.D.

cognella®

SAN DIEGO

Bassim Hamadeh, CEO and Publisher
Amy Smith, Senior Project Editor
Casey Hands, Production Editor
Jess Estrella, Senior Graphic Designer
Kylie Bartolome, Licensing Coordinator
Natalie Piccotti, Director of Marketing
Kassie Graves, Senior Vice President, Editorial
Jamie Giganti, Director of Academic Publishing

cognella® | ACADEMIC PUBLISHING
3970 Sorrento Valley Blvd., Ste. 500, San Diego, CA 92121

Also by Jeffrey A. Kottler

Jeffrey A. Kottler is one of the most prolific authors in the fields of psychology, health, and education, having contributed over 100 books to the literature across multiple disciplines. His trademark wit, vulnerability, and approachable writing style have enriched the academic market and the lives of thousands of students and readers.

Kottler, J. A. (2023). *Healthy Aging in Action: Roles, Functions, and the Wisdom of Elders*. Cognella.

Kottler, J. A. (2022). *Unexplained Mysteries of Everyday Human Behavior*. Cognella.

Kottler, J. A. (2022). *On Being a Therapist* (6th ed.). Oxford University Press.

Kottler, J. A. (2022). *Critical and Provocative Issues in Human Development*. Cognella.

Kottler, J. A. (2021). *Practicing What You Preach: Self-care for Helping Professionals*. Cognella.

Kottler, J. A. (2021). *Essentials of Psychology: Basic Concepts Revealed Through Compelling Stories*. Cognella.

Kottler, J. A. (2021). *Excelling in College*. Cognella.

Kottler, J. A., & Balkin, R. (2020). *Myths, Misconceptions, and Invalid Assumptions of Counseling and Psychotherapy*. Oxford University Press.

Kottler, J. A. (2019). *Fallen Heroes: Tragedy, Madness, Resilience, and Inspiration among Famous Athletes*. Cognella.

Kottler, J. A., & Safari, S. (2019). *Making a Difference: A Journey of Adventure, Disaster, and Redemption Inspired by the Plight of At-Risk Girls*. Cognella.

Kottler, J. A., Banu, S., & Jani, S. (Eds.) (2019). *Handbook of Refugee Experience: Trauma, Resilience, and Recovery*. Cognella.

Kottler, J. A., & Englar-Carlson, M. (2019). *Learning Group Leadership: An Experiential Approach* (4th ed.). Cognella.

Safari, S., & Kottler, J. (2018). *Above the Mountain's Shadow: A Journey of Hope and Adventure Inspired by the Forgotten*. Cognella.

Kottler, J. A., & Sharp, L. (2018). *Understanding Research: Being a Competent and Critical Consumer*. Cognella.

Kottler, J. A., & Montgomery, M. (2019). *Theories in Counseling and Therapy: Experiential and Practical Approaches*. Cognella.

Kottler, J. A. (2018). *What You Don't Know About Leadership but Probably Should: Applications to Daily Life*. Oxford University Press.

Kottler, J. A. (2018). *Living and Being a Therapist: A Collection of Readings*. Cognella.

Kottler, J. A. (2017). *Secrets of Exceptional Counselors*. American Counseling Association.

Kottler, J. A., & Balkin, R. (2017). *Relationships in Counseling and The Counselor's Life*. American Counseling Association.

Brew, L., & Kottler, J. A. (2017). *Applied Counseling Skills: Transforming Lives* (3rd ed). Sage.

Kottler, J. A., & Carlson, J. (2016). *Therapy Over 50: Aging Issues in Psychotherapy and the Therapist's Life*. Oxford University Press.

Kottler, J. A. (2015). *The Therapist in the Real World: What You Never Learn in Graduate School (But Really Need to Know)*. W. W. Norton.

Kottler, J. A. (2015). *Stories We've Heard, Stories We've Told: Life-Changing Narratives in Therapy and Everyday Life*. Oxford University Press.

Kottler, J. A., & Carlson, J. (2015). *On Being a Master Therapist: Practicing What We Preach*. Wiley.

Kottler, J. A., & Shepard, D. (2015). *Introduction to Counseling: Voices from the Field* (8th ed.). Wadsworth.

Kottler, J. A. (2014). *Change: What Leads to Personal Transformation*. Oxford University Press.

Kottler, J. A., & Kottler, E. (2013). *The Teacher's Journey: Building Relationships and Flourishing Throughout Your Career*. Corwin.

Kottler, J. A., Englar-Carlson, M., & Carlson, J. (Eds.) (2013). *Helping Beyond the 50 Minute Hour: Therapists Involved in Meaningful Social Action*. Routledge.

Kottler, J. A. (2012). *The Therapist's Workbook: Self-assessment, Self-care, and Self-improvement Exercises for Mental Health Professionals* (2nd ed.). Wiley.

Kottler, J. A., & Chen, D. (2012). *Stress Management and Prevention: Applications to Daily Life* (2nd ed.). Routledge.

Kottler, J. A., & Carlson, J. (2011). *Duped: Lies and Deception in Psychotherapy*. Routledge.

Kottler, J. A. (2011). *Lust for Blood: Why We Are Fascinated by Death, Horror, and Violence*. Prometheus Press.

Kottler, J. A. (2010). *The Assassin and the Therapist: An Exploration of Truth in Psychotherapy and in Life*. Routledge.

Minichiello, V., & Kottler, J. A. (2009). *Qualitative Journeys: Student and Mentor Experiences with Research*. Sage.

Kottler, J. A., & Carlson, J. (2009). *Creative Breakthroughs in Therapy: Tales of Transformation and Astonishment*. Wiley.

Kottler, J. A., & Marriner, M. (2009). *Changing People's Lives While Transforming Your Own: Paths to Social Justice and Global Human Rights*. Wiley.

Kottler, J. A., & Kottler, E. (2008). *Students Who Drive You Crazy: Succeeding with Resistant, Unmotivated, and Otherwise Difficult Young People* (2nd ed). Corwin Press.

Kottler, J. A., & Carlson, J. (2008). *Their Finest Hour: Master Therapists Share Their Greatest Success Stories* (2nd ed.). Crown Publishing.

Kottler, E., Kottler, J. A., & Street, C. (2008). *English Language Learners in Your Classroom: Strategies that Work*. Corwin.

Kottler, J.A. (2008). *A Basic Primer of Helping Skills*. Sage.

Kottler, J. A., & Kottler, E. (2007). *Counseling Skills for Teachers* (2nd ed.). Corwin Press.

Kottler, J. A., & Carlson, J. (2007). *Moved by the Spirit: Discovery and Transformation in the Lives of Leaders*. Impact.

Kottler, J. A. (2006). *Divine Madness: Ten Stories of Creative Struggle*. Jossey-Bass.

Kottler, J. A., & Carlson, J. (2006). *The Client Who Changed Me: Stories of Therapist Personal Transformation*. Routledge.

Jones, W. P., & Kottler, J. A. (2006). *Understanding Research: Becoming a Competent and Critical Consumer*. Prentice-Hall.

Kottler, J. A., Zehm, S. J., & Kottler, E. (2005). *On Being a Teacher: The Human Dimension* (3rd ed.). Corwin Press.

Hazler, R. J., & Kottler, J. A. (2005). *The Emerging Professional Counselor: Student Dreams to Professional Realities* (2nd ed.). American Counseling Association.

Kottler, J. A., Carlson, J., & Keeney, B. (2004). *An American Shaman: An Odyssey of Ancient Healing Traditions*. Routledge.

Kottler, J. A., & Jones, W. P. (Eds.) (2003). *Doing Better: Improving Clinical Skills and Professional Competence*. Routledge.

Kottler, J. A., & Carlson, J. (2003). *The Mummy at the Dining Room Table: Eminent Therapists Reveal Their Most Unusual Cases and What They Teach Us About Human Behavior*. Jossey-Bass.

Kottler, J. A., & Carlson, J. (2002). *Bad Therapy: Master Therapists Share Their Worst Failures*. Routledge.

Kottler, J. A. (2002). *Students Who Drive You Crazy: Succeeding With Resistant, Unmotivated, and Otherwise Difficult Young People*. Corwin Press.

Kottler, E., & Kottler, J. A. (2002). *Children with Limited English: Teaching Strategies for the Regular Classroom* (2nd ed.). Corwin Press.

Kottler, J. A. (Ed.) (2002). *Counselors Finding Their Way*. American Counseling Association.

Kottler, J. A. (2000). *Doing Good: Passion and Commitment for Helping Others*. Routledge.

Kottler, J.A. (1999). *Exploring and Treating Acquisitive Desire: Living in the Material World*. Sage.

Moss, J., & Kottler, J.A. (1999). *The Last Victim: A True-Life Journey into the Mind of the Serial Killer*. Warner Books. (New York Times Bestseller)

Kottler, J.A., & McEwan, E. (1999). *Counseling Tips For Elementary School Principals*. Corwin Press.

Kottler, J.A. (1997). *Travel That Can Change Your Life*. Jossey-Bass.

Kottler, J.A. (1997). *What's Really Said in the Teachers Lounge: Provocative Ideas About Cultures and Classrooms*. Corwin Press.

Forester-Miller, H., & Kottler, J.A. (Eds.) (1997). *Issues and Challenges in Group Work*. Love Publishing.

Kottler, J.A. (1996). *The Language of Tears*. Jossey-Bass.

Kottler, J.A. (1995). *Growing a Therapist*. Jossey-Bass.

Powell, R., Zehm, S., & Kottler, J. (1995). *Classrooms Under the Influence: Counteracting Problems of Addiction*. Corwin Press.

Kottler, J., Sexton, T., & Whiston, S. (1994). *Heart of Healing: Relationships in Therapy*. Jossey-Bass.

Kottler, J. (1994). *Beyond Blame: A New Way of Resolving Conflict in Relationships*. Jossey-Bass.

Hazler, R., & Kottler, J. (1994). *The Emerging Professional Counselor: Student Dreams to Professional Realities*. American Counseling Association Press.

Kottler, J. (1993). *Advanced Group Leadership*. Brooks/Cole.

Kottler, J. (1992). *Compassionate Therapy: Working With Difficult Clients*. Jossey-Bass.

Kottler, J. (1992). *Self-Guided Exploration for Beginning Counseling Students*. Brooks/Cole.

Kottler, J. (1991). *The Complete Therapist*. Jossey-Bass.

Kottler, J. (1990). *Private Moments, Secret Selves: Enriching Our Time Alone*. Ballantine.

Kottler, J., & Blau, D. (1989). *The Imperfect Therapist: Learning From Failure in Therapeutic Practice*. Jossey-Bass.

Kottler, J. (1983). *Pragmatic Group Leadership*. Brooks/Cole.

Kottler, J. (1981). *Mouthing Off: A Study of Oral Behavior, Its Causes and Treatments*. Libra.

Van Hoose, W., & Kottler, J. (1977). *Ethical and Legal Issues in Counseling and Psychotherapy*. Jossey-Bass.

Brief Contents

Preface

Every beginning counseling or therapy student learns within the first few weeks of the program that there are major learning, growth, and significant changes that lie ahead. This does not just cover the exhaustive curricular offerings that introduce theories, ethical decision-making, assessment, diagnosis, research, clinical, and interpersonal strategies but also the incredible personal growth that usually takes place as a result of helping others deal with their demons, decisions, and difficulties. In addition, many, if not most programs, include experiences and components that intentionally encourage deeper exploration of ongoing personal difficulties whether in the context of group sharing, process-oriented supervision, or an assortment of activities and assignments that require internal searching and intimate relational engagement. In many cases, students and interns are strongly encouraged to find their own counselor or therapist to help them deal with the inevitable personal issues that are likely to crop up along the journey, not to mention the invaluable experience of sitting in the client's chair.

There's a very good reason for this integrative approach since there are few other careers beyond the mental health professions that so infuse personal and professional roles in such powerful and meaningful ways. After all, *everything* we've ever learned in our lives helps us to better understand the nature of human experience and informs us about ways to connect with others. In addition, most of what we have learned in our training to help clients is just as useful and effective when relating to anyone else in our personal lives, including colleagues, supervisors, instructors, and most of all family and friends.

The reciprocal connection between what we learn at work—and during our daily lives—creates so many opportunities to examine their mutual effects and influence. This makes our respective roles quite complementary but also really confusing in other respects. Consider those times when we forget for a moment that we are in working mode and we let slip in a session some personal detail of our lives, an impulse we immediately regret. Or when we are talking to a friend or family member and realize we just slipped into "therapist mode" of trying to fix them—and we are frustrated because they are not properly deferring to us as clients would.

Once people find out what you do for a living, they are not exactly shy about trying to dump their problems onto us for a quick consult. Yet when all is said about these parallel roles and the confusion they engender, over 90% of mental health practitioners say they are actually grateful for the ways their own psychological wounds have significantly informed their ability as healers (McBeath, 2019). It may very well be the single greatest gift that we enjoy as part of this profession.

Academic Learning, Professional Development, and Personal Transformations

Regardless of the discipline to which one owes primary allegiance as a psychologist, social worker, counselor, family therapist, psychiatrist, psychiatrist nurse, or mental health worker, the curriculum likely had two components that were required by professional accreditation standards. The most explicitly mandated requirements include academic content considered essential to do the job such as theoretical models, diagnostic procedures, and research methodologies, among others. Second, training programs also include exposure to aspects of professional development such as ethical standards, legal background, primary clinical skills, and standards of care. Although it may not be as consistently and universally required in all programs, there is also a third domain that encompasses the kinds of personal changes that also take place during these training years, a process that might be less formalized and structured but is still an absolutely essential part of one's development as a practitioner.

It does not take more than a few weeks as a student to realize that the things you are learning in class will be just as useful to apply to yourself. There is an intriguing phenomenon operating on both unconscious and intentional levels during which one's personal experiences, attitudes, perceptions, and behaviors are all profoundly influenced and transformed as a result of this preparation. You not only develop a deeper understanding of the problems and challenges that confront those you help but also your own unresolved issues that require continued work. Similarly, all the new techniques, processes, theories, ideas, and skills that become part of your repertoire to build solid alliances with clients are just as useful in enhancing intimacy with family, friends, colleagues, and partners. *Everything* you learn in such a program impacts not only your professional competence but also your personal development.

Just as interesting, *all* your previous experiences in life, both joyful and traumatic, affect the ways you function as a clinician. You are constantly triggered by clients who resemble others you've encountered, or who present difficulties that are all too familiar. Every day, you will face the kinds of problems that consistently disrupt people's lives, reminding you of some personal demons that have yet to be banished.

All practitioners can identify an assortment of ways that they have become utterly transformed as a result of the things they've learned, the stories they have heard, the clients they have encountered, the themes they have explored, and mostly the significant lessons they have learned that could be applied to their own lives.

There are so many significant lessons learned while preparing for this noble profession. Many of them do relate to academic pursuits such as theoretical structures, research paradigms, diagnostic systems, and other core knowledge in the curriculum. There are still other skill-based lessons that directly relate to clinical situations—how to defuse conflicts, negotiate therapeutic contracts, and address sensitive personal issues. In addition, there are so many other lessons learned that are affected by and, in turn, shape your personal experiences. After all, almost everything you study and practice as part of your training is just as effective in all other realms of life. There is just so much significant growth that is associated with this journey.

Of course, not everyone is in the market for major personal growth associated with their professional studies. Things may seem perfectly fine in your life just the way they are already aligned. Nevertheless, it is almost impossible to deny, ignore, or downplay the sorts of internal and behavioral changes that take place during this journey. You will begin to think differently and decipher and decode actions according to precise models that have been field tested. You will begin to notice aspects of people's behaviors, as well as your own, that had previously seemed invisible. You will respond to others in different ways now that you have an assortment of potent relational skills.

Overview of the Contents and Themes

This book is intended for a number of different courses in the helping professions, whether to introduce beginners to what lies ahead or to alert more advanced students and practitioners as to the processes that will likely follow them for the rest of their lives and careers. As such, dozens of questions are explored throughout the chapters of this book, most of which reveal some very interesting, provocative, and actually essential changes that most likely take place during the life and career of a practitioner.

Consider what you would predict are some of the most valuable lessons and learning that take place during the training years, most of which can be internalized as a "way of being" in the future. Obviously, that would include such things as becoming far more skilled at persuasion and influence, convincing people to do things (or yourself) that have been avoided. After all, that is what we do for a living! In addition, a sampling of other such takeaways that are reviewed include (1) a deeper understanding of how groups function; (2) how to work through disappointments constructively; (3) enhancing *all* one's relationships through deeper intimacy; (4) dealing with stress and trauma more effectively; (5) increasing patience, empathy, and compassion toward others; (6) expanding flexibility and one's worldview to be more sensitive and responsive to diverse people; (7) taking a greater stand for social justice, especially as an advocate on behalf of the marginalized and dispossessed; (8) navigating interpersonal conflicts more effectively; (9) becoming more forgiving of lapses and failures; and (10) becoming a "better" person, parent, partner, neighbor, friend, and colleague as a result of so much advanced training in what it means to be helpful to others. This might seem like an impressive list of personal benefits, but these just scratch the surface of possibilities.

The chapters explore dozens of additional themes that are frequently reported as the aftereffects and consequences that accrue to most self-reflective counselors and therapists. Since the content of these issues is rather personal, intimate, and often intensely private,

it seemed reasonable and fair that as the author of this provocative survey, I first introduce the topics through my own very personal disclosures prior to highlighting possible
applications to work and life. With a certain amount of courage, and sometimes a touch of
shame, I reveal the most challenging, difficult, painful, and traumatic experiences I have
survived that have directly or indirectly been triggered by my sessions with clients. In spite
of enforcing strict boundaries, as well as disciplined objectivity and detachment, there have
been times when the walls between myself and others have collapsed, and I was left with
no other choice but to face my own difficulties. If that is the "bad" news then the counter-
point is that some of the best interactions and experiences I have ever enjoyed in my life
have been the result of the lessons I have learned as a teacher, therapist, researcher, and
supervisor. It has always seemed impossible to me to talk to others about their problems,
challenges, and difficulties without applying those lessons to myself. Even now, this very
moment, as I am talking to you, I am of course also talking to myself as a reminder of my
capabilities during times of adversity.

How to Read This Book

Whether this book was assigned as a text, supplementary reading, or was chosen for personal
entertainment, it is not a volume to be skimmed casually. The discussions are designed with
a single goal in mind—and that is to stimulate further insights and reflections on how therapeutic work not only leads to positive outcomes for our clients but also the innumerable ways
that we also profit from the interactions. This makes the educational process of "growing" a
mental health professional a fascinating process that weaves the two strands of professional
development and personal learning together. Each aspect of our daily experiences affects
the ways we conceptualize our work just as everything we learn in training and on the job
impacts our personal lives.

After you review the introductory personal examples, they will likely arouse considerable contemplation over how this lesson could be applied in some meaningful way. While
reading about how our clients can teach us to be more adventurous and courageous in the
risks that we take, we cannot help but reflect on how this might lead to constructive action in
our own lives. Just as we must demonstrate extraordinary levels of interpersonal sensitivity
and responsiveness in sessions, there is a distinct carryover in our ability to do so with loved
ones. This is also true with respect to a host of other skills and abilities related to developing
greater patience, resilience, empathy, creativity, and sense of well-being and life satisfaction.

Each chapter closes with "Takeaways," some practical ideas that can be adapted to your
own life, whether to improve professional functioning or personal growth. There are also
questions posed at the end of each chapter for further reflection and discussion, either in
class, as a course assignment, or to process with family and friends. This is, therefore, not a
book to be read "lightly," so to speak. It does not include the sort of content that you would
find in a multiple-choice exam in which there are only five possible answers, one of which is

labeled "correct." Rather, this is a joyous, as well as a "painful" exploration, of the aspects of this profession that are often ignored, if not denied. One of the realities of this work as helpers and healers is that we really have nowhere to hide from the issues and life challenges that people find most distressing. We spend all day talking about private secrets that may have never been spoken aloud previously. There is little doubt that the sacred, honored space that we occupy in clients' lives often leads to the kinds of personal transformations that make us the most fortunate professionals alive.

Jeffrey Kottler
Houston, Texas

Reciprocal Changes in Helping Relationships

Be yourself. Everyone else is already taken.

—Oscar Wilde

The Voice Inside My Head

It is not that I'm psychotic or anything (well, maybe a little), or enfeebled and forgetful (okay, maybe more than a little), but I talk to myself—and other people—a *lot* inside my head. So do you.

Consider all those times you rehearse what you want to say ahead of time, trying out different versions until you settle on the choice that seems optimal. Then there are all those instances when you relive a distressing conversation from the past, wondering how things might have turned out differently if you had tried another alternative. Such "mentalizing" of lived or imagined experiences is perhaps the most unique and fortuitous ability of our species, more significant than opposable thumbs or an upright stance. After all, it is precisely such internal dialogue that not only makes it possible to anticipate and plan for the future but also helps to make sense of prior events: "What did that guy mean when he said that?" "I wonder what would happen if I tried something else?" "Why the heck did I say that?"

The origins of mental activity evolved as a means by which to become more intentional, strategic, and effective when making critical decisions. This internal voice inside our head also acts as a coach, as well as a critic, providing both reassurance and support when needed. "Come on! You can do this! It's not that hard." Once I reached adolescence, the internal dialogue took one of several forms, the first of which involved compulsively rehearsing what I really wanted to say to a friend, teacher, bully, or anyone else who intimidated me. The second version was similar, but with a different goal intended to forgive myself for those times I was less than courageous or assertive: "Hey, it's no big deal. You'll do better next time."

Once I entered university as a psychology major, I received strong encouragement to become far more self-aware and self-reflective, both of which demanded continuous and exacting internal processing of every thought, feeling, revelation, or internal disturbance, whether joyful, indifferent, or distressing. The theories we were first introduced to, whether philosophers like Rene Descartes and Martin Heidegger, psychoanalysts like Sigmund Freud or Carl Jung, psychologists like Jerome Bruner or William James, developmentalists like Jean Piaget and Erik Erikson, writers like Fyodor Dostoyevsky, Virginia Woolf, and Ivan Turgenev, all stressed the significance of one's internal world, as well as the conversations that take place within that private space.

One of my early mentors encouraged—no *insisted*—that I begin keeping a journal of my innermost thoughts and feelings on a daily basis. He believed this was the hallmark of anyone who aspired to become an exceptional communicator, rattling off all the classic examples of correspondence and journaling from the likes of Anaïs Nin, Franz Kafka, Mark Twain, or Sigmund Freud. We will discuss the importance of recording such thoughts, reactions, insights, and discoveries in one of the last chapters.

Training to become a psychotherapist magnifies the frequency and depth of this type of self-reflective dialogue to extreme levels. We analyze and attempt to make sense of *everything*, frequently asking ourselves, "So, what is the person *really* saying (or doing)?" And then once we are in session with clients every single thing we say or do is followed by persistent questions regarding what we could have said or done instead that might have been a better choice. It may seem like this is unusually self-critical, but this is also the means by which any of us improve our performance through honest self-scrutiny of behavior that may have been improved.

One of the most popular models for helping people in the throes of emotional disruption is among the first introduced to beginning therapeutic practitioners. Cognitive behavior therapy (CBT), and all its other permutations (rational emotive therapy (REBT), mindfulness-based therapy (MBT), dialectical behavior therapy (DBT), acceptance and commitment therapy (ACT)), share a few key concepts, the most important of which is that emotional reactions are the result of internal perceptions and interpretations we make about anything we encounter. Almost all the work that takes place involves learning alternative ways to talk to oneself during times of trouble, challenging beliefs that are simply not based in reality, and substituting other beliefs that are more clearly supported by evidence and more sober, objective observations. There have since been a multitude of other therapeutic approaches (narrative, constructivist, feminist, Adlerian) that focus on the internal narratives, beliefs, attitudes, stories, and thought patterns that shape perceptions and behavior.

Once someone becomes a teacher or supervisor of one's craft, much less a researcher and writer who attempts to explain complex phenomena, there is no other choice except to permanently occupy another dimension of reality that leases space inside the cerebral cortex. There are other regions of the brain, as well, where memories are stored or emotional reactions are triggered, but the frontal cortex region directs the integration and meaning making of our experiences, most of which take place during the conversations we have inside our heads.

I have spent most of my life engaged in conversations with clients—and myself—about the ways perceptions and interpretations of events have been distorted, exaggerated, or otherwise misconstrued in such a way that most of the accompanying misery was self-inflicted.

It is a habit that you may have already adopted in the earliest stages of your training; over time, the process will continue to evolve quite naturally. It is part of the predictable process implicit in Oscar Wilde's quote that began this chapter, especially for neophyte practitioners who try so hard to imitate and emulate mentors instead of discovering their own unique voice and style.

In later life, a stage I currently occupy, I find these internal talks with myself and others have become increasingly dominant. Time is running out for me, leading to reminiscences about the past. I frequently think about the mistakes I have made, regrets I have harbored, injuries I've inflicted on others, or those I've suffered myself. I find myself telling people things in my mind that I never found the opportunity or courage to do in person or in writing. I imagine myself handling things differently. I debate with myself about things I might do or perhaps *should* do, even though I have been avoiding action. Mostly I review all the lessons I have learned from spending almost all of my adult life passionately, compulsively, and sometimes futilely, trying to help others overcome their misery. This has not been solely a selfless, altruistic pursuit of me trying to save the world but rather a desperate attempt to save myself. It is the only thing that can possibly explain why I have lived and worked in so many places around the world. It's as if that voice inside my head would never stop badgering me to keep striving, exploring, learning, and growing at a relentless pace.

Staring Into the Abyss

What compels any of us to choose such a difficult and challenging career and life path that virtually requires us to consistently and relentlessly stare directly into the existential abyss of despair that leads to so much distress and confusion? In my case, it was while I was still in middle school that I was drafted to become my mother's savior and head of our household after my father left. My mother was never a model of happiness, but she became even more despondent after her marriage ended, drowning her troubles in alcohol and cigarettes, both of which combined to end her life before her 50th birthday. During the early years, sometimes I would come home from school and find my mother locked in her room crying. At age 12, I had already memorized her psychiatrist's emergency phone number to call for consultations when she refused to leave her room. Let's just say I was indoctrinated early in life to believe my value lay in being useful to others, a discouraging realization since I was convinced I had so little to offer anyone.

From the trials and tribulations of adolescence that followed, to a half-century later when the conversations inside my head have spawned so many books about dozens of different subjects, let's just say I'm intensely fascinated with the multitude of ways that reciprocal changes take place within therapeutic relationships. When we talk so much to others about their troubles, we just cannot help but reflect on our own thoughts and feelings that crop up during such dialogues. As a result, I still "talk" to some of my former clients, students, lost friends, colleagues, and collaborators who I miss and mourn; those who "ghosted" me;

nemeses who betrayed me; and past friends who remain very much alive in my memories. I still talk to my grandfather who died decades ago and sometimes to my deceased parents, as if they are still very much alive in memories (which of course they are). Interestingly, as you are reading these very words right now, you are also engaged in a conversation with me, as well as with yourself, about reactions to how this fits with your own experience.

What are some of the secrets that have been revealed after intimate discussions with tens of thousands of confused, overwhelmed, sometimes desperate people in the throes of personal crises? How have these themes become internalized in such a way that they remain so vibrant and influential? And most importantly of all, how might we talk to ourselves differently, engaged in internal discussions that are far more self-fulfilling and self-enhancing?

A Matter of Interpretation

Whether you ever choose to align yourself with one of the cognitive-based approaches, there are aspects of these approaches that have become somewhat universal across all systems and approaches. It is one of the most "magical" things you will ever learn, or at least become reminded of, that how you react to events and circumstances depend on the particular way you choose to interpret their meaning. It is one of the first and most important things you learn when training to become a helper and healer: that misery, suffering, disappointments, anxiety, depression, and all the rest, are simply (or not so simply) the result of perception.

Two students each receive a "B" on an assignment. One feels relieved, the other devastated. Class is canceled: Some students are disappointed, while others are joyful. Sitting in a lecture class, some students are bored out of their minds; others are fascinated. What's the difference that determines these reactions? It is almost always some variation of what we are telling ourselves about what is happening.

Albert Ellis, a founder of one of the cognitive approaches (rational emotive therapy), once declared in a lecture that the more often he talks others out of their crazy, distorted thinking the more clearly he talks to himself afterward. Such logical, analytic, scrupulously constructed, evidence-based thought patterns are indeed contagious! As you learn to talk clients out of their self-destructive behavior, there is another part of your brain that is also paying attention: At some point, this voice will pester you mercilessly until you challenge your own distortions. What a gift this becomes—the ability to better ground yourself in reality by making different interpretations of what you are experiencing at any moment in time.

This skill (and it *is* a learned skill) is among the most valuable resources you will ever learn and strengthen over time. It is like a superpower, almost as useful as X-ray vision (but probably not as fun as the ability to fly). Talking sensibly and rationally to yourself during times of adversity or stress is the equivalent of a magic potion that allows you to completely transform annoying, disturbing, or uncomfortable emotional reactions. Just as you will wield this power in service to others when they are spinning out of control, you have the capacity to better manage your own emotional regulation when being (or feeling) tested.

Dynamics and Processes of Reciprocal Therapeutic Changes

Therapeutic relationships are obviously never intended to be reciprocal in nature. During such encounters, there is an exchange of services for compensation, whether it is offered by the client, the agency, the institution, or the funding source. There are clear ethical boundaries that protect clients from professionals meeting their own needs in the relationship. And yet even though clinicians are careful to ensure that they restrain themselves from any form of self-indulgence, focusing all their attention and energy on the client's welfare, there are still some vicarious processes that take place during the sessions. The reality is that we sometimes learn as much from our clients as they learn from us, a phenomenon that goes far beyond merely discussing countertransference reactions.

The nature of this vicarious learning and growth is both mysterious and complex. How is it that we manage to learn important lessons through unconscious (or at least unintentional) observation of the behavior we witness? This is actually the process by which many new skills are acquired, first watching others before you try something new yourself. In the context of counseling and therapy, practitioners are expected to remain fully present while clients share stories of suffering, despair, discouragement, trauma, and debilitating fear. In spite of enforcing clear boundaries, it often seems difficult, if not impossible, to metabolize such tales, much less process and "repair" them, without becoming profoundly affected by the emotional intensity and the messages contained therein.

It may be true that while the meter is running, we do our level best to resist getting into our own issues, monitoring carefully any potential self-indulgence, but once the client walks out the door we are left to sort out lingering feelings, confusing thoughts, doubts, and uncertainties, some of which relate directly to the case at hand and others that are attached far more intimately to our own behavior. We know, for example, that when treating severe trauma, the clients are not the only ones who might experience some degree of persistent effects over time. Although most research has been devoted to the so-called negative consequences of treating trauma (vicarious trauma, compassion fatigue, secondary trauma), there are also many examples of growth that are associated with helping others (Deaton et al., 2022; Hyatt-Burkhart, 2014; Kottler, 2022a; Kottler & Carlson, 2006; Manning-Jones et al., 2017).

It is hardly surprising that we would be affected profoundly by repeated exposure to stories of trauma, abuse, neglect, and chronic suffering no matter how hard we attempt to protect ourselves. Less appreciated—or at least rarely acknowledged—are the times that such experiences energize or motivate us to examine more closely significant lessons we can apply to our own lives. This is often reported by practitioners to include a much greater appreciation and gratitude for one's own life circumstances, as well as respect and wonder at the power of human resilience in the face of so much adversity and suffering. In addition, it is often reported that practitioners feel an increased commitment to improving intimacy in their personal relationships and friendships. There are deeper explorations of themes and issues that are brought up in sessions, leading to greater meaning and purpose. This often results in improved well-being and life satisfaction as a result of making a difference in people's lives.

Takeaways

First and foremost, we must protect our clients from any sort of self-indulgence, exploitation, or personal agendas that are not clearly part of their therapeutic goals. There is never an excuse for meeting our own needs, working on our own problems, or talking needlessly about our own issues in sessions that are supposed to be exclusively for the welfare and betterment of our clients. That is why we must constantly monitor tendencies to drift away from the client's own needs, curtailing inclinations to talk about ourselves or engage in excessive personal sharing. The most essential question that remains foremost in our minds is how what we are doing at any given moment is actually helpful. If we cannot provide a legitimate rationale for why we are saying or doing something, then it is often because it is misguided.

With that said there are nevertheless endless opportunities for clinicians to occupy an enriched environment in which we are constantly questioning the choices we make, the behaviors that may not be in our own best interest, and especially the meanings that we ascribe to our actions. This mostly takes place for those who are interested and committed to ongoing self-development. The reality is that some professionals are perfectly satisfied with the status quo—or they are lazy and complacent, unwilling to apply to themselves what they ask of their clients. For the rest of us, the gifts of this work just keep on giving—but only if you are paying close attention.

Questions for Reflection or Discussion

1. Think of a recent conversation or interaction you had with someone you were trying to help in some way. Even though your attention and motivation were concentrated on serving the other person, what did *you* learn from the encounter that you found interesting or instructive?

2. What are some examples of how and when you talk to yourself during times of stress? Compare an instance when such self-talk or cognitive restructuring led to neutralizing some discomfort versus another one in which you made things far worse through continuous self-criticism.

3. The chapter explored some of the post-traumatic growth benefits that can result from processing life difficulties in constructive, affirmative ways. Think of a time in your life when surviving adversity made you stronger and more resilient.

2

Knowing What Makes a Difference

Reality is merely an illusion, albeit a very persistent one.

—Albert Einstein

Making Sense of Things

For someone like me who felt pretty worthless and incompetent during early life, it is not all that surprising that I selected a career that made me seem like I know and understand things that might have escaped others. I really had nothing much going for me as a kid. I sucked at sports, relegated to right field during baseball games—and for good reason since I rarely caught any balls hit my way. I could not run very fast either. But far worse was my marginal performance in school, barely able to maintain average grades. If that did not take a toll on my self-esteem, it surely hurt my willingness to tackle new challenges. I was a mess.

It was only much later, about the time I entered high school, that I discovered the origins of my limitations: I just could not see very well. All my life, the world appeared blurry. I just assumed it was that way for everyone, that life was generally a very shadowy and indistinct place. That explains why I could not hit or catch a ball very well, why I sat so close to the television, and especially why I had done so poorly in school. In fact, I had never learned much of anything in class that was ever written on the blackboard—because I could not *see* the hazy scribbles.

Consider all the ways that might have affected and handicapped me. I never learned much about basic math or algebra because whatever the teacher wrote on the board was just a blur. Whenever I was called up to the front of the room to "solve" an equation, I would just stare helplessly at the numbers and letters that finally came into focus. For some reason, we were supposed to move those integers and numerals around, from one side of the equal sign to another, but I could never figure out how or why to do that. Even more surprising was that I never learned grammar, or at least the pieces that required one to identify the parts of a sentence, adjectives, adverbs, and such. Whenever the teacher drew lines from nouns or verbs to other parts of the sentence, I was likely staring out the window in the back of the room. To this day, I'm not exactly certain which words are adverbs if they do not end in "ly." Of course, it is precisely that lack of concern about how sentences are supposed to be constructed that has made it possible for me to become such a fluent, effortless, and intuitive writer, able to churn out dozens of pages of prose as a first (and virtually final) draft. I learned how to write just like I talk. No hesitation whatsoever. I have never encountered "writer's block" any more than I would ever find oral speech on mute.

You might wonder why my vision had not been corrected, or why my parents or school authorities did not have my vision checked routinely, especially since I literally sat just a few feet from the television screen at home. The truth was that I was embarrassed I could not see things that apparently others could view just fine. I memorized the eye chart during required examinations at school, sort of proud it was one of the few tests I could actually pass, even if I could not really see the letters on the chart. It was not until I was attending a Detroit Lions football game with my father that my disability was revealed. There had been an exciting play on the field, resulting in a touchdown, but I had been staring into space.

"Did you see *that*? Did you see that play!" my father screamed and then turned to see my puzzled expression. Then he pointed out toward the fog that enveloped my world. "Check out number 89," he said and then pointed once again toward the field. I just shrugged. This was the moment that we both realized that something was very wrong.

I did eventually get glasses. And that did indeed make a huge difference in my life. The whole world was revealed in shapes, colors, and especially clarity that I never imagined could be possible. I became aware for the first time just how much I had missed most of my early life, why I could not see the ball in baseball, and why I missed so much in school. It was far too late for me to make up all the grammar and math that had slipped by my notice, but at least I had an explanation for why I always felt so far behind. Perhaps you can also appreciate how that might have been a turning point in my passionate desire to make up for lost time, maybe even to become smart, wise, and knowledgeable. It is certainly no accident that I picked a job in which what we do for a living is learn and teach things to others, especially really valuable stuff like how to make sense of what we experience in life.

Therapists and Counselors Know Stuff

If you would describe to a child (or an alien) what we do for a living, one of the descriptions would mention that we know and understand a bunch of things that seem inscrutable or confusing to others. Examples might include such topics as what matters most in life, how to create greater meaning and satisfaction, how to more effectively get what you want and achieve desired goals, and why people do the things they do even if they do not seem to make sense. We know all kinds of cool stuff—the different types of personalities, the endless ways that the mind goes haywire, predictable stages of development, how people tend to learn best, what mistakes most often get them in trouble, cultural variations, cognitive errors. The list of our specialized knowledge and heightened understanding goes on and on.

Regardless of the personal reasons and motives that led you to make a difference in others' lives, you have got to admit that it is an amazing journey to learn all the valuable ideas, skills, and knowledge that help unravel the greatest mysteries of daily life. We understand (mostly) why people engage in behavior that is not in their best interest. Even more critically, we know a lot of things that anyone (including ourselves) can do to change those patterns. If ever given the opportunity, we have the best advice to offer, guidance that reflects our extraordinary wisdom.

When reviewing the curriculum of study that is required for this profession, some of the requirements may certainly seem boring, tedious, and even only tangentially relevant to what you intend to do. And yet every single course offers, to varying degrees, new insights, handy skills, and useful information that helps explain the nature of the human condition and why things sometimes fall apart. We are introduced to an encyclopedia of knowledge that provides us with a background in assessment, diagnosis, human development, ethical conduct, psychopathology, social behavior, group dynamics, family configurations, cultural variations, addictions, career trajectories, plus a range of interpersonal, leadership, and advocacy skills that make us extraordinary conversationalists, influencers, leaders, decision-makers—and healers. We are useful precisely because we do know and understand so much about the problems of everyday life, as well as the most disturbing behavioral dysfunctions.

We are the gurus, wizards, sages, and experts in contemporary culture that deal with the kinds of personal struggles that disrupt people's lives. We well understand those choices that end up futile and frustrating, as well as those most likely to make a real difference in behavioral functioning. Over time, we become even more experienced and expert at selecting the courses of action that may be most potent for a given person at a particular moment in time.

Even more useful as far as our own emotional, behavioral, and interpersonal functioning is that our work offers a window into the most common and salient difficulties that plague people's lives. We become intimately familiar with all the things that spouses and partners complain about to each other. We hear endless stories about the annoyances of parents regarding their children's incorrigible behavior; then we hear alternative narratives from the kids discussing their own frustrations. We are exposed every single day to all the kinds of things that drive people a little (or a lot) crazy. We listen to them talk incessantly about their unrealistic expectations for themselves and others, their seeming inability to let go of things they cannot control, and their persistent obsessions about insignificant things that hardly matter.

Just think about all the things that people allow to drive them to the limits of their frustration tolerance. It is one thing to feel somewhat disappointed if you do not get the job or promotion most desired, if your favorite political candidate does not win, if dinner is not ready when expected, or if someone does not deliver what was promised and quite another to allow such displeasures to destroy your equanimity. People tell us all kinds of things that knocked them off their emotional kilter—traffic congestion, weather anomalies, a rude comment, airline delay, canceled appointments, or a long line to purchase some cherished new product that is hardly essential.

While these conversations are taking place, we review the options for how to best respond helpfully. Is it time to confront the person or just simply listen carefully? Is this an opportune moment to make some connections to the past? Would a roleplay be useful to work this through? Or maybe it might be best to deal with some of the underlying issues that appear to consistently undermine progress. As these sorts of clinical decisions are being sorted out, there's another voice in our heads asking other questions that are best left for another time: "What is this person talking about that directly relates to your own experiences?" "In what ways have you been avoiding these same issues in your own life?" "How are you really going to help this guy when you haven't figured out how to deal with this yourself?"

Not every practitioner insists on overpersonalizing therapeutic conversations, but there is still a temptation, maybe better said as an *opportunity*, to continually upgrade our own personal development, as well as professional expertise, by engaging in ongoing self-reflection. Every time a client brings up a problem, difficulty, or issue that you haven't yet fully resolved, it is time to get back to work on your own personal functioning. And to be clear, this may not be so much a choice as an obligation—if the goal is to truly get the most from the lifestyle of being a counselor or therapist.

Exploring the Unknown and Other Curiosities

There is so much that we do not understand, so many mysteries that confound us. Every single day, we are faced not only with the puzzling nature of our clients' disorders and difficulties but also those related to so many aspects of human behavior. Just as an experiment try to brainstorm all the unexplained mysteries of human existence that have never made much sense to you. Have you really thought seriously about how to account for peculiar phenomena such as how and why laughter, crying, blushing, yawning, or kissing evolved? Why do teenagers take such seemingly stupid risks? Why are humans about the only creatures that survive after childbearing years are over? Why would people knowingly risk their lives for perfect strangers? What's the appeal of violent entertainment media? What causes mental illness? What are dreams really for? Why are blue eyes considered more attractive than brown eyes? What are the universal origins of prejudice and racism? What are the purposes of feelings anyway? Such questions abound (explored in Chapter 15), most of which we cannot really provide definitive answers to (Kottler, 2022b).

Welcome to the life of a mental health professional in which we explore mysteries for a living and in doing so never lose the passion for learning and accumulating greater wisdom. Every single session we ever conduct offers some new life instruction—that is, if we are really paying close attention and choosing to apply what we hear to our own lives. Just think about all the arcane facts and knowledge that are captured in our brains, stuff that earns us credit as walking encyclopedias of human behavior. Just rattle off a list of your own random recollections: Telling stories is 22 times more memorable to a listener than just providing facts and statistics alone. During and after trauma, brain functions become fragmented and lead to recursive, disturbing memories. Three-quarters of dreams involve some sort of physical or social threat. Gossip evolved as a means to control outliers and enforce social compliance. People tend to be most satisfied with their lives during old age and least satisfied during adolescence. Therapeutic techniques actually account for less than 10% of positive outcomes. Most self-care programs or prescriptions only increase daily burdens and lead to inevitable relapses. Ninety percent of people who pay for monthly gym memberships never, ever actually use the facilities. Statements such as these, without supportive evidence or sources, can be easily refuted with alternative studies or sources. In spite of debates about what qualifies as an "alternative fact," the main point is that we have at our command so many interesting ideas about the nature of human existence and experience.

It is certainly true that not every mental health professional feels passionately committed and devoted to upgrading their own personal growth and behavioral functioning alongside the progress of their clients. If we are honest about this state of affairs, many practitioners view themselves as too busy, too "otherwise occupied," or just not that interested in spending much time thinking about the direction of their own lives. That is one reason why we hear, more often than we would like, about clinicians whose own lives have fallen apart. They work too hard. They do not take care of themselves very well. They do not believe it is even important that they practice in their lives what they teach—and preach—to others. They do not view themselves as hypocrites so much as just a bit lazy.

Takeaways

There is little doubt that training as a professional helper provides us with an assortment of insights, knowledge, and skills that permit us to gaze deeply into many of the issues, difficulties, and mysteries that plague human experience. As such, we are potentially able to pull together ideas and knowledge from diverse sources, including personal experience, in order to make greater meaning and sense from challenges along the way. We may not always know what would make the greatest difference in anyone's life (including our own), but we are privileged to understand what often matters the most in different circumstances.

One of the most important takeaways from this chapter is a single overarching question that will likely rule your life and career for many decades in the future: What kind of person and professional do *you* wish to be?

Questions for Reflection or Discussion

1. What are a few of the most extraordinarily interesting things that you now know and understand as a result of your training and experience?

2. Review the curriculum of every course you had in your training (at least those you can remember) and mention one critical, significant lesson you learned in that class that you've applied ever since to some aspect of your life.

3. Recall a relationship, or even just a single conversation, with someone you helped in some capacity that resulted in a major breakthrough in your own life.

3

Mastering the Skills of Persuasion and Influence

The best way to show that a stick is crooked is not to argue about it or to spend time denouncing it, but to lay a straight stick alongside it.

—D. L. Moody

On Self-Persuasion

When someone has felt powerless and inept during early life, there is a tendency to lose confidence in the ability to convince others to do things that you believe are necessary, or at least preferable. I spent a lot of time immersed in fantasy during my childhood years, sitting in class staring out the window. I thought about what it would be like to be different than I was, far more capable, smart, athletic, and attractive. I imagined enticing interactions with some of the cute girls in my class. I pictured myself on adventures around the world. But one of my favorite reveries, ignited by Disney movies, was imagining I had certain abilities that were far beyond what I ever thought was possible. Sure, I wanted X-ray vision, super strength, and a lot more friends, but more than anything, I wondered what it would be like to be a really good talker, the sort who could get people on his side, or get them to do things that were important to me. Or maybe just to be nicer to me.

Obviously, I was not very good at talking to people in those days. Or at least I did not think so. My grades in school seemed to be a clear indicator of my limited potential in the future. When I had trouble getting into college, *any* college, my worst fears were confirmed. When I showed up for one admissions interview without my parents (who had already determined I would not amount to much anyway), the admissions director was so impressed he decided to admit me for one semester on probation. This was one of the first experiences in which I noticed that I had actually been pretty convincing with an authority figure who potentially controlled my future. I do not remember what I told him exactly, but I am pretty sure that it was offered with conviction.

Once I attended classes, both in undergraduate and graduate school, I found them mostly less than inspiring—with a few notable exceptions. The classes in psychology and counseling that I found most interesting seemed to have little to do with the actual subject and far more with the charisma and passion of the instructor. How else could I explain that I fell in love with courses such as "Factor Analysis," "Learning Theory," or "Freud as Literature." It was the teacher. Or I should say it was the teacher's excitement and willingness to bring me along on his or her journey.

I soon realized that there were so many different ways to captivate people, to earn their respect and trust, to have a direct impact on them. I may not have been (or felt) very smart and capable, but I did have an excess of energy and desire to be really good at *something*. It is so interesting how we learn over time that half the battle in developing expertise and excellence relates not necessarily to native ability but rather to motivation and commitment to the cause. Once I decided that I wanted to become not only a therapist but a really exceptional one, the path that I would follow seemed clear: I would just flat out work harder than anyone else to make up for all my other limitations. I suppose that means I learned that persuasion begins with ourselves first, providing convincing reasons and rationale for why the sacrifices and labor will eventually be worth the effort.

One of the outcomes of the decision to become a professional communicator and influencer (which is really what we are in addition to the role of a change agent) is that the ability to describe, explore, and explain phenomena transcends the ability to speak persuasively. I realized over time that writing fluently was simply an extension of persuasive speech. Whether writing a journal article, book, blog, or even case notes, the goal is to present convincing evidence for a point of view that is packaged in an accessible structure. The same is true with respect to public speaking in front of an audience. Once again, I learned over time that unless I could command attention from those in the room, provide some sort of novel experience, make them laugh *and* cry to activate emotional resonance, I was pretty much wasting my time. When I would look over the audience in the room (or nowadays on the screen) and see individuals distracted, playing with their mobile devices, mumbling to the person next to them, I realized how important it is to shake things up, often to do the unexpected.

For someone who had been chronically shy, insecure, and inhibited most of my life, I gave myself permission to be wild and a little crazy, to become provocative, to say things out loud that others would only think privately, if at all. I once read in a review of one of my books that I was described as the "conscience" of the profession, a truth teller. One of my longtime heroes has always been the boy who pointed out that the emperor was not wearing any clothes, the one person in the crowd who refused to go along with the deception and lies. We now live in a time that has been called "post-truth," when even established facts, supported by overwhelming scientific evidence, are disputed and considered subject to debate, if not correction, according to one's preferred ideology. We have had political leaders who proudly lied tens of thousands of times while in office, without a ripple of pushback from their legion of supporters. Warnings about global warming from 99.9% of environmental scientists do not appear to make a dent in the beliefs of a sizable portion of the population who find this really inconvenient and annoying, enough so to completely ignore or deny the evidence altogether. The whole notion of what is real, what is true, what actually happened is up for constant debate.

It has felt like the values and beliefs that I hold most sacred are now being challenged and replaced with new and different standards that seem like they are resurrected from the Dark Ages—restricting women's rights, expanding access to firearms, encouraging racism and prejudices, banning books, oppressing those who are most vulnerable and desperate, just as serfs were treated a thousand years ago. It is in this context that I have tried even more than usual to be as honest and direct with myself and others as I possibly can. Even with this desire and commitment, I know that I am lying to myself—and to you. After all, image management is what all memoirs and autobiographies are really about, leaving behind a highly selective and edited version of a life in which many of the blemishes are covered up and excuses are offered to explain away anything that doesn't fit neatly in the sanitized narrative.

Being a Good Talker

When reviewing all the things that counselors and therapists do in their jobs, first and foremost involves convincing people to do things that they would rather not have to do. Clients have plenty of excuses for avoiding such action: None of this is really their fault. It is really not much of a problem anyway. Besides, it is just too hard. They do not really feel like it anyway. Just not in the mood. And even if they did try, it probably would not change much anyway. What's the point?

People can become remarkably persistent and stubborn maintaining habits, choices, and behaviors that end up sabotaging their articulated goals. In some cases, this reflects their own ambivalence about change, especially all the adjustments and hard work that is involved when altering established patterns. In spite of what anyone says, hardly anyone really means it when they say they want to make constructive changes. What they *really* want is for *us* to do the work on their behalf, or at the very least agree with them that they really do not have a problem after all; it is others who are the problem.

So, how do we convince reluctant or resistant people to do certain things that we know are good for them, but they still resist the hard sell? Well, encapsulated in Moody's quotation that headed this chapter, we do not persuade people merely by telling them what to do. That is another lesson well learned in graduate school: Giving advice hardly ever works. And when anyone does listen to what we have offered, it only makes them more dependent on similar advice in the future. After all, they don't really trust their own judgment.

When showing them a "crooked stick" to demonstrate just how dysfunctional and useless such a tool can be, we are hardly surprised at the excuses that often follow: "The stick isn't really crooked; it just looks that way," or "I *like* crooked sticks," or "Even if the stick was straight it still wouldn't make much of a difference." Naturally, all of these defensive and avoidant responses ensure that things will remain very much the same in spite of complaints about how annoying and distressing that is.

Once we discover ways to help clients compare their current choices, habitual patterns, dysfunctional behavior, or "crooked sticks" to other alternatives that aren't accompanied by such devastating side effects, there arise the first glimmers of interest in possibly trying something new and different. As we will explore in future chapters, astute, experienced practitioners rarely resort to direct advice and admonishments in order to disrupt existing processes. If that were the case, our job would be as simple as just telling people not to do the things they are currently doing and to do something else instead. I cannot remember the last time (or *any* time) in which that worked out very well.

Instead, clinicians have within their bag of tricks an assortment of far more subtle, indirect, sometimes disguised approaches that bypass resistance and reluctance. Some practitioners favor the use of metaphors, narrative reconstructions, or mindfulness exercises. Some use imagery, movement, poetry, art, dance, and other nonverbal means to circumvent the usual denial or disowning of difficulties. Still other therapists prefer to use hypnotic inductions, misdirection, enactments, dream interpretation, paradoxical techniques, or storytelling, all of which are designed to help bypass resistance.

Regardless of the particular strategy employed, an important lesson learned is not to argue with someone who seems overly entrenched in a position. That signals a time to back off, to de-escalate any disagreements or conflicts.

"I'm not sure I understand what you want," the therapist says with a touch of exasperation.

"What do you mean?" the client replies knowing exactly what she meant.

"Well, on the one hand, you said you were tired of being stuck in this dead-end job and abusive relationship that leaves you feeling trapped."

"Yeah? So what?"

"I notice that every time we approach a point where you might actually say something to your partner or boss, you immediately retreat and say that you don't know how, or it wouldn't work, or it will only make things worse."

"You gotta admit that might be true."

"Sure," the therapist readily agrees, refusing to get sucked into the argument. "So, then, perhaps it would be best for you not to mess with things after all. Maybe instead it would be best if we worked on helping you to just accept the status quo and to stop pretending you want something else."

In many different therapeutic approaches, there are variations of this theme, variously called "reverse psychology, "paradoxical intervention," "prescribing the symptom," "curious questioning," "unique outcomes," among others. Regardless of the chosen name, each strategy avoids direct confrontation and instead acknowledges the importance of the client's readiness and current capacity for making changes.

After all, the goal is to help clients just to "compare sticks."

Takeaways

If giving advice, direct confrontation, or just using a louder voice fails to make much of an impact on our clients, then the same is obviously true when we find ourselves in conflict with a partner, friend, colleague, or family member. We may sometimes find ourselves trapped in such difficult situations and frustrating relationships, but once we take a step back and inhale deeply a few times, we are reminded that we really do know how to handle such predicaments much differently if we so choose.

That is one of the important lessons that are worth remembering. The same strategies and skills that extract us from futile conflicts with clients also work (almost as) well in our personal lives. I inserted "almost" because there are also clear differences in that we hardly enjoy the same level of authority, respect, and deference with friends and family that we do with those we are paid to help. The reality is that some attempts to apply such strategies with loved ones may actually be quickly called out: "Quit doing that therapy crap with me!" Nevertheless, it is so incredibly useful to catch ourselves stuck in a conflict or disagreement because we failed to recognize the dynamics at play. Once we remember the other options at our disposal, including backing off, surrendering, deescalating, distracting, or just "comparing sticks," we are potentially on our way to a possible breakthrough. Even if the outcome does not change much, such an approach significantly reduces internal frustration.

The same can be said with respect to clinical work since the main reason why practitioners often fail with certain clients is because of their own stubbornness and refusal to stop doing what is clearly not working very well and instead try something else. Like "civilians," sometimes we just get overinvested in familiar strategies with which we are already comfortable, regardless of whether they are suitable or effective in a situation. It takes a certain amount of self-persuasion to abandon a favorite approach in lieu of something else that is entirely new and different—with quite uncertain results.

Whether during meetings, embroiled in conflicts, debating different points of view, or just engaged in passionate conversations, we have at our disposal all the optimal tools by which to present clear and cogent arguments or perspectives that are designed to have the most impact. Just as importantly, we are also quite aware of those times when it is best to just back off when we realize the futility of arguing with someone who has no intention of listening to alternative opinions. In the immortal words of French novelist Alexandre Dumas, "Never argue, you won't convince anyone. Opinions are like nails; the more you hit them, the more you push them in."

Questions for Reflection or Discussion

1. Think of a time when you were feeling reluctant to make a change in your life as a result of pressure from others. What was most helpful in overcoming your resistance?

2. Imagine that someone you are trying to help becomes unreasonably stubborn and defensive. Instead of arguing with the person, or repeatedly attempting to convince the person to change their mind, what are some alternative ways that you might attempt to break through that resistance?

3. What are some of the reasons why some clients declare they want to make major changes in their lives but then appear to block attempts to influence them?

4

Heightening Relational Intimacy and Engagement

Sometimes just to annoy my therapist I ask him, "So how does my lack of progress make you feel?"

—Tweet from a therapy client

Those We Will Never Forget

As I look back on a half-century of clinical practice, I cannot help but recall most vividly that some of the most important relationships I have ever experienced in my life were not just with my family, friends, and colleagues but also included so many of my clients. Some of the most intimate, provocative, revealing conversations I've ever had have taken place during sessions. I would hear stories that were absolutely astounding and still haunt me to this day. If I close my eyes for a few moments and let my mind wander, I cannot stop myself from thinking about many of the individuals I have helped, especially those with whom I enjoyed a long-term, truly honest, and engaged relationship that resulted in a satisfactory outcome for both (or all) of us. Perhaps even more memorable are those clients I have disappointed or failed.

These fond and painful recollections are just as significant to me as any experiences I ever had with my son, wife, or grandchildren. Although I am a bit surprised to admit it, some of the most impactful, significant personal discussions I've ever had were not with my friends but with clients. It seemed like the usual guardrails were dismantled that discourage people from being completely open, transparent, and honest. It certainly helps that there are also clear boundaries and safeguards in place to protect client privacy, confidentiality, and ongoing support. In such circumstances, it is no wonder that we end up talking about things that would not (or could not) take place anywhere else.

An older Vietnamese woman once told me about the fall of Saigon at the very end of the war. She had been hiding with her fiancé inside her house when the enemy invaded. Even though this occurred 50 years earlier, she was still haunted by memories of a soldier who beheaded her fiancé and made her hold the decapitated head on her lap. Such cruelty was horrifying, of course, but the image I cannot get out of my mind was this lovely, kind woman sitting in my office, still understandably traumatized by this experience. I can still see what she was wearing and the expression on her face as she told me about this. I remember feeling so honored and grateful that she trusted me enough to revisit this terrible event in my presence.

Other clients immediately come to mind for very different reasons, perhaps because I disappointed them in some way. Some become unaccountably angry, if not enraged. Others may have tried attempts at manipulation or seduction, attempting to break through our professional demeanor. Some clients suddenly do not return, and we never know why. There are those who are disgruntled and make sure we know that every time they have the chance to remind us of our limitations. Other clients spin out of control or even take their own lives. In each case, depending on the duration and intimacy of the relationship, we are left wounded and wondering what went wrong and why.

Most of the clients who still occupy a special place in my memories were with me for quite a long time during the days when there were few limits on frequency and length of treatment. There were several children and adolescents I worked with when they were young who remained in contact with me for the rest of their lives, providing updates and reports on their continued progress. Even after so many decades, I still think about them, still worry about them, still wonder how they are really doing.

Indelible helping relationships don't necessarily have to last a long time to have profound and enduring effects. While it is true that intimacy takes time to develop since trust is such an essential component, there are sometimes instances when relatively brief encounters can also have profound effects, depending on their unusual features and the emotional arousal that is felt by the participants. I was part of a trauma team working in an isolated, earthquake-ravaged region of Nepal where tens of thousands of people were killed and hundreds of thousands were left desperate and homeless. There were hundreds of people streaming out of the hillsides with broken bones, internal injuries, respiratory problems, and catastrophic trauma. They lined up outside my "office," a dilapidated school classroom that had only partially survived the devastation. I arranged my chair very close to the door so I could escape during the repeated aftershocks.

Among the dozens of people standing in line for mental health services was a very old man of indeterminate age. He could have been 50 or 90 but more likely closer to the latter considering his milky eyes and missing teeth. I was curious about what I could do for him when he finally walked through the door and sat directly opposite me with our knees touching. Since he only spoke the local dialect of the Sherpa language, without much understanding of English or Nepali, I wondered how exactly we would communicate. Before I could begin, the elderly gentleman held out his hands and grabbed mine tightly as he stared into my eyes. We had yet to speak, so it was quite strange and uncomfortable just staring into eyes that were clouded with glaucoma. The silence went on for some time, perhaps 5 minutes that felt like an hour. I tried to focus and remain fully present, but it was difficult when I could see all the restless people waiting outside for their turn. He must have noticed my distraction and impatience because he nodded his head and released his hands, coupling them into the tent-like acknowledgment of respect and acknowledgment. He then bowed deeply and said, "Namaste."

"Namaskar," I replied, using the more formal version reserved for elders. Then he walked out the door and proceeded to go to the back of the line to wait patiently for another "session." What did I actually do? I wondered. What the heck happened during that interaction? We never said a single word to one another until the very end. I never heard his story. I never learned about his life and struggles. And yet it was one of the most intimate, spiritually transcendent encounters I have ever had in my life. I feel chills at this moment as I think about what happened, even though I cannot explain it. It was clear that something miraculous happened for me, and presumably for him, when we connected so deeply with one another. It not only seemed to be healing for him in some way, but remarkably, I felt healed myself. All through the previous weeks, I had been subjected to the most terrifying, confusing, chaotic situations filled with dead bodies and desperate, wailing people. I felt overwhelmed and lost. I could not sleep at night because I was frequently awakened by aftershocks and images of broken bodies. Yet after this "conversation" with the elderly man, I somehow felt clearer and calmer. It was as if he was there to reassure me that we would all be okay eventually. What we needed to do was hold hands and gaze into one another's eyes.

This changed *everything* for me, not only during the weeks that followed treating hundreds of other trauma survivors but long afterward when I felt a renewed respect and appreciation for the power of relational engagement. I knew this already of course. So do you. But I had never fully appreciated that sometimes that is all we have to give. And sometimes that is enough.

The Primacy of Relational Engagement

There's been considerable research and discussion about the so-called common factors that have been found to be universal across theoretical models (Bailey & Ogles, 2023; Elkins, 2019; Grencavage & Norcross, 1990; Wampold, 2015). Regardless of the particular approach, whether classified as cognitive, psychodynamic, humanistic, constructivist, or whatever else, certain features have been identified that are associated with positive outcomes. Surprisingly, the chosen model itself is likely the *least* important variable, accounting for a tiny percentage of the effects. Likewise, specific techniques do not seem to matter very much, even though practitioners are often obsessed with collecting them. So, what *does* appear to matter most? Besides the client's own personal characteristics, which include motivation, commitment, personality traits, and specific presenting complaints, it is the quality of the relational bond that determines about half of the results.

Interestingly, this perception of a solid alliance and trusting relationship primarily relates to the *client's* perceptions, not those of the clinician (Kottler & Balkin, 2017, 2020). This has profound implications, not to mention considerable reassurance for beginners in the field, since it is highly unlikely you will ever completely grasp the nature of what is actually happening with anyone you ever treat. Here's the good news: It may not matter that much whether *you* truly understand your clients *as long as they feel understood.* In addition, your favored theoretical model may also not be nearly as important, as all the attention justifies making the "optimal" choice.

Obviously, there are so many different theoretical orientations, each of which describes a particular kind of helping relationship best suited to that approach. Some attempt to create a corrective emotional experience, while others prefer authentic engagement, collaborative partnership, compassionate confidant, or working alliance. Regardless of the model, there are certain features that are usually most helpful to a relational bond that is experienced as empathic, respectful, and trusting. Second, the structure and style of the relationship are mutually negotiated in terms of the goals, choices, and unique needs of the client. Nevertheless, in spite of so many investigations and correlational studies that examine the variables most associated with client satisfaction, we still cannot ultimately determine which specific or common factors are definitively at play (Cuijpers et al., 2019). It is still very much a mystery, one that is considered to be absolutely essential that we prioritize for the future of the profession (Gaines et al., 2021).

In spite of the debates, arguments, and conflicts over which therapeutic approach is superior to the rest, and which aspects of those models are most potent, whether examining the past, present, or future, cognitive, emotional, or behavioral features, there is surely a consensus among most clients that if any useful work is going to take place they have got to feel a degree of caring, trust, compassion, and empathy from their helper. Above all else, we are relational specialists, able to engage almost anyone who seeks our services, regardless of their background, complaints, or preferences. After all, the best among us are adaptable if nothing else, able to negotiate with almost anyone some working alliance that permits constructive engagement.

As mentioned previously, there are a lot of different relational variations that are possible. Some people need a lot of structure and direction, while others work best under conditions of maximum freedom and flexibility. Some clients need clearly enforced boundaries; others must feel like they are the ones in control. Every individual case dictates a somewhat unique, mutually negotiated type of interaction that capitalizes on the client's preferences and signature strengths. At least in theory, that is likely true, although there are certainly quite a few practitioners who insist on operating essentially the same way with almost everyone, regardless of their issues, preferences, and needs. This is likely far from ideal.

Relationship Specialists

Given our training, skillset, and experience, it is fairly obvious that therapists and counselors do indeed have a "superpower," an ability that allows us to virtually connect with almost anyone. Beyond everything else we can do, we know how to build trust in relationships. We are intimately familiar with all the intricacies of human interaction. We are excellent listeners, able to respond helpfully to whatever is expressed. We know how to defuse conflicts and de-escalate arguments. We are experts at drawing people out, helping them to tell their stories, exploring features that have been ignored or denied. If given the chance we can get almost anyone to trust us—or at least give us a chance to help them. We try to be scrupulously honest and open, creating alliances that feel safe and secure. There is really no other profession that better equips someone with the knowledge and abilities to create and maintain deep human connections. So, here is the key question: Why don't we do all this more often with the relationships in our lives that matter most?

If there is one remarkable advantage and skill within our behavioral repertoire, it is the capacity for creating intimacy with others. Yet sometimes we still find ourselves estranged from those we love, as well as caught up in family drama or interpersonal conflict. You would think we would know better, or at least immediately recognize such situations and figure out how to better manage them. Of course, we do know better, but we still feel helpless and frustrated at times to alter dysfunctional patterns. There are good reasons and legitimate excuses for this since in such personal relationships we do not enjoy the sort of power, control, and authority we have in our professional roles.

I sometimes marvel when I am in session, on stage, in a classroom, or in front of an audience how people sit silently attentive, taking notes on what I say, yet hardly anyone in my family thinks my contributions are any more important than their own. When I write books like this, offering my presumed wisdom and knowledge, students are required to learn the content; they are even tested on the material. But when I introduce these same ideas in daily conversation, hardly anyone really cares or listens. During counseling sessions, I explain complex issues and unravel confusing puzzles, hired as a specialized expert for this explicit purpose. Once again, however, hardly anyone in my normal daily life outside of the office is all that interested in my informed opinions on matters. This is the reality of a mental health professional's life, and that helps explain why we are not able (or willing) to apply in our own relationships what we do so well when we are helping others.

Takeaways

Whether capitalizing on the opportunities or not, mental health professionals have the opportunity to apply more diligently to their personal lives many of the things that we do so well with our clients. Sure, sometimes we just don't feel like it. Or we don't know how in a given situation. Or when we attempt to swing into "therapeutic mode," others become annoyed or frustrated: "There you go again, doing that counseling crap with me!"

Being called out in such a way just means that we were inept or awkward, not that the attempt to be more responsive was ill-advised. We each have our limits of patience and tolerance, especially after having to be on our best behavior all day. We are never permitted to lose control, to indulge ourselves, to tell someone to back off or take a hike. We sit stoically, endlessly patient and (seemingly) empathic and understanding.

"Yes, I can tell you are rather upset and angry with me right now," we might say in the calmest, most measured voice, even though the client is turning bright red and screaming at the top of his voice. A part of us would love to just tell the person what we really think, but instead, we take a deep breath and remain in control. It is no wonder that the reservoir of patience becomes depleted once we return home.

Of course, we cannot be expected to maintain Herculean efforts of self-control and relational excellence continuously, but we always retain the ability to question our own behavior in such circumstances. Just as we would with clients, we might challenge ourselves by asking how the interactions that appear to be unfolding between us reflect a familiar pattern in our own lives that we have encountered previously. Or perhaps we might ask ourselves what we might be doing (or not doing) that is making matters worse instead of improving. What we have learned from our clients is how important it is to take at least partial responsibility for encounters that have gone awry rather than blaming others or external factors beyond our control.

Questions for Reflection or Discussion

1. If you were to seek help for some personal problem, what would be most important to you in a relationship with a therapist or counselor?

2. What do you believe is most often neglected or ignored when negotiating an alliance with a new client?

3. How has what you've learned in your training significantly affected the ways you relate to friends and family?

Understanding Group Dynamics and Leadership Behavior

Never doubt that a small group of thoughtful citizens can change the world; indeed, it's the only thing that ever has.

—Margaret Mead

If your actions inspire others to dream more, learn more, do more and become more, you are a leader.

—John Quincy Adams

You are not here merely to make a living. You are here in order to enable the world to live more amply, with greater vision, with a finer spirit of hope and achievement. You are here to enrich the world, and you impoverish yourself if you forget the errand.

—Woodrow Wilson

Being Held Accountable

"What do I do *now*?" I wondered. I was losing the audience and could easily read the signs they were disengaged. A few people were sneakily checking their phones. I could see a few yawns and people slumping in their chairs. Eyes looked glazed. It seemed as if we were pretty much all wasting our time together.

It used to amaze me when I was a student how we would all be sitting in class and the professor in front of the room was standing behind a podium reading from his yellowed notes in a wrinkled file folder—and in those days it was *always* an elderly man. He would drone on and on, covering the same content we had already reviewed in our texts. I would glance over my shoulder and notice that everyone in the room was just as bored and disinterested as I was feeling. Even the instructor looked bored with himself. I looked at the clock on the wall, still an hour off because it had never been changed after daylight savings time.

Nevertheless, it clearly indicated we still had another hour and 21 minutes before we would be released from this prison.

As I sat there stewing in frustration it never ceased to amaze me that if I could readily tell that nobody was paying attention, then why couldn't the instructor tell that nobody was really listening? After all, *he* was the one standing in the front of the room with a perfect view of all our bored faces. So if he looked up from his notes and scanned the room, couldn't he see what was really happening? If what he was doing failed to interest us, why wasn't he doing something else instead? Isn't that supposedly what we were learning in this program— how to help and lead others by providing them with relevant knowledge in digestible form?

I was having second thoughts about my decision to continue these studies since I had first undertaken this program as much to bolster my own personal functioning and well-being as to make a difference in others' lives. Sure, I wanted to help people. But I had also hoped that what I was learning and those who were teaching the subjects would be models for what I wished to become. I wondered how this teacher in the front of the room, who seemed so clueless about what was really unfolding, could possibly have been very effective as a counselor. This led to other thoughts, given how often I had experienced similar poor instruction and supervision from others who had been in positions of leadership.

Fortunately, the other class I was taking that semester was an experiential group in which we were expected to work on our own personal issues led by a world-class expert. We were required to keep journals and write a paper about our own personal development. We were also encouraged to identify any of our unresolved issues that might compromise our professional effectiveness. It was during such self-scrutiny within the context of this group that I made a few momentous decisions. I had been engaged to a woman out of a sense of obligation. I was stuck working in a job I hated, but it provided generous compensation. In truth, I was pretty miserable, which is why I enrolled in graduate school in the first place.

Interestingly, most of the progress I made on these issues took place in my own mind rather than aloud during a group session. It was silent, private work that I was still too uncomfortable to bring out in a public forum. Yet I still felt supported in these efforts by those present in the group, even if I had not yet told them about my future plans. I would do so once I was ready to take constructive action.

At the very end of a group meeting, I quietly announced that I would not be attending class the following week, as I would be out of town. What I did not tell them was that I made secret plans so that when they saw me again in a few weeks, I intended to be a profoundly different person than the one they currently encountered. I had decided that I needed to change my life in a dramatic way, and this group, and especially the leader, had inspired me to take extreme measures. I purchased a series of recordings that had been published by the group leader as part of a collection. There were exactly seven of them. I decided to sell my car and use the money to book a plane ticket and pay for accommodations on a Caribbean Island. I would then find a comfortable spot underneath a shady tree near the beach where each morning I would listen to one of the recordings and then reflect on the themes throughout the day and how they applied to my life.

Once I arrived home, I was excited about some monumental decisions I had made while I was gone. First I informed my fiancé that although I was still interested in seeing her, I was definitely not ready to be married. She, in turn, decided to end the relationship, which let me off the hook. Second, I told my boss I was quitting my job, in spite of the generous salary, so I could attend graduate school full time. When I returned to the group, and we began our usual check-in process, I casually disclosed all the major changes in my life that I had initiated since they had seen me last. I received an enthusiastic round of applause, cementing the pride I felt in finally extracting myself from the rut I had been stuck in.

This group experience changed my life in so many profound ways and made me a true believer that such settings were the ideal spaces to promote significant changes. I became fascinated with the complex dynamics and processes involved in such group work; there was so much more going on than in individual sessions. I loved the unpredictable drama of the encounters and the chaos at times since there was so much happening all at once. All the while someone was talking, others were glancing at one another, revealing varied reactions, taking sides, engaging in behavior that was distracted, disinterested, or overwhelmed. It just seemed amazing to me that although I had never really spoken or shared much in the group thus far, the leader still managed to inspire me sufficiently to make the sort of personal life changes for which we all yearn.

As much as I wanted to lead such groups myself, I realized that no matter how hard I studied and how hard I tried, I would never, ever fully grasp the full complexity of what was happening at any moment in time. There was just so much going on. I loved this! I was determined to be good at it, to learn not only how to run a therapeutic group but all the ways I could apply such knowledge to social situations.

Practicing Leadership in Everyday Life

All this got me thinking—and I have yet to stop—about all the different ways that what we know and learn in order to lead therapeutic groups can be applied to so many other aspects of life. It turns out that I am hardly the only one who believes that the subject of leadership is the single most popular and studied aspect of human behavior. There are leadership courses in almost every discipline imaginable, obviously management, political affairs, advocacy, and human resources but also any other context and setting in which coordination and effective functioning are important.

Mental health professionals learn a particular process and structure for conducting groups designed to promote growth, learning, and development. I remember when I was first learning the basic skills and strategies involved in leading groups, I was given an extensive list of instances when some intervention was required. I made a "cheat sheet" of the 20 critical incidents that could occur, each of which suggested a particular response. For instance, if a member repeatedly interrupted others while they were talking, the leader would block such behavior to enforce norms of mutual respect and make sure each person has a voice.

Effective leaders usually intervene to protect the safety of those present, to prevent any form of disrespect or abuse that could result in casualties. My list also mentioned several other critical times when some decisive action is required to (1) cut off digressions, distractions, or needless rambling; (2) enforce norms of respect and caring; (3) correct irrational or dysfunctional thinking; (4) cue a group member to help another; (5) provide additional structure as needed; (6) block complaining; (7) confront inconsistencies; (8) provide constructive feedback; (8) clarify, interpret, or reflect feelings or content; (9) summarize or draw closure after lengthy discussions. There are probably several others that you would wish to add to the list, depending on your own style, preferences, and approach.

Every practitioner has a "cheat sheet" of sorts, whether in their mind or actually recorded, that guides their intervention choices when someone does or says something that is potentially instructive or counterproductive. Common examples of this might occur when someone is disruptive, in the throes of decompensation, or acts out in ways that undermine trust and cohesion in the group. In addition, leaders are inclined to intervene when there is a need to make sure everyone present has a voice, feels heard and understood. One of the most consistent challenges that leaders face in any situation, whether in social work or therapeutic groups, is to control the interactions in such a way that quieter members are drawn out and more verbose participants are discouraged from taking over the conversation.

When reviewing this list of possible interventions, it is relatively easy to imagine all the ways we might use a few of these same responses in other situations, whether conducting a meeting, planning a social event, or even sitting down to dinner with family or friends. All too often, conversations devolve into the most superficial or predictable drudgery—talking about the food, sporting events, or favorite recipes. Yet we know how to deepen conversations and promote more meaningful interactions. We know how to stop one person from dominating the discussion just as we are equally proficient at drawing out others who have been silent or feel marginalized. We know how to help everyone in a room (or on a screen) feel like their voices have been welcomed.

Advice for Really, *Really* Bad Leadership

In spite of all the resources, training programs, continuing education, blogs, books, and videos devoted to teaching exceptional leadership, it is surprising how poorly many in these positions actually perform. This is not just about the ultimate productivity that results but also the perceptions of their followers, employees, supervisees, members, and clients. In recent times, there have been many controversies related to prominent corporate and tech CEOs who have displayed florid symptoms of narcissism and self-serving decisions, not to mention abuse and neglect of those they are paid to serve. Success and achievement are often measured exclusively in terms of the financial bottom line with absolutely no concern whatsoever for employee well-being, job satisfaction, and morale.

It is more than a little ironic that in spite of such interest and required training for most professional leaders, it has been estimated that half of all corporate managers and organizational leaders are viewed by their followers as incompetent in their roles. Even worse, close to three quarters of employees say the worst part of their job is dealing with a terrible supervisor who represents the single greatest source of stress in their lives (Hogan et al., 2010; Kottler, 2018). Yikes.

As mental health providers, we should be especially astute at applying what we know on the job to other aspects of daily life. Nevertheless, those who have spent much time in large organizations or toxic work cultures are already well aware that many leaders in positions of authority remain in those roles not because of their superior abilities but rather because of their thirst for power and control. In addition, they are able to remain in these positions in spite of their essential inability and lousy leadership because of entrenched dysfunctional cultural norms. They engage in behavior that is consistently annoying and ineffective because of their own arrogance and unwillingness to adapt to the needs of others. They do all the things that we know we are supposed to avoid doing when leading groups. They talk *way* more than they ever listen to others. They are never, ever willing to admit they were wrong or made mistakes, never inclined to apologize. Whenever possible, they tend to blame others, luck, fate, the economy, weather, or other external factors when things fall apart. If they are ever caught lying, manipulating, or failing, they will inevitably distract or change the subject, or else go on the attack. They take credit for all successes and progress rather than acknowledging the contributions of others. In these and so many other ways, their actions are discouraging, dispiriting, and frustrating, even though they should know better.

You have likely witnessed such a style of toxic leadership, whether in the political or social arena, as well as in the workplace. During the last few years, well-known political and corporate leaders in positions of authority have been challenged because of their inclinations to become abusive, disrespectful, deceitful, and manipulative toward others. They have engaged in the kind of name-calling toward opponents that would be expected by immature, threatened children. The greatest tragedy of all is how they will resort to *any* means to hold onto their power.

Yet someday *you* will likely rise to a position of authority and leadership as you move up the ranks, whether within an agency, organization, community, or the larger culture. Once deputized to mentor, guide, and support other people, you will find yourself in the perfect position to create and maintain an enriched context for not only achieving goals but also enjoying the work. After all, that is what we are uniquely trained to do, whether in a therapeutic setting or one in which we promote the growth, development, and productivity of others within our care.

Takeaways

There are two principal ways that therapeutic group leaders can potentially excel in applying their knowledge and skills to social, family, and other everyday interactions in groups. First and foremost we know that one of the major advantages of group settings is not only the enlivened interactions but also the opportunities to provide people with valuable feedback about their behavior. After all, participants present have been witnesses to the particular (and peculiar) ways that everyone has chosen to behave. We often make assumptions that someone's consistent actions in a group likely reveal established patterns that may get them into difficulty in the outside world. As such, we often structure opportunities for people to hear from others about how they were perceived, coupled with feedback on the effects of their actions on others, as well as suggestions for how they might respond differently in the future. That is one reason why therapeutic-type groups are so incredibly powerful: They help individuals to hear honest reactions about their characteristic behavior.

It is not surprising that there are many other group settings in which helping people give, hear, and respond to feedback only enhances cohesion and stimulates further learning and growth—if the person can actually take in the comments without feeling unduly defensive. That is why it is so important to assist group members to offer their perceptions in such a way that it is truly useful. In any situation, we can better help people to more constructively process feedback from others when it is offered with caring, kindness, sensitivity, and compassion rather than feeling like it is a criticism or an attack. The best examples of this occur when what is offered to someone is delivered in such a way that it is both concise and clear, as well as highly specific rather than general. This is just part of the way we normally operate in our jobs that can be adapted to other group situations that are functioning less than optimally because of one or more individuals who are consistently annoying, blocking, or discouraging others who are present.

A second useful adaptation is the standard "check-in" that we would typically initiate before any group dives deeply into action. Imagine you are planning a social gathering, dinner party, or just getting together with friends or colleagues over coffee or a drink. Now, recall how you would begin any group you might lead, always starting with a "check-in" to make sure everyone has a chance to say something, as well as to "check the pulse" of members as a preliminary assessment. This sets the stage for session planning and "triage" processes to determine who needs time the most and what dynamics might be operating that day. Just as this standard procedure is so valuable to invite equitable contributions from everyone present, it is just as useful in any other situation when we might find ourselves in the presence of others.

There is a popular exercise that is often introduced around the end of the new year. Those present are asked to look back on the preceding 12 months and share something meaningful that occurred in their lives. They may be asked what was the best and worst thing that they experienced, or something they regret, or sometimes to declare an important goal they wish to achieve during the next year. It is interesting how this same process can be applied to almost any other situation. Everyone around the table can be asked to share something significant that happened to them during the preceding week, or something they have never shared before with those who are present, or perhaps just a humorous or embarrassing incident that would lighten things up. The point is that we are uniquely qualified and skilled at leading others in such a way that intimacy is heightened and relationships are further enhanced.

It may sound interesting to lead "check-ins" at social gatherings to invigorate social interactions and interpersonal connections, but it takes courage to disrupt habitual patterns that have been solidified over time. Imagine, for example, that you were asked this very moment as a "homework assignment" to put this plan into action. The next time you find yourself in a social situation with a group of others and you notice that the conversations taking place are both predictable and dreary, try to shake things up a bit. Ask each person to share something that is present in their life right now, some struggle, something that bothers or annoys them, something they hadn't yet mentioned to others but still weighs on their minds. This is not about counseling others in such situations but rather that we invite people to be more honest and authentic with one another.

There's one other thing that we know is crucial when leading groups and that is that we do not let participants depart before asking what they learned that they are taking with them: "What's going to stick with you?" "What did you hear (or read) that struck you as most useful and interesting?" "As you think back on our conversations, what do you believe will truly stick with you over time?" Finally, as you review the ideas covered in this chapter, what will *you* find most useful?

Questions for Reflection or Discussion

1. Who is the best leader you've ever known, whether in the context of school, a job, or daily life? What were this person's qualities that you most admired?

2. If you were going to take on a major leadership role at some time during your life and career, what form would that take?

3. What do you believe is the most neglected aspect of being a leader if the goal is to inspire people to take constructive action?

6

Taking Inventory of Personal Biases, Prejudices, and Entrenched Beliefs

The only man I know who behaves sensibly is my tailor; he takes my measurements anew each time he sees me. The rest go on with their old measurements and expect me to fit them.

—George Bernard Shaw

Not My Yacht Club

I was being given a tour around town by one of my new colleagues who I had been hired to replace as the department head. He was a formal, aristocratic, elegant gentleman who spoke in clipped speech with a soft, Southern accent. I found him both somewhat eccentric and a bit intimidating. I noticed when he spoke to me he would barely make eye contact. I sensed he didn't much like me, but since we'd just met, I knew I couldn't have done anything yet to annoy him. I wondered if he resented that I was now going to be in charge of our unit. Maybe I was just being oversensitive?

As we were driving around, he would occasionally point out some historical building or cultural artifact, including a statue of his own ancestor who had apparently arrived in this country on the *Mayflower* or something. He didn't seem all that interested in answering the many questions I had about my new job, especially regarding what the other staff members were like or what some of the difficulties had been in the past. He'd just shrug in response to my queries, and I couldn't figure out if he was being rude or, once again, if this was just part of his peculiar nature.

"See, over there?" he said pointing out the window toward a building on the harbor.

I glanced where he was directing my attention and just nodded, although I wasn't sure exactly what I was looking at except a bunch of boats.

"That's my yacht club," he explained and then paused for a minute and seemed uncomfortable. "But your people go somewhere else."

My people? Who are *my* people? I immediately wondered. What was he telling me? Did this place have a special yacht club for newcomers as opposed to longtime residents? No, that couldn't be it. So, then, who exactly *are* "my people?" Given that we'd just met for the first time, how could he even know who my people might be?

Then it hit me when I remembered where I was and the legacy of racism and antisemitism that had always been part of this place. Somehow, some way, he figured out I was Jewish. I'm not sure how exactly he determined that. I don't have horns on my head. Maybe the curly hair gave me away? And what was he actually telling me, that Jews weren't allowed in his special club?

Although I'm not particularly religious and have never identified very strongly with my cultural heritage, somehow this guy identified me with this "tribe" in a way that felt creepy. He was letting me know that I wasn't part of his elitist culture and would never be permitted entrance through the gates of his special club. I wondered mischievously if I could ask him to take me in there as a guest sometime, just to mess with his head a little. But the truth is that I was dumbfounded.

I went to inner-city public schools in Detroit all my life. *Everyone* was a minority. I had never been subjected to any form of prejudice or oppression in my life, at least that I'd ever been aware of. But then again I have white skin and blue eyes, often indicators of privilege. I felt singularly unprepared to deal with such an offensive comment, but I decided it would be best to just let it go and ignore what he'd said. That turned out to be an ill-advised mistake since his behavior would escalate over the next several months, eventually leading me to quit the job and move on. Even though the administration had specifically hired me to deal with this racist clown, I just didn't feel like this was the best environment for me to flourish.

I mention this incident as just about the only instance of antisemitism I ever experienced in my life. Lucky me. All my life, I had been insulated within diverse communities so as to have been shielded from at least direct behavior like this. Most of the racism and prejudice circulating in my world was couched in teasing and ridicule. But now I felt the effects directly, even in this rather mild, seemingly inconsequential form. Once I recovered from feeling sorry for myself, apologizing to my family because we'd have to relocate once again in less than a year, I was faced with the prospect of examining more closely my own biases and prejudices that I denied or ignored. I liked to promote myself as an icon of tolerance and acceptance of difference, but I knew this was a lie. Like almost everyone else residing on this planet, I prefer to hang out with "people like me" and avoid "people not like me." By this, I don't mean similar to me in appearance, skin color, sexual orientation, economic status, or religious identification, although I must confess that those features certainly do affect my perceptions. After all, almost all of my friends are therapists and teachers, so what does *that* really say about my biased preferences? Not an engineer or accountant in the mix.

If any of us delves very deeply into the motives and reasons for why we chose a profession that so passionately encourages advocacy and justice for the marginalized and oppressed, there is an interesting historical legacy perhaps buried deep in our early lives. I know that in my case, I harbor such shame about my behavior as a child. In fact, I just can't get certain images out of my head.

There was a group of friends on my street that would play together almost every day, whether "cowboys and Indians," "pirates," or *Combat*, a popular World War II show on television during this time. We'd hide and run all over the neighborhood chasing one another. There was this one kid—I can still see him standing at a distance. There was something not quite right about him. He didn't talk "right," and his behavior was always weird. At the time, I didn't understand fully what it meant to be "retarded" or "cognitively challenged" in contemporary parlance. I suppose that's my excuse, but it seems so feeble and inadequate. Whenever we'd see the boy, we'd call him names and chase him. Every time. He was never allowed to join our group. In many ways, we terrified him. I've never lived this down. I've never really come to terms with my meanness and insensitivity. I've never been able to fully forgive myself for how I mistreated him. Even now as I revisit this time, I can feel myself burning in shame, becoming upset once again: How could I have ever been like this? How could I have been so inhumane?

This might sound a little improbable, but I attribute this memory as the origin of my commitment to rectify the past, to make up for my actions during this time when I didn't seem to know any better. Perhaps that is a gross simplification since motives and intentions are the result of so many different influences and factors, but I still choose to hold onto this painful memory as a path to redemption.

The Functions of Prejudice and Racism

As George Bernard Shaw remarked in the quotation that began the chapter, biases and prejudices represent prejudgments, those not based on "actual measurements" but rather outdated beliefs, distorted perceptions, and convenient "truths" that ignore the realities of individual and cultural differences. These attitudes mostly relegate "others" to positions of inferiority compared to those who occupy our own identified status group. This has not only led to the oppression of certain groups but also to tribal conflicts and world wars, some of which have endured for centuries. Throughout all of human history, those who enjoyed lofty positions wielded their power to provide advantages for their brethren and allies, excluding those who didn't share their birthright or connections. The same has always been true throughout most of the animal kingdom (and queendom) in which "alphas" control access to the best food and resources for their own kin and compatriots, excluding others from such privileges. Humans have done much the same with their invented class and caste systems, determining at birth who is worthy of the most opportunities, based not on ability or fairness but to preserve the inequitable status quo that favors those already in control. In some ways, this has been the most "natural" consequence of forming human communities and cultures, regardless of its seeming injustice.

Evolution prepared and protected us against potential threats it had "learned" to avoid over millennia. When approached by a stranger our brains had mere seconds to decide if this was an "enemy" or a "friend," someone who represented a threat or an ally. If you hesitated too long, indulged in indiscriminate "friendly" behavior toward anyone around, you likely wouldn't have lived long enough to produce offspring. Such naivete or carelessness was punished by a death sentence. That's why throughout the ages, it was perfectly reasonable and appropriate to become suspicious of people who were different, who were outsiders, who were "not like us." Strangers were potentially dangerous as spies for neighboring enemy tribes. Anyone different in appearance, who spoke a foreign language, who behaved strangely, was viewed as a potential threat. Their behavior was often viewed as confusing, bizarre, and inappropriate given the prevailing cultural standards of the tribe. If you really think about this phenomenon, it doesn't make a lot of sense that any human would help others outside the tribe. Within nature, species are so "ethnocentric" and "racist" that they literally kill and eat any member of their group that doesn't share their genetic material.

Within this context, it's no wonder that humans developed a tendency to prejudge others who didn't look or act like them. They were judged rather harshly and in many cases killed outright, exiled, or enslaved. They were called "aliens," "outsiders," "uncivilized," and other names denoting inferior status. Whether in Nazi Germany, Rwanda, Cambodia, Armenia, Bosnia, Sudan, or among Indigenous peoples of North and South America, there have been tens of millions of people murdered in the name of ethnic cleansing. Rather than being exceptions, these have become the norm every decade or two. In most cases, they represent attempts to maintain power and control to benefit one's own family and allies. The initial warning signs of increased oppression we can easily witness today with democratic systems being eroded, free elections sabotaged or undermined, increased racism, and even a resurgence of authoritarian leaders who seek to impose their own will for personal and financial benefits.

This discussion is *not* an excuse to justify continued racist and oppressive behavior but rather to understand better its origins and purposes during earlier times. This is our legacy no matter how much we might choose to deny it. That such attitudes and policies are now counterproductive in many ways, at least for the majority, doesn't change the reality that a few unscrupulous individuals will do anything they can to maintain their hold on power.

So much of the anxiety, disenfranchisement, depression, and other mental health issues that we treat are a direct result of the disempowerment that many people feel, regardless of their ethnic background, religious beliefs, and skin color. They feel trapped in their sense of helplessness and unable to upgrade their lives, they feel unworthy, or, in some cases, they feel the futility to change anything given all the forces that appear to stifle progress.

Our Own Internalized Racism

Prejudices, biases, and other similar distortions are examples of cognitive errors that mislead one's ability to clearly recognize and respond to situations because of flawed information and misguided assumptions. Although buried within such processes may be belief systems that marginalize certain groups, they also represent overgeneralizations based on limited previous experiences. If you believe that you have been ignored, bullied, mistreated, or disrespected in the past by someone with certain characteristics, then it may lead to making absolute critical judgments about anyone else who resembles this person or identified group. This can result in viewing members of a particular race, religion, ethnicity, or certain appearance as being "less than" or inferior to others in some way. As one small example of this that can develop, it feels like I have been repeatedly cut off on roads by huge, hulking, black pickup trucks that seem to tailgate and drive recklessly more than other vehicles. Now, I do not know if that is actually true or not (maybe unlikely?), but it nevertheless affects my perceptions: Nowadays, every time I encounter such a truck, I automatically keep my distance and (here's the biased part) mutter some obscenity to myself. Of course, I have other biases and prejudices if I see someone wearing a red MAGA hat, but that is a belief system, however overgeneralized, that I have no interest in challenging, even if it is not true.

In the context of therapy, we recognize many of these cognitive error processes as defense mechanisms such as denial, projection, and rationalization, but they are actually just one facet of the tendency to engage in dysfunctional thought patterns. Some of the most common forms include making overgeneralizations ("Because I got a 'B' on the assignment, I'll never do well in this class); overpersonalizing ("This sort of thing always happens to me"); dichotomous thinking ("Either I get this job or I'll never amount to anything"); and mind reading ("I can tell the teacher doesn't like me because he ignored my question in class"). There are also dozens of other cognitive distortions that we often encounter, especially those that involve blaming external factors, jumping to conclusions, discounting the positive, and filtering information and experiences in such a way that one holds beliefs that are not necessarily based in reality. Among the most common harmful examples, not only to the individual but to everyone else in the vicinity, are those that display racism, homophobia, ageism, sexism, and other absolute judgments about a whole class of people.

Mental health professionals make a very big deal out of challenging institutional racism and denigrating cultural diversity. We are required to complete multiple courses in these subjects, to study the ways that different groups of people react in varied ways to life circumstances, as well as the best ways to be helpful given these unique values and characteristics. In order to publish a journal article or present a program at a national conference, it's usually a requirement to include objectives related to diversity issues. Likewise, annual required continuing education programs often encompass aspects of cultural competency. In spite of this priority of our profession, a central tenet of our commitment to help those most in need, recently there has been a backlash launched by certain politicians, some of whom have literally outlawed teaching "critical race theory," cultural identity, ethnic studies, African American or Latinix studies, and even the historical legacy of racism.

With the best of intentions, the approaches in our field usually imply that each distinct cultural group requires slightly (or radically) different strategies that mesh with their values, priorities, and unique features. We are admonished to adapt our methods to fit the supposed vast differences evident in client populations. Thus Vietnamese Americans, Native Americans, or Ukrainian refugees would receive some form of specialized treatment best suited to their experiences. All of this sensitivity to how people are unique and different is quite useful, allowing us to better customize and personalize strategies. However, often left out of the mix are the ways our own hidden biases, disguised prejudices, and internalized racism and homophobia remain in place. After all, if prejudice is conceived as the prejudgment of individuals based on prior experience, then that is surely something very difficult to completely eradicate. The reality is that most of us still retain some semblance of our own prior attitudes and beliefs toward certain groups of people (or black pickup trucks) based on what we've observed and how we've been treated in the past.

Each of us is triggered in different ways, in spite of claims that we are perfectly neutral and unbiased. Imagine, for example, you encounter two people on the street, the first of whom is sporting the words, "Make America Great Again" on a red cap. Now tell me you don't have some visceral reaction to that person based on this single observation. A few minutes later, you run into someone wearing a white hat that reads, "Make America Kind Again." Now, once again, which one is a member of your "tribe," and which person might you be inclined to judge harshly versus generously? Certainly, one of these persons feels like a member of your "tribe," while the other is viewed as an outlier.

Whenever we hear someone say certain things, dress in a particular way, react to situations in particularly unusual ways, we cannot help but form strong opinions about the relative appropriateness of such behavior. Mostly these judgments reflect differences from what we might do or think is best. Are we proud of this rush to judgment based on limited or skewed data? Of course not. But the reality of subjective human experience is that it is almost always affected by prior events that shaped our attitudes and beliefs.

Counselors and psychotherapists are presumably among the *least* prejudiced, biased, or racist professionals considering that our essential job is to encounter each client in such a way that they feel respected and honored. Without such features within the relationship, we would not be able to accomplish very much. Yet in spite of *appearing* so accepting and nonjudgmental, there is a question about the extent to which we are being truly genuine, honest, and authentic. Does anyone, *ever*, reach a point of perfect unbiased, completely neutral, all-accepting attitudes and beliefs toward others, especially those who seem most different from what is most familiar? We are all works in progress.

Takeaways

If the bad news is that prejudices and biases can never be completely eliminated, that does not mean we cannot continuously challenge such beliefs that compromise our ability to better connect with diverse individuals. Regardless of our own cultural background, racial or religious identity, dominant language, or family origin, each of us has experienced times in our lives when we have been relegated to minority status, when others made assumptions about who we are based on how we look, dress, talk, or who we remind them of. It is precisely such encounters that remind us how important it is to continuously question and challenge the assumptions and judgments we make about others, not only when we are in helping roles but also in our daily lives.

This was a difficult subject for me to write about honestly and somewhat transparently, to own and admit my tendency to be so critical of others "not like me." I rail against injustices. I talk a good game about advocating on behalf of the dispossessed. I push agendas that provide greater opportunities for those who have been marginalized. I carefully engage in image management to come across as one of the "good guys" who stand against exploitation and oppression. But crawl inside my head, and you will hear a constant running commentary criticizing others as "stupid," "ill-informed," "clueless," or "inappropriate" because they do not act the way I would or embrace my most cherished beliefs and values.

It is by acknowledging our own hypocrisy, by honestly confronting lingering biases and prejudices, that we demonstrate to our clients, as well as to our families and friends, that our espoused beliefs are more than platitudes. It is only after acknowledging shortcomings that we are ever in a position to improve them.

Questions for Reflection or Discussion

1. The chapter discussed the idea that racism and prejudices are somewhat universal, based on maintaining power and sticking with those who are most similar to us in significant ways. If you were really honest with yourself (and others), which groups are you most inclined to admit holding biases or prejudices toward?

2. What has been a seminal experience in your life in which you experienced distressing prejudice, racism, or bias based on your appearance, culture, religion, or values?

3. What are some steps you could take to become more sensitive and responsive to people who are quite different from you in significant ways?

7

Processing Disappointments and Failures

You build on failure. You use it as a stepping stone. Close the door on the past. You don't try to forget the mistakes, but you don't dwell on it. You don't let it have any of your energy, or any of your time, or any of your space.

—Johnny Cash

Perceptions of Success and Failure

I was delivering the keynote speech at a professional conference to a huge audience numbering in the thousands. I put my nervousness aside as I walked on stage, thinking this could very well be one of my last performances. The pandemic had canceled most in-person conferences, virtually putting me out of a job since this had become my specialty. I had transferred my clinical skills to that of a public speaker, always searching for ways to apply what I know and understand to entertain and inform large audiences. As you well know, this is not very easy to do since most such presentations are tedious and put people to sleep with all the endless slides on the screen.

I had figured out that the best way to engage people in memorable ways was through dramatic stories that make people laugh *and* cry. If there is some emotional arousal activated, if I can introduce some novel or unpredictable features, if I can use media, photos, music, and especially dramatic enactments to make my points, I would increase the likelihood that the talk would have some enduring effects. It always struck me as a waste of time to do a modest, predictable program or talk that would likely be soon forgotten.

I took a few deep breaths and reminded myself that, given my advanced age and far more limited opportunities, this might be my last appearance for quite a while. I was highly motivated and intensely determined to make this my best speech ever! I know that sounds unrealistically ambitious, but I felt desperate to get back to work in front of groups after such a long hiatus. I wanted people to remember this talk if it was going to be my closing curtain call and final legacy. I thus decided to give myself permission to be more wild and crazy than usual, to push myself to the limit.

Sure enough, I was practically vibrating with energy and passion. Rather than just talking about things, I acted out stories on stage, at one point even rolling around on the floor to punctuate a point. I was relieved throughout the presentation to hear lots of laughter at the appropriate times, complete silence and stillness during moments of tenderness. When I looked out through the blinding stage lights, I could indeed see some people who were shedding tears. I felt even more emboldened and decided to up my game further, trying things I have never done before, saying things out loud that were intentionally provocative. I reassured myself that was indeed just about the best I could do. If this was to be my retirement, so be it: What a satisfying way to go out on top. Or so I told myself.

By the time I walked off stage to a standing ovation, I was euphoric. People walked up to me to confirm how awesome I was. Members of the audience wanted to give me hugs, shake my hand, take my photo, and have me sign copies of their books. I was absolutely delighted and proud of my overwhelming success.

Since the title of this chapter gives away its primary focus and theme, you can readily guess what is coming next—things were not necessarily what they seemed to be, at least with respect to the excellence of my speech as far as *everyone* was concerned. I seem to have overgeneralized based on the limited sample I chose to consider. Miscalculations and mis-interpretations of situations like this are often based on a lack of sophistication or complete understanding of what was really going on behind the scenes. During these times when technology has evolved so quickly, when distance-based communications exist on screens to replace showing up in person, there is indeed lots of room to miss the complexities and variations of audience experiences.

I am certainly an expert at working a room. Whether in a classroom, therapy session, or conference program, I am constantly scanning reactions, making adjustments, connecting with the listeners. But this Zoom or screen-based stuff? I do not fully understand what people are truly experiencing. I cannot see their eyes. I cannot read their nonverbal behavior. Heck, I can't even see them very well, especially the rest of their bodies. I had been told there were also hundreds of other people "attending" the program from all over the world, an exciting prospect but one I could not really grasp very well. Who were these other people that were invisible? Where were they in the world? What were they doing while watching the presen-tation? All of this data was lost to me.

Apparently, unknown to me and long forgotten, when people are often participating in a program online, they are most likely also multitasking. All the while they are watching and listening to the presentation, participants are also reading and replying to messages, munching on snacks, talking to roommates or family members, googling something of interest, planning their grocery list, or just taking a brief snooze. Let's just say that in such circumstances, the presenter has less command of the situation and the viewer's attention. So that was a clear miscalculation on my part to assume that one setting was equivalent to the others. Actually, if you think about it, *every* remote participant was in a completely different setting, space, environment, and context.

Second, and far more significant, is that I also forgot that during screen-based programs, the technology permits viewers to "chat" and send out public messages. In some cases, questions might be sent to the speaker to ask for elaboration, although most of the time people are inclined to just write spontaneous comments, the sorts of things they might ask the presenter in person after the talk is over. Of course, people are far more inclined to say things in a relatively anonymous chat that they would never say in person. I was mostly shielded from such dialogue because I was otherwise occupied, unable to see what people were writing.

I only learned much later that day, while I was still celebrating my glorious achievement, that things were not necessarily as I imagined them to be. Someone confessed to me that during the talk, a few people who were online (she wouldn't tell me how many) were writing the most scathing, critical, derogatory comments about me and what I was saying. A few were offended by my "expressive" language. A few others disagreed most vehemently with points I was emphasizing. Some were downright offended because I had made an offhand comment that remote learning just is not the same as attending in person; they might be roughly equivalent but they are hardly identical experiences. A few others were just plain rude and disrespectful (because they could get away with it without being held accountable—except for others who pushed back and told them they were inappropriate). The accumulative result of this phenomenon, about which I was unaware at the time, was that among the hundreds of people who were watching the program from afar, their experiences were thoroughly "polluted" by this small group that did not much like what I was doing and were not shy about saying so. I was also informed that at one point, a few people were so disrespectful in their comments that the organizer had to shut the chat feature down altogether.

Whatever elation and satisfaction I once felt came crashing down. Although I have always struggled with feeling inadequate and not being good enough, feeling like a failure throughout my life has been my cross to bear. Whenever I would read the participant or student evaluations after a lecture, presentation, or class, I would usually completely ignore the vast majority who enjoyed and profited from the program and instead home in on the few who thought I was a clueless fraud. Secretly I believed that *they* were really the ones who saw me clearly.

I have spent most of my career discussing this subject, including in several books about coming to terms with failure (Kottler & Balkin, 2020; Kottler & Blau, 1989; Kottler & Carlson, 2002; 2011; Kottler, 2022a), all of which emphasize that mistakes and disappointments in this job (or any job) are inevitable, and even incredibly useful to provide feedback on what we are doing that is not very helpful. Even though I know this stuff all too well, I still found myself failing to process my disappointment and shame that I so missed what was going on underneath the surface of my speech—at least for a few people. I was clearly engaged in a spectacular cognitive distortion by making absolute judgments about my performance, switching from one extreme of elation to the other of disappointment.

I write and talk about these themes constantly, admonishing practitioners to embrace their failures, learn from their mistakes, and own their imperfections so that they might grow as a result. Yet what had felt to me to have been an overwhelming success on stage now felt like an unforgivable lapse. And of course that is not exactly true: Just because a few people were unhappy does not mean that my performance was indeed a "failure," but that exemplifies how exaggerations, distortions, and perfectionism lead us (or at least me) to either become unforgiving of errors and miscalculations or else deny mistakes altogether. For so long throughout my career, nobody ever seemed to talk about screwing up or not knowing what they were doing most of the time (my default position). I always felt it was my role and responsibility to go in the opposite direction—to try to fearlessly and honestly acknowledge my foibles and limitations, no matter how uncomfortable it is to do so.

The Avoidance of Acknowledging Failures

Making mistakes or misjudgments is not only embarrassing but often gets us in trouble. Such lapses can be judged as evidence of incompetence, especially by beginners who are already feeling somewhat insecure about their abilities. We tend to bring up cases in supervision about which we are only a little uncertain and confused but sufficiently informed that we can respond adequately to queries and address concerns. Admitting that we absolutely bungled a session or acted in a less-than-stellar manner may hurt our standing. Even when we are not sure what's really going on (which is the usual state of affairs), we are expected to pretend otherwise.

For these reasons, and so many others, professionals in almost any field engage in image management, highlighting the things we do well and sweeping the mistakes under the rug. When things do go awry, we tend to blame factors that are outside of our control—toxic family dynamics, lack of resources, the client's lack of motivation, intrusive parents sabotaging progress, all the familiar excuses. When sessions are stalled, it's easy to blame the client as resistant, defensive, obstructive, or ambivalent about making changes. Even when it's acknowledged that progress is disappointing, it's not uncommon to interpret these setbacks as only temporary. Relief is just around the corner if you're sufficiently patient.

Another strategy to avoid acknowledging mistakes or failures is to define the outcomes in ways that let one off the hook. In a series of interviews in which we asked a few dozen famous theoreticians in the field their particular definitions of failure, the responses were all over the map (Kottler & Carlson, 2002). Some believed that failure occurs when therapists do not listen to their clients and instead follow their own agendas, while others said it relates more to being inflexible and refusing to make adjustments. Still others said that failure occurs most often when the practitioner is arrogant and overconfident or uses methods that are obsolete or not supported with evidence. Additional theorists instead referred to making invalid assumptions about what is going on in sessions, losing control of the countertransference issues, or being unable to establish a solid alliance. Finally, another theorist defined failure as "not knowing where you are going." Clearly, each of these particular conceptions reflects their own individual priorities, values, and preferences that are embedded in their approaches.

There are indeed many different reasons why things do not work out very well, often the result of the client's own unrealistic expectations, internal ambivalence, poor coping skills, or self-sabotaging personality traits. It is also true that a lack of a support system, sabotaging peer group, or enmeshed family structure can ensure that any progress will be blocked.

While some of these variables are somewhat out of our control, there are certainly other factors that relate directly to our own functioning. We may also hold unrealistic goals for what can be accomplished. Our own rigidity, arrogance, and narcissism may act to blind us to our foibles, making us unwilling to accept responsibility for our mistakes. Countertransference issues may capture our attention in such a way that we lose perspective, leading to misdiagnoses and poor clinical decisions. Finally, burnout, depletion of energy, and lack of self-care may contribute to increased errors in judgment.

Rather than attributing negative outcomes to either the client or the therapist, it's far more helpful to remember that *all* conflicts are really interactive effects in which both participants share responsibility for the unsatisfactory results. Perhaps there are incompatible personalities, the pace is too fast or slow, or the chosen treatment approach is just not all that appropriate in this situation.

Regardless of the particular cause and reasons for the failure, and who is most to blame, there is much to learn from such situations. It is during those instances when things go wrong that far more time and effort are devoted to figuring out what happened and why, as well as what could have been done differently. In many ways, we learn far more from our mistakes than we ever do from our successful encounters—but only if we are open to the lessons that are offered.

Exceptional therapeutic practitioners, similar to professionals in almost any field, intentionally and systematically process their mistakes, errors in judgment, invalid assumptions, and failures in such a manner that they do not repeat them—at least the same way. Several valuable questions might be considered in such circumstances, a kind of self-supervision protocol that might help us to uncover what went wrong and why, as well as the lessons that were learned as a result (see Table 7.1).

It is the last question in Table 7.1, what can be learned from the mistakes or miscalculations, that is a main theme of this book. One's attitudes about failure largely determine the extent to which further attention will be devoted to analyzing what went wrong and why. It is pretty evident that we often spend a lot more time thinking about our failures than our successes—and for very good reasons in that such ongoing reflections (if not excessive) provide valuable feedback regarding future actions, encourage greater flexibility, and foster increased experimentation and creativity. Perhaps most important of all, these mistakes teach us greater humility.

TABLE 7.1 **Protocol for Processing Failures**

What are the signs that therapy isn't working? How do I know that results are less than desirable?
Where was the turning point when things started slipping downward? Was there a critical incident or particular conversation, event, or situation that drastically changed the trajectory of progress?
What "benefits" or secondary gains are the client celebrating as a result of the failure? How does remaining stuck provide useful excuses for avoiding action?
How has the identified problem been defined in a way that it cannot be resolved? How might it be reframed in such a way that it creates other options?
How have I been attempting to disown responsibility for what is going on? What have I been assigning blame elsewhere?
What interventions have been most and least helpful? What have we been doing together that has been working best, and what should I probably stop doing because it consistently annoys the client?
What have I been expecting that is unrealistic or beyond the person's ability? What have I missed that would be useful to consider?
Who has an interest in sabotaging the treatment? Which significant others in the client's world are most supportive of the changes taking place, and which people have been attempting to actively undermine progress?
How have I been negligent? What have I ignored or minimized that might be having a negative impact on the relationship?
What in me is getting in the way of being more effective? Whether identified as countertransference, projective identification, compassion fatigue, or any other personal issues that are going on, how are they interfering with outcomes?
What can I learn from this to help me grow?

Takeaways

What are some of the benefits, lessons, and "gifts" that we might receive as a result of honest scrutiny of what went wrong? Obviously, reflecting back on one's mistakes leads to a deeper exploration of the interaction, hopefully highlighting critical points that could have been handled in alternative ways. This sort of internal processing can be extraordinarily constructive if the assessment results in improved effectiveness rather than harsh self-criticism. In addition to acknowledging self-perceived failures, it is also important to be forgiving of lapses just as we would advocate for our clients. This is especially the case with respect to the work that we do that involves a continuous recursive feedback loop, treating various failed or ineffective interventions as added data that would be incorporated into subsequent attempts. It is rare that an initial interpretation, reflection, or offering is enthusiastically accepted by clients—until such time that we make adjustments in light of additional input.

Failures are also known to become an impetus for increased innovation, creativity, and flexibility when solving problems. Failed attempts simply eliminate possibilities of what does not work, freeing up time and space to experiment with other alternatives. Tech geniuses like Bill Gates and Steve Jobs, for example, faced devastating disappointments in their initial efforts to launch favored ideas, yet persisted in their efforts in spite of continued obstacles. Jobs was even fired from his own company, a circumstance that he later attributed to the major breakthroughs that followed. He claimed it was the best thing that could have ever happened to him.

Well, nobody is really all that grateful they were rejected, dismissed, or otherwise failed miserably at something important to them, but such experiences can and do provide important life lessons if we are open to that feedback. After all, one definition of "failure" is that it's simply useful information about options that probably shouldn't be repeated in such situations. Most exceptional athletes, or performers in any domain, study their mistakes in such a way that they are less likely to repeat them. When composer Igor Stravinsky first premiered his new ballet *Rite of Spring* during the turn of the 20th century, the Parisian audience became so offended and upset, a riot broke out that had to be restrained by the police. Likewise, Jimi Hendrix and Elvis Presley were both booed off stage when they first performed. Yet such experiences only led them to refine their craft, although not necessarily abandoning their unique and novel musical visions.

In the context of the usual situations in which our efforts might prove less than optimal, practitioners tend to respond in two very different ways, either with frustration, disappointment, and discouragement or else improved resilience, patience, and tolerance for such temporary setbacks that will only improve with experience. This only enhances our humility and willingness to sometimes embrace a position of not knowing and not understanding, even though we feel so much pressure to demonstrate expertise and confidence.

After interviewing hundreds of expert and notable practitioners during the last few decades, it has become clear that the best among us metabolize their mistakes and failures by, first of all, reframing these experiences as only constructive feedback. They attempt to monitor their own sense of complacency and laziness during times when they are functioning on autopilot. They are also not afraid to admit their fallibility, to model their fallibility and willingness to own imperfections and limitations. This helps us to challenge our own unrealistic expectations and demands for perfectionism. It is only by accepting inevitable failures as a natural part of therapeutic work that we can learn these important lessons, upgrading our efforts in the future.

Questions for Reflection or Discussion

1. When you think about the failures in your life, which one bubbles to the surface as having been the most disappointing to you? In spite of the regrets and dissatisfaction, what important lessons did this experience teach you?

2. What is a recent experience in which you found yourself making excuses and pointing blame at others when things didn't go as expected?

3. Think of a time when you tried your absolute best to help someone who was struggling. You exhausted every option you could think of to assist this person, but nothing worked. How did you process that experience afterward so that you were better prepared the next time?

8

Coming to Terms With Grief and Loss

You will lose someone you can't live without, and your heart will be badly broken, and the bad news is that you never completely get over the loss of your beloved. But this is also the good news. They live forever in your broken heart that doesn't seal back up. And you come through. It's like having a broken leg that never heals perfectly—that still hurts when the weather gets cold, but you learn to dance with the limp.

—Anne Lamott

Haunted by Unacknowledged Grief

It was a typical evening during the pandemic, like hundreds of others that followed the same script. We had just finished dinner, cleaned up, and watched the news, after which we put on our favorite television show, maybe one of the best ever: *This Is Us*. It was about a somewhat dysfunctional family that was also quite loving and interesting in all kinds of amazing ways. There were three siblings who compete, fight, and support one another at various times, just like me and my brothers when we were younger. The characters were all relatable in different ways, each of whom offered important life lessons. In some ways, I thought about them as my "clients," even though I could not really do anything to help them. And they sure needed a lot of help coming to terms with their respective losses and grief. Each of the parents, children, and their spouses suffered unimaginable wounds, which is why some critics called the show a kind of "tragedy porn" because it so blatantly went after viewers' propensity to react emotionally to the characters' dilemmas and losses.

There was not an episode I had ever seen that I did not shed at least a few tears. I kept a tissue box close by because I just knew that something in the show was likely to take hold of me. The episode I had been watching that evening was a bit disappointing in some ways because it had gone off script. Rather than following the usual characters who had been left hanging from the previous week, this episode had gone back in time to explore one of the characters (Randall) who had been trying to connect to his past as an orphan, not having known his biological parents. It was kind of a low-energy but poignant hour, interesting but not as engaging as usual for me—until the penultimate scene.

The character, Randall, had recently rediscovered his father and was now trying to find out more about his mother who gave him up for adoption. He knew she had been a drug addict and was quite troubled, but he still wanted to find out more about who she was and why she had chosen to abandon him. By the time he tracked her down, he was told that she had died a few years earlier. It was too late to connect with her—at least in *this* world. In one of the final scenes, Randall discovered the place where his mother liked to spend time, and he literally waded into a lake to connect with her for the first time by speaking to her ghostly image that was reaching out to him. Just as he hoped, his mother confessed to him she was sorry for all the time they missed together.

I completely lost it. It so reminded me of my own mother who struggled with addictions. There was so little time we had together. She never really knew me as an adult. She was never alive to meet my son or know about my career achievements. I was never able to really understand her problems and disappointments. And although I so resented the burdens that she placed on me throughout my childhood, and felt some relief after she was gone, watching Randall trying to connect with his deceased mother was just too much for me. I began sobbing so deeply, so noisily, so completely that I was scaring myself and afraid of disturbing my wife who was looking at me with increasing concern. It was as if some creature had inhabited my body and was making these weird noises coming out of my mouth. I did not understand what was happening to me, but it felt like I was no longer in control of my body.

Afraid of upsetting my wife further, and concerned I might be having a stroke or heart attack, I fled outside. I was also feeling ashamed and a bit fearful that something so distressing was happening inside me without warning or immediate explanation. For several minutes, I just sat on the curb and then started howling like a crazy person. I could not stop. I just kept crying with such total abandon I could feel the hurt deep in my chest.

I started whispering to myself, an attempt at self-soothing, until I realized I wasn't speaking to myself at all; I was talking to my mother who I hadn't spoken to in 50 years. All that I remembered about her after all these years was how unhappy and troubled she always seemed. I could not remember how she felt or smelled, but I could vividly recall the scent of Scotch that was usually by her side. I blamed her for ruining my childhood, and I felt bad for both of us. Finally, she kicked me out of the house when I was 16 because I refused to follow her rules. The last straw had been when I refused to take out the garbage, a deliberate act of defiance that was intended to get me out of the house so I could live with my father instead. After that, until her death, my mother and I had a somewhat cordial but distant relationship.

Ever since I saw that show on television, I have been trying to remember what it felt like to hug my mother, nor could I recall any particularly interesting conversations we had together. I tried to recall any fun we had together—surely we must have since it was evident in early photos that we all appeared to be reasonably happy. Part of the losses must be the result of aging, but another part relates to the way my recollections are colored by my resentment.

While sitting on the curb sobbing uncontrollably, I found myself telling my mother how much I loved and missed her. I can feel the tears returning right now as I relive this experience that completely shocked me. It transformed me. I feel differently about her now. Where had been my compassion for her, my understanding? Why couldn't I give her a break?

It just seemed so strange, disturbing, and yet so interesting what happened. I felt such loss and pain in my heart. I wonder now if it changed how I think about her, how I talk about her. I wish so badly I could "know" her, spend time with her now, talk to her about things. I feel regret that I didn't—or couldn't—when I was younger and she was still alive. The last few years, before she died of cancer in her 40s, I do recall that we had a friendship of sorts, even if we didn't talk or see one another very often.

During this particularly emotional outpouring of grief and loss, I had been triggered vicariously by fictional characters in a television show. Yet this was not a completely unfamiliar experience to me, or any mental health professional, who is continuously exposed to the tragedies and heartbreaks of our clients. Even within our most dispassionate and protected boundaries in place, we are still sometimes profoundly affected by the stories we hear, not only because of empathy and caring but also because of the ways we might be reminded of our own losses.

Sorry for Your Loss

One of the most common reasons that people might consult our services is to help them to deal with devastating losses, especially of loved ones. The death of a parent, child, sibling, or partner is considered one of the most difficult adjustments in life, one that sometimes leads to ongoing depression, despair, and lingering grief. Some individuals never recover from such a loss; others may move on in their lives but with a constant ache of regret.

What can one possibly say to someone who has lost a loved one to disease, divorce, or disability? What is the best way to respond to someone who just lost the most important person in their life? One of the most frequent automatic replies, an ingrained habit by the general public, is to say something like, "I'm so sorry for your loss." This is both a sincere acknowledgment of the pain that must be felt, as well as an expression of commiseration. Most of the language chosen in such situations is euphemistic and carefully polite, as if mentioning actual death might send the grieving person into a panic. Thus people often prefer, "He's passed on," or "She's in a better place." Anything to avoid saying, "She's dead. Gone. Not coming back. And that's too bad."

Our clients have taught us over time that they often have very good reasons for holding onto their deceased family member. As long as they continue to mourn the loss they have experienced, it feels like they are honoring this person with all their love and care. They may enjoy other benefits as well, such as remaining stuck in a victim's role, gaining sympathy from others, or having a ready excuse to avoid unpleasant tasks or responsibilities ("Sorry, I'm in mourning"). Heck, well-wishers even bring food and ask what they can do to help.

There are many things we can do to assist such a grieving person to come to terms with their loss. There are often a lot of unresolved, confusing feelings associated with the death, perhaps lingering guilt, anger, regret, resentment, or emptiness. We try to provide clients time and space to talk about the deceased person, as well as to adjust to life afterward. We are sorry; they are sorry; everyone is sorry for the loss.

But here is the astounding breakthrough that we learn in our work with grief issues: People do not actually *lose* a loved one after they die (or "pass on" if you prefer). According to Neimeyer (2016, 2022) and other grief specialists, instead, we just negotiate a different kind of relationship with the loved one. After all, we did not actually "lose" that person, or even misplace them. They still exist in our memories. The person still speaks to us in our dreams and fantasies. We still hold conversations with them in our minds. They still live in all their glory in our spirits. It is just that we relate to them somewhat differently than we did previously when they occupied the same physical space.

This is just one of the many concepts we have learned that seem to turn everything upside down. Such an idea does not take away the feelings of grief over what happened, but it does offer a rather different way of processing the feelings that are much less devastating. *That* realization is the gift that keeps on giving long after a client is done with us. It is almost magical how the simplest of notions that we introduce to people can become utterly transformative for them—and for us. And this one is a biggie!

People sometimes remain stuck after losing someone or something important to them. So do we. One example of this that continues to haunt us long after the incident is over is when a client inexplicably never returns for a scheduled session. Everything seemed to be going quite well. Progress was steady. Mutually agreed goals were consistently met. The relationship seemed open, honest, and trustworthy. The alliance was solid. The client repeatedly expressed gratitude for what had been accomplished thus far. But then one day the appointment is canceled, and we never, ever learn what happened or why. Did the person feel like they were already satisfied, if not cured, and did not require any more sessions? If so, why would they not stick around to say something about that and at least say goodbye? And if they were unhappy about something, distressed or frustrated with the way sessions had been going, then why would they not mention something about that as well so adjustments could have been made? Instead, we are left with uncertainty, doubt, and confusion, all of which we must learn to endure. We will never learn the answers and must accept that, if not try to make sense of it. It is in so doing that we try to shrug off the mystery and move on to those who are still left within our care.

Therapists and counselors also experience their own grief and loss when clients end their sessions, whether suddenly or as part of the treatment plan. We do not talk about this very much, but the level of intimacy in some of our relationships approaches, if not exceeds, that of some of our closest friends. It is such a pleasure and honor to know some of our clients, to truly *know* them in deep and special ways since we are privy to their most precious secrets and sacred experiences. There are things they have told us that they have never revealed to anyone else. They have chosen to trust us with the most tender parts of their lives, a privilege that we take to heart. And when they are ready to move on, we may feel great pride and satisfaction, but also sadness, and yes, a sense of loss that we may never see them again.

Don't you wonder what ever happened to someone you helped and made such significant progress? Isn't there a bit of regret that we are no longer a part of their lives once they are launched? For anyone who has children who have grown into adolescence or beyond, there is a similar feeling of pride in their independence and autonomy but also grief and sadness over no longer knowing everything about what they think, feel, and desire. Instead, there is often escalating conflict in the relationship and increasing resentment about the ways we are so intrusive in their lives.

There was a character in a novel I read who once observed that if adolescents did not fight with their parents and become embroiled in conflicts with them, then they would never leave home. And then the world would end. That is likely not only true but a profound recognition of the ways that people develop their sense of self, their unique identity, their personal path, by declaring their independence from family and authority figures. This, in turn, requires the therapist, parent, or elder to also come to terms with the losses associated with this developmental transition.

Takeaways

Struggles, losses, suffering, and sacrifices are all an inevitable part of life; they are often the most memorable experiences, even if they involved considerable unpleasantness at the time. During the period in Sigmund Freud's life when he was struggling the most to gain credibility and support for his seminal ideas in spite of the brutal criticism from his colleagues, he disclosed in a letter to Carl Jung, "One day, in retrospect, the years of struggle will strike you as the most beautiful" (Freud, 1907/1992, p. 258). This may be a bit overromanticized, but it nevertheless highlights how we often look back on our darkest periods as those that were indeed the most interesting and transformative, even with the sometimes devastating losses that occurred.

Each of us has lost *something* in the past for which we still grieve. It may be the loss of innocence or confidence. Most of the time it is the result of missing someone we once loved (or *still* love). Whether as a consequence of death or divorce, estrangement or conflict, neglect or disappointment, there are close friends and family members with whom we are now out of touch. It is hard not to obsess about these forced or voluntary separations, nor to stop feeling sorry for ourselves about what was lost along the way. We often see extreme cases of this in which people become absolutely fixated on someone or something that was once important to them and is now completely gone, with little prospect of ever returning.

During those times when we grieve for those who are no longer with us or feel despair over the loss of a relationship or precious possession, we are so well prepared to counter these feelings with an assortment of skills and strategies that help us come to terms with situations out of our power to control. We learn that we may not be able to bring someone back from the grave, or even rehabilitate an estranged relationship, but we sure can make ourselves move on from this in a similar way that we talk to our clients about their own losses.

Questions for Reflection or Discussion

1. Who is someone in your past that you've "lost," either through death, relocation, or relational conflict, who still weighs heavily on your mind? If you so desired, how would you help yourself to move on from this and to let the unresolved feelings go?

2. Imagine a time in the future when someone very dear to you dies (or passes away if you prefer). How do you think you'd deal with that loss and grief given what you understand about the processes involved?

3. What do you think would be the absolutely most challenging cases to work with, given some of your own unresolved losses?

Dealing With Difficult People

Knowing your own darkness is the best method for dealing with the darknesses of other people.

—Carl Jung

Beyond Blaming and Complaining

I could see the blue vein in his forehead pulsing like the signal indicator on a car's dashboard. It should have been enough to warn me about the upcoming nuclear reaction, but I was not paying sufficient attention to him because I was searching for a quick exit. That an explosion was coming was no longer up for debate: There seemed to be nothing I could do to avoid the fallout.

I had joined this department several months earlier, having fled from a previous job with another unpredictable and toxic supervisor. This seemed to be my greatest burden in life, failing to do my due diligence regarding the morale and interpersonal relationships among staff. It was as if I could never escape these noxious work cultures, no matter how many times I relocated and quit jobs. This time, however, I was not the target of this narcissistic, abusive, controlling, power-hungry individual who resembled a certain former president in his temper tantrums.

Clyde (as I'll refer to him) was volatile, unpredictable, and inclined toward rage when something upset him—and almost *everything* upset him if it was not what he preferred or expected. His default position when surprised or disappointed by anything was to lash out at anyone who was nearby, regardless of their role in the predicament. I once overheard him brag that he had made every female member of our department cry at one time or another. He was especially proud of that achievement.

I was quite familiar with the reminder from 12 Step support groups about allowing someone "to live rent-free in your head." I had invited this guy to homestead rather permanently in an apparently unoccupied space in my brain. I railed against him in my mind. I complained to myself, and anyone else who would listen, about his inappropriate behavior. He would scream at staff whenever the urge struck him, but so far he'd avoided a direct attack on me. Maybe he was a little uncertain or afraid of how I might react. That would change.

I was sitting in my office catching up on paperwork when I was startled by some papers that were thrown onto my desk. I looked up and could see that little blue vein in action: "Warning. Warning. Impending explosion!" Sure enough, my supervisor's beet-red face and aggressive posture signaled he was about to lose control. Again.

"What the fuck is this?" he screamed at me, pointing to the papers that were spread on the desk, a few sheets having fallen on the floor. I was so startled by this intrusion, I opened my mouth but nothing came out. I do not think anyone had actually screamed at me since I was a kid, so I was completely at a loss. Finally, after taking a deep breath, I scanned the papers and saw they were phone records.

"Excuse me?" I finally replied, not really feeling all that excusable. "Ah, what's this?"

"Phone records you dumb shit!" he yelled back even though he was standing a few feet away. I could hear other office doors closing once the staff around me realized that we were now in "Defcon 4."

So, why was he showing me phone records, I wondered? Once Clyde noticed my confused look, he pointed to one of the sheets. "See? See all these long-distance phone calls?"

"Ah, yeah, I guess so," I answered in a timid voice, disappointed that I was being so deferential to this crazy person.

"Well," he explained, crossing his arms to demonstrate his authority and power, "*you* made most of these phone calls, hundreds of dollars in long-distance charges." This was when long-distance calls on landlines were rather pricey.

"Yes, that is probably true," I admitted. "Remember, you asked me to follow up on our alumni to conduct a survey for our next accreditation visit?"

There was a long silence after that. He looked around my office as if searching for someone else to blame for his impulsive explosion. "Oh," he said. "I forgot. Sorry about that."

Of course, he was not sorry at all. This was the way he treated almost everyone, at least those with whom he could get away with it.

Clyde, or various other incarnations of him, have been my nemesis throughout most of my life, and the reason why I had been so unsatisfied in several jobs. I just have a very low tolerance for being around mean people. I have trouble brushing off their annoying behavior. I become indignant at their abuse. While others around me seem to have found ways to either ignore or forgive abusive outbursts, I seem incapable of that. Or probably just unwilling, given the injustice of it all.

What surprises me most about this is that I am such an expert at diffusing conflicts when they belong to others. I sometimes actually enjoy the drama of interpersonal tension because it so often leads to breakthroughs. Like most other practitioners, I am highly skilled at working through such intense encounters. If a client loses control and starts acting out or going after me, I know how to depersonalize the situation, remain calm, avoid defensiveness, and allow the process to unfold. So, here is the question that plagues me: Why have I been so timid and unprepared to handle interactions with difficult people in my daily life? Why do I let certain individuals get underneath my skin? Why do I give them so much power and control, if not during our interactions, then when I obsess about them afterward? They disrupt my sleep and invade my fantasies.

You'd think with all my training and preparation, all my experience working through conflicts with the most difficult clients imaginable, sporting all kinds of personality disorders, manipulative games, and dysfunctional behaviors, I would also be pretty good at dealing with frustrating people outside of work. But I tend to take things *way* too personally. I hold unrealistic standards and expectations for how I believe others should act—and when they do not comply with these norms, I become indignant. Naturally, just like my clients, I usually complain about the ways I have been treated and then blame others for my plight—most often the person I believe is an abusive bully because I do not understand how anyone can treat others with such disrespect.

Processing Difficult Counseling Relationships

When making sense of why clients (or anyone else) may behave in ways that are less than cooperative, we often begin with an analysis of the underlying benefits and reasons for these actions. Of course, there is a motive behind such behavior even if it seems, at first, to be inscrutable. All behavior persists because it is somehow useful or rewarded in some way. These benefits are often referred to as "secondary gains" and reveal the agenda that may be operating beyond the person's awareness. Such a phenomenon was first identified by hospital staff when they noticed that certain patients seem to revel in their "sick" role, refusing to improve in spite of no medical reason for languishing in bed. Looking closer, the staff noticed they appeared to "enjoy" all the attention they were getting. They seemed to like complaining a lot, using this as an excuse for getting out of any task or activity that was not to their liking: "Gee, I wish I could do that, but as you can see, I'm still in a bad way. Maybe after I recover—if I ever do." Such a response may also provide lots of sympathy and additional aid.

Within our own domain, we also notice the ways that certain clients seem to revel in their misery, using their chronic depression, anxiety, or dysfunctional behavior as an excuse for getting out of things they do not wish to do. Our job is to help them to uncover these benefits, making them far more explicit since it is hard to get away with acting in these ways once you realize what you are really doing. In a sense, we "ruin" their favored strategy since it only works when they can at least pretend they do not realize how they are acting.

We are talking about individuals who engage in consistently annoying, disruptive, and seemingly self-sabotaging actions. The client says she wants closer intimacy with her partner but then does things that push him away. Someone else declares that he would like to become more self-sufficient but then appears to do everything possible to remain enmeshed and codependent within his family. Another client frequently undermines progress in sessions by showing up late or forgetting appointments altogether. Still another refuses to talk much at all, just sits in the chair scowling with arms folded, daring the therapist to try to break through. In these cases, and so many others, it seems bewildering that people would decide to ask for help and then do everything possible to make certain it is not very useful. Of course, such a *conscious* decision is never actually made since processes are taking over that have developed precisely because they are hidden or disguised.

One useful idea counteracts such client resistance and obstructiveness by decoding the mysterious reasons why anyone engages in behavior that doesn't seem to be in their best interest. Such an exploration usually begins by wondering how this behavior is actually useful and functional for this person. It's indeed interesting to speculate about what benefits this person is "enjoying" as a result of remaining stuck and helpless.

In therapeutic groups, it is fun to bring this into the open for collective discussion and brainstorming: "It seems that Mika keeps ending up in these dead-end relationships, almost as if she does it on purpose and ends up hurt once again. When we asked her what she really gets out of this habit, all she could do was shrug, denying that there could possibly be any benefit to her. Let's see if we can help her by listing some of the payoffs of being in dead-end relationships. Surely, there must be something going on or Mika wouldn't keep making the same mistake over and over."

If you try to answer the questions for yourself, it might occur to you, as it did to members of this group, that Mika may actually be afraid of real intimacy in spite of what she claims. As long as she picks partners who seem incapable of connecting with her, she can hold onto the illusion that none of this is really her fault. She can always blame others for their inadequacy instead of looking at her own ambivalence and fears. It may also be the case that she may be enjoying the role of a victim with the sympathy and attention she gets from others. Since she is frequently recovering from a romantic breakup, she has a great excuse to avoid doing other things that are annoying. There are many other possibilities as well, each of which is designed to maintain the status quo. In spite of what many people claim, it is so much easier to remain stuck than it is to invest hard work in changing and the even more challenging tasks of maintaining that progress in the face of potential relapses.

When digging into the origins of someone's ongoing resistant and difficult behavior, a few common themes are usually identified. First, such patterns allow clients (and others) to continuously procrastinate, put off action, and avoid doing new things that are best avoided. They maintain the status quo at all costs. The person may be miserable and dissatisfied but at least there are no surprises. In addition, the person can avoid responsibility for the plight, blame others, and claim that it is other people's fault if only *they* would act differently. They revel in their sense of power and perverse control in that they can sabotage things on their own terms. Finally, they get to feel like victims and solicit sympathy and attention for their predicament. With all of these potential "benefits," it is no wonder that it is sometimes so difficult to promote lasting changes.

Who Is Really Difficult Anyway?

In addition to understanding the particular reasons why a client appears difficult or uncooperative, it is also important to acknowledge that we do not all necessarily agree about who qualifies as a member of this challenging group. There is not even necessarily a consensus about how to even define what it means for someone to be "difficult" or "resistant." It is all in the eye of the beholder.

When dozens of famous theorists were asked to describe what it meant to be "uncooperative" or "difficult" in sessions, their responses were all over the place and often pointed more toward the practitioner's behavior rather than to that of the clients themselves (Kottler, 1992; Kottler & Carlson, 2002). Arnold Lazarus (multimodal therapy) mentioned cases when people just did not listen, stubbornly following their own agendas. Michele Wiener-Davis (solution-focused therapy) said it is when people just keep making the same mistakes over and over again even though it's clear that these choices are not working. John Norcross (integrative therapy) agreed that inflexibility and reluctance to make adjustments not only lead to client disappointment but also contribute most to consistent therapist failures. William Glasser (reality therapy) believed that therapists actually make their clients difficult through their own arrogance, narcissism, and overconfidence. Susan Johnson (emotionally focused therapy) pointed instead to a failed alliance that compromised trust and cooperation. Each and every prominent figure had a slightly different reason to explain why people become resistant, almost always the result of some interactive effects.

Although many practitioners would certainly nominate clients who display florid symptoms of borderline personality disorder, or who are seriously addicted to drugs and do not see that as much of a problem, there are also a number of personal preferences. Some clinicians actually enjoy working with belligerent adolescents, argumentative couples, or narcissistic personalities and find "ordinary" adjustment reactions to be rather uninspired cases to treat. Nevertheless, most clinicians might agree that we are most challenged when the people we are trying to help have (1) extremely unrealistic expectations for possible outcomes, (2) unconscious desires toward self-sabotage, (3) poor motivation to actually initiate any changes in their lives, (4) limited capacity for insight because of cognitive dysfunctions or other organic factors, and (5) self-destructive personality traits (rigidity, negativity, impulsivity, toxicity).

In another sense, however, there really are no so-called difficult clients, only those who cooperate in ways that are not exactly to our liking. Everyone, even those who are consistently annoying and obstructive, are still just doing the best they can under the circumstances. They may push back against our efforts because they just are not ready yet to make the moves we think are so urgent and necessary. It is for this reason that it could be said there really are no "difficult" clients, only difficult therapists who are unwilling or unable to demonstrate the patience, flexibility, and responsiveness that are necessary to meet people where they are, not where we wish them to be.

Takeaways

Just as we repeatedly urge resistant clients to assume greater responsibility for their lives, we must do the same when in the middle of our own interpersonal conflicts and interactions with difficult people. We have all the tools at our disposal to minimize, if not avoid, getting sucked into such soul-destroying skirmishes. We teach others to focus on the things that are within our power to control—which is our own behavior and the ways we process what is happening.

Whenever we find ourselves stuck at an impasse, unable to alter the nature of a frustrating relationship, we must resist the temptation to focus on and talk about the other person. This makes perfect sense but is really hard to do because it is often so easy to point to the peculiar, annoying, disruptive things that others do. We are faced with situations every day that include tailgaters, complainers, loud talkers, entitled narcissists, screaming babies, racist assholes, rude and disrespectful strangers, and we may become easily triggered by such behavior, sometimes losing control. And yet we have all the tools at our disposal to remind ourselves that whereas we cannot control other people's behavior, we sure can manage more level and appropriate responses to it.

Most conflicts, without exception, involve contributions from *both* parties. Once reminded of this reality, we are encouraged to wonder what assumptions we are making about other people that might not be valid or what we are doing persistently that is only making things worse. Then there are the ways we might be overreacting to situations as a result of personal issues being reminded of someone else who this person seems to resemble. In addition, what expectations are we demanding of others that they may be unwilling or unable to meet?

As much as all this might make sense and seem familiar as the process by which we work through difficulties in supervision about a case, it is just so challenging to put this into practice in our own lives. The truth is that, on some level, it is fun to complain about others, to solicit support and sympathy from others, to commiserate about how frustrating and annoying others can be (or seem). It takes tremendous effort to step back and apply to our own lives that which we teach to others.

Questions for Reflection or Discussion

1. If you were attending sessions, how would you predict that you would be most difficult as a client, given some ambivalence you might feel about making needed changes?

2. What sort of person would be the most difficult client for you to work with in sessions?

3. Describe a difficult relationship that you are currently experiencing in your life, with a colleague, supervisor, friend, or partner. Given what you know and understand about the nature of interactive effects within interpersonal conflicts, what is *your* role in making things considerably worse?

Metabolizing Stress, Adversity, and Trauma

10

No experience is a cause of success or failure. We do not suffer from the shock of our experiences, so-called trauma—but we make out of them just what suits our purposes.

—Alfred Adler

Cascade of Traumas

I consider myself somewhat of an expert on trauma and post-traumatic stress reactions. I have spent most of my working life helping immigrants and refugees come to terms with their losses after escaping violence, chaos, and oppression in their home countries. Many of them have been subjected to torture or unimaginable abuse. Some of them have spent years in camps or shelters, separated from their families. They have lost their homes, most of their possessions, even their core identities. They are now relegated to the absolute bottom of economic prosperity, even if they once enjoyed status as professionals. They are subjected to hate-filled discrimination and told to go back to where they came from.

You would think that with all my experience helping these desperate people come to terms with their life catastrophes I would be highly skilled at dealing with my own chronic stressors or traumatic events. Whereas that has mostly been the case throughout my life, although more recently things have seemed to fall apart after a series of accumulative events that left me helpless and gasping for breath. Even worse than all the disruptive symptoms and despair has been feeling that I am a complete hypocrite for being unable to help myself—or ask for help from others. I suppose I can only admit this now after I have (mostly) recovered.

In 2015 there was a 7.8 earthquake in Nepal that killed tens of thousands of people. I arrived in Kathmandu a few days later with a trauma team composed of a few friends who had training in nursing, pharmacy, and hospital administration, and even a Navy SEAL medic. The very day we arrived, there was a second 7.6 earthquake that, in some ways, was even more devastating: all the buildings that had been on the verge of crumbling now collapsed. Bodies were buried under the rubble. Roads and pathways in the Himalayas were impassable. There were no medical or rescue services. We were the only team that had been allowed into the country when the government shut down—and to say we were "allowed" is a misnomer since we actually snuck into the country since there were no officials at the airport when we arrived with nine duffel bags filled with medical supplies.

There was no clean water, no safe housing, and no prospect of immediate assistance. The monsoon rains had begun. Government officials went into hiding, leaving the population to fend for itself. Then the aftershocks began—a dozen each day—making it impossible to spend time inside a shelter or to sleep at night. There was devastation, chaos, and suffering everywhere. Even years later, I still have disturbing images of the crushed bodies and horrific injuries. Mostly, I still feel the terror after weeks of isolation and uncertainty about whether I would ever manage to escape.

After several weeks of working to help restore basic services and treat the injured, I returned home to resume my normal routines and responsibilities that had been put on hold. Our young granddaughters were spending the night with us when, close to midnight, there was an explosion in the house under construction that was adjoining our home. The fire raged through our bedroom windows, allowing us just a few precious minutes to escape with whatever we could take on the way out the door. I managed to grab my 3-year-old granddaughter in one arm and my laptop in the other. I did not have time to put on shoes.

It is interesting to me, and somewhat bizarre, that I *still* feel the cobblestones of our street on the bottom of my feet. We lost most of our possessions and the house was destroyed, but the most alarming effects took place inside my own agitated mind. I began to think about, then obsess over, how close we came to losing our granddaughters in the tragedy. We survived, but I began to fantasize about how close I came to having to tell my son that I "lost" his mother and children. This fantasy began to grow as the days continued, eventually taking over my whole being. I just could not get the idea out of my mind, no matter what I tried—talking to friends, exhausting myself through exercise, practicing mindfulness. I had thoughts of suicide, even though I knew I could never bring myself to consider such a "selfish" escape that would so harm everyone else I loved. Instead, I began to plan my disappearance. I know this sounds irrational, if not downright crazy, but hey, I wasn't thinking very clearly. I even researched online "how to disappear" and leave my identity behind so nobody would ever find me again. Of course, none of this made sense, and, eventually after several months, I once again (mostly) recovered. But as I well understood, traumatic incidents are often accumulative.

I had only recently moved to Houston after retiring from full-time teaching in California, so I did not have much in the way of a support system beyond my family. My job at the medical center was interesting but I never really had much opportunity to meet and interact with colleagues, all psychiatrists who seemed overworked and overwhelmed in their own lives. Then Hurricane Harvey destroyed the city. This time, the origins of my stress were not the result of my own loss (our house survived the torrential rain and flood after being rebuilt) but a consequence of the stories I heard from the patients I was treating at the convention center that was converted into a homeless shelter harboring tens of thousands of displaced residents.

This narrow escape from the flood would last only until the notorious "freeze" that brought temperatures in this tropical region into the teens. The energy grid broke down, leaving us with no heat, no water, no means to flush toilets or prepare food. The streets were too icy to drive, or even walk. There was no mobile phone access, no internet signal, no news available without electricity. We put on all our winter clothes and lay in bed in the dark for almost a week. This seemed to hit me worst of all, perhaps because it seemed like the last straw, like the world was ending. Given the news about all the political corruption, demise of democracy, and election of autocratic leaders around the world, it really did seem like all hope was lost. It seemed as if the 10 historical plagues of Egypt were being reincarnated in Houston. At least thus far, we'd managed to escape locusts, boils, and eternal darkness.

Then the pandemic hit. There were so many other losses one after another, leaving me reeling. My father died. My best friend died. I lost all my work when in-person conferences ceased altogether. Maybe worst of all was that with so much discretionary time on my hands, I spent *way* too much of my attention focused on the state of political chaos that was taking over the country. I did not recognize America any longer and felt such a loss of faith in so many of my fellow citizens who seemed willing to support and embolden policies of oppression and bald-faced lies.

On top of all this, I turned 70 years old and, seemingly all of a sudden, felt even more mortal. It felt like I was not only "retired" but suddenly invisible. My health and fitness may have still been quite extraordinary, but that did not change the reality that my life span was now quite limited. How much time do I have left? Another decade? Another year? Maybe this is my last day? I have lost so many friends and family members much younger than me. Heck, I've already survived my mother by 20 years.

As if this has not been enough trauma and suffering to meet my allocated quota, it is as if fate has a sense of perverse humor, announcing: "You ain't quite done yet!" I had decided to take a week off from my writing routine on this project after completing the previous chapter. I decided I had earned a break to go skiing, one of my absolute favorite things to do. There had been a huge dump of fresh powder and, in spite of my age, I was carving turns better than ever. It was glorious! Then disaster struck once again: a freak accident that resulted in a fractured leg and torn anterior cruciate ligament (ACL). The agony. The frustration. The injustice. The dang inconvenience of it all, limited to crutches and wondering if I will ever again resume the athletic activities that so define my life.

I mention all this not to gain sympathy but rather to highlight that in spite of all my knowledge and experience dealing with trauma, I had reached my limit in managing my own life challenges. I do not want to make excuses for this even as I claimed earlier that my reactions were completely understandable given the numerous hits I took, one after another. I wish to acknowledge that I did not really learn the lessons that I use to help others to metabolize their own trauma and stressors. Instead, I felt sorry for myself. I lapsed into feelings of helplessness and depression. Surprisingly, I now feel (almost) grateful to have survived these events since I have learned so much personally about what I have taught to others. It is one thing to spout our favorite therapeutic admonishments to clients and quite another to truly "know" them intimately in our own lives. For most of us, there will come a time when it seems like everything we know and take for granted will appear to have changed in unanticipated ways, testing the limits of what we are capable of handling. Sometimes we learn these lessons directly, but just as often we discover them via the growth and development of our clients.

Growth From Vicarious Trauma

It is so interesting what we learn from our clients about all the different ways that people respond to adversity. We see a fair number of people who completely fall apart after facing difficulties, which is not really all that surprising. What is even more fascinating are those who somehow manage to take tragic experiences in stride, or even rise to the occasion and discover something new and amazing about themselves. Even more astounding are the ways that a family or group can be exposed to identical traumatic circumstances and yet become affected in such different ways, depending on their level of adaptation.

It has been estimated that somewhere between half and two thirds of all adults will experience some form of trauma during their lifetime. Whether the result of combat, catastrophic natural disaster, debilitating chronic disease, loss of loved one, neglect, abuse, or act of violence, the residual effects can continue unabated for many months or years (or a lifetime). We are hardly immune from such tragic or challenging life experiences. In some ways, we are exposed to even more than our fair share of accumulative stress and trauma since our job requires us to hear such stories vicariously almost every hour of the day. Surely these narratives sometimes penetrate our psyche, wear down our resistance, and sometimes make us more vulnerable to our own daily stressors. That, in fact, is what often leads to burnout and compassion fatigue.

It is surprising to realize how we can be so profoundly affected by listening to the trials and tribulations of someone else who is suffering. Yet our brains are uniquely equipped to treat the stories we hear as just as real as anything we might actually experience directly. Of course, that explains the appeal of dramatic films, novels, plays, and other media that arouse such strong emotional reactions, sometimes to the point that they result in lingering nightmares. In a later chapter, we will explore more about this phenomenon of a "storied brain." For now, we likely agree that some of the things that clients talk about during sessions are far more captivating, alluring, interesting, arousing, and at times disturbing than anything we would ever watch on a screen or read in a book. We are *there*, in the room, utterly captivated, sometimes feeling so privileged and honored that we are allowed to be present and hear the sacred tales.

Sometimes we become severely "wounded" from the things that we hear and experience in the room. People share secrets that are sometimes quite disturbing; others might be best kept to themselves. But we become the receptacles for anything or everything they wish to dump on us and allow us to sort out the garbage. That is one reason why we might be inclined to seek our own help to work through the material, whether in supervision or our own counseling sessions.

It is much less acknowledged and understood how exposure to the plight of others during helping efforts can also lead to major personal transformations. We talk a lot about post-traumatic growth in the context of how resilience and hardiness can develop as a result of surviving and flourishing during times of adversity. This would be no less true in the case of mental health professionals who devote their lives to assisting others during their trauma recoveries. Each story we hear reveals its own unique features of suffering, as well as attempts at recovery.

It is hardly unusual to find oneself reeling long afterward with residual effects from a traumatic narrative that was particularly disturbing, perhaps featuring acts of violence, sexual assault, fatal health issues, or a catastrophic natural disaster. If the relationship with a client was especially close and intimate, the vicarious effects can become even more potent. It is within the throes of this self-reflection that many gifts are potentially revealed, offering important lessons for dealing with struggles in the future. It is not uncommon for practitioners to realize that when some of their sessions are over, they also have a lot more work to do processing what occurred. Sometimes it is about feeling greater appreciation for one's own relatively privileged, comfortable life.

As any self-respecting Buddhist, masochist, or endurance athlete will tell you, there is often potential value in suffering. Our culture may be pain avoidant at all costs, relying on drugs, alcohol, and distractions to dull any discomfort, but there are also important lessons and learning that can accrue from traumatic or painful experiences, depending on how they are processed. After all, people sometimes intentionally choose to undergo deliberate suffering when they join climbing expeditions—or for that matter when they seek to undergo psychotherapy with all the uncomfortable things likely to become stirred up. They do so for some greater good that appears worth the price of a certain amount of pain, inconvenience, and annoyance. People also choose to make sacrifices, undergo painful procedures or rituals, or even subject themselves to daily suffering when they participate in exercise routines or sometimes continue to show up at a job that is less than fulfilling.

It is inevitable, if not a certainty, that sometime in life there will be bouts of suffering to endure—and hopefully to manage effectively. This may not necessarily lead to a "cure" or banishing of the pain as much as reaching a point where the condition or situation can be better tolerated and understood. Existential philosophers like Friedrich Nietzsche were fond of pointing out that "to live is to suffer" and yet also "to survive is to find some meaning in the suffering." That, of course, is what we often do for a living

Takeaways

There is an interesting historical legacy among some of the most prominent figures in the field, many of whom struggled with extreme adversity, emotional and health difficulties, and other life challenges from which they eventually recovered, or at least learned to adapt to them. Sigmund Freud had a host of mental health issues related to his assortment of psychosomatic complaints, phobias, fears of death, addiction to cocaine, and even his insistence on smoking his infernal cigars long after his jaw was removed because of cancer. He eventually took his own life with self-administered morphine because of the intolerable pain. Alfred Adler barely survived childhood with his pneumonia, poor eyesight, and feelings of inferiority—which became one of the foundations of his theories. William James, the first "official" psychologist, likely set a record for the most distinct personal problems that included both vision and hearing problems, stomach ailments, chronic back spasms, and repeated failures as a painter, medical student, and anthropologist. All the while his brother, Henry James, became one of the world's most notable writers. Poor William became so depressed and despondent that he seriously considered suicide. Each of these seriously wounded individuals, who struggled mightily with their own traumas, losses, and disappointments, somehow found a way to convert their suffering into constructive action. These influential theorists have since become models for us in the ways we might capitalize on our own failings, disappointments, and losses for some greater good.

After all, we are experts at stress management. We command extensive knowledge of the latest research on the mechanisms of anxiety and other related mental disorders. We know the differences between "helpful" stress (a.k.a. *eustress*) that improves performance in certain situations, and the other sort that wreaks havoc within our endocrine and nervous systems. This is just one of several important insights that help us to better understand how to manage life challenges, whether among our clients or in our own lives.

Good and bad stress. We understand how some types of stress are nature's way of ramping up our systems to optimize functioning, whether in athletic competition or daily life when facing adversity or dangers. It represents both a psychological and physiological reaction to either real or imagined threats. In mild doses it provides a boost of hormones, blood, and oxygen flow, as well as increased focus and concentration that actually improves performance: we become stronger, faster, more decisive. In that sense, it is a type of survival mechanism that is designed to increase awareness of danger and kick in all the body's resources for protection.

It is about self-control. Like most things in life, it is not really necessary to *be* in control; you just have to *feel* that way. Many things are way beyond your power to influence them. You are required to take certain classes that you would rather skip altogether. You have no influence whatsoever over the weather, economy, or even most people's behavior. Yet personal habits, routines, structures that have been put in place may help to organize behavior and provide a semblance of control, but they are still subject to the whims and influences of other forces. We teach self-control to others and have thus learned how important it is to strengthen our own abilities.

Most stress is self-inflicted. Although we might be inclined to attribute negative reactions to the effects of trauma, conflict, or disasters, we know that so much depends on how we process them in our minds, and what we tell ourselves about what they mean. Whether we are talking about sports performance, academic achievement, or public speaking, there are vast differences between what people think to themselves before, during, and afterward. Once again, we teach people to engage in "positive appraisals" whenever possible, to choose an attitude that capitalizes on learning and growth rather than the inevitable annoyances and discomforts that are usually associated with novel experiences for which we are not fully prepared.

Creating meaning. We are well aware of how people are able to tolerate all kinds of suffering, stress, and life difficulties, as long as it seems to have some larger purpose and ultimate good. After all, what is aerobic exercise (running, swimming, cycling, etc.) except a form of self-inflicted suffering for some greater good? Watch someone strenuously working out or running along the side of the road; they are likely grimacing, not smiling with joy (even with the "runner's high"). We can put up with all kinds of annoyances and inconveniences if we believe they are for some worthwhile purpose, whether standing in a crowded, noisy, stressful line for coffee; driving in rush hour traffic to get somewhere important; or putting up with the stress associated with additional education for some ultimate prize at the end—plus all the great things you learn about yourself, others, and the world at large.

Questions for Reflection or Discussion

1. At some point in your life, you must have experienced some major traumatic, or at least harrowing, experience, something that still sticks with you today. How have you been aware that this incident has continued to affect you?

2. What have been some of the important lessons and growth that you've experienced as a result of surviving some adversity?

3. Spending time with people who share their stories of tragedy, trauma, disaster, and loss can have accumulative effects over time, for better or worse. What are some of the ways you've been impacted vicariously as a result of hearing and holding such narratives?

11

Assessing and Diagnosing Difficulties

Before you diagnose yourself with depression or low self-esteem, first make sure that you are not, in fact, just surrounding yourself with assholes.

—William Gibson

Questioning Standard Systems

It became one of the most consistent pleasures in life after taking courses in psychopathology and psychodiagnosis. All of a sudden I had the means by which to make sense of behavior that had long been incomprehensible. At the very least, I now had at my disposal a bunch of fancy-sounding names to describe strange behavior I witnessed: "mood dysregulation disorder," "schizoaffective disorder," "histrionic personality." Finally, I had the means by which to label certain annoying relatives or acquaintances.

Once I began seeing clients and was required to assign a diagnosis for each case, I became increasingly concerned about the shame associated with these categorical labels. They all sounded so dismal and discouraging, especially those like impulse disorders or certain personality configurations because they seemed impervious to change. That is why my absolute favorite choice was "adjustment reaction with mixed emotional features" because it seemed to cover almost *anything* I would ever encounter. I loved how these words rolled off my tongue, making me sound smart and knowledgeable about such things that were mysteries to others. Maybe I could not very well explain how and why these conditions exist, but I could insert them into conversations to demonstrate my new specialized training. For perhaps the first time in my life, I felt like I had been provided with a window into a world of secret knowledge that might very well change almost everything for me.

Like most beginners, I began applying my new assessment skills to members of my own family and peer group, fascinated by the enhanced level of understanding of why certain people close to me seemed to struggle so much. One of my siblings had always been moody and overemotional, but now I realized he had bipolar disorder. My mother seemed sad and unhappy most of her life, but now I realized she had been clinically depressed although I couldn't figure out the distinction yet between so-called major depression and "dysthymia." My grandmother's behavior appeared erratic at times until I discovered that she may have been abusing prescription medications, displaying an addiction disorder. Then I turned my diagnostic attention to a few friends, classmates, and even a professor or two who seemed rather bizarre to me. Well, this might be familiar to anyone who has completed such coursework.

Most of my life, I've been somewhat obsessed with my own mental (in)stability. One of the first papers I ever wrote in an advanced psychopathology course as an undergraduate was called "History of Abnormal Behavior." It was a lengthy treatise about people throughout history who got into a lot of trouble because they were "different" from everybody else. They ended up in mental institutions, prisons, or exiled to foreign lands, a destination that I fully expected to end up in someday. I believed myself to hold some kind of "alien" status. I did not seem to think in the same manner that others did. I understand now, of course, that almost *everyone* in their early 20s believes themselves to be totally unique, but I seriously wondered at the time whether I was doomed to develop eventual mental illness because I seemed so moody. It is no surprise that I spent way too much time always trying to diagnose myself and figure out which category of craziness I belonged to.

Let's just say I was convinced there was something seriously wrong with me and that I had best try to hide my true self or I would never have any friends or a partner. Of course, almost everyone who takes these classes becomes obsessed with how these labels might be (mis)applied to anyone they encounter. But then I had a major change of heart and mind. It seemed to me that not everyone could easily be cataloged into one of these finite classifications. I started to resent labeling people based on just one aspect of their behavior. I found myself in trouble at times pushing back against supervisors and faculty who insisted I provide names for what I was observing in my clients' behaviors.

"But it's more complicated than that!" I would try to explain. "He's *more* than just his symptoms of panic disorder," I would insist. I realized that I was not just explicating a more nuanced diagnostic process that would not dehumanize my clients, but I was also defending my own unique proclivities that did not seem to fit into neat little boxes. I did not like how it felt to be labeled, as if that was sufficient to explain one's actions. It was about that time that I decided I would pretend to adopt this system of using "diagnostic decision trees" and the *DSM* "bible" but instead I would secretly employ alternative methods that more fully captured a person's spectrum of behavior. This first hit home when I was referred a client who was extremely disturbed because of his impulse to dress up in his wife's underwear, clear evidence of a "paraphilic disorder" or "transvestic fetishism." After telling me about how he liked to wear certain alluring garments I was either too cavalier or surprised to respond other than to shrug. I even said to him, "Yeah? So, what's the problem?"

Apparently, in my naivete or inexperience, that may very well have been the single most potent and successful therapeutic intervention I have ever wielded—although that certainly had not been my attention. The client later told me in a subsequent session that after my initial, casual reaction to his shameful disclosure, he felt totally relieved. He had believed himself to be the victim of some terrible affliction that would ruin his life but after my throwaway remark, he started wondering if maybe this was simply just a fun, harmless indulgence. It did not bother his wife at all; he said she found it kinky. But the remarkable thing, which may not even be directly related to my actions, was that he reported that this tendency to continue this behavior started to diminish over time and eventually the impulse ran its course.

Like most cases that we attempt to unravel in retrospect, I really have no definitive idea what happened in our sessions that he found so helpful and reassuring. I prefer to think it was my refusal to pathologize him, my complete acceptance of him without apparent critical judgment. Truthfully, I really was being genuine and honest with him. Compared to the other patients I was seeing on this psychiatric unit, the nature and severity of his problems were so mild and inconsequential compared to active hallucinations, paranoid fantasies, and sociopathy. I decided, once and for all, I would supplement medically based diagnostic schemas with other assessment processes that covered additional aspects of a person's experience. This was a valuable lesson that I further expanded to challenge other standard policies and universally accepted practices that did not address some other aspects of functioning that I considered important. I now felt permission and encouragement to question other standard models and principles that did not seem especially applicable to the cases I was seeing. Why, for example, was everyone in the field arguing with one another about which single theoretical approach was better than all the others when each of them seemed to have something valuable to offer? Or, even more curious, how did it happen that our field delivers standard 45- (or 50-) minute dosages of our treatment to *everyone*, regardless of their age, presenting complaints, economic resources, cultural background, expectations and goals, access to transportation, and a bunch of other variables? Think about it: What other medical or health procedure administers the same exact dosage to every patient who walks in the door, regardless of their age, gender, size, culture, health status, physical condition, and presenting symptoms? Yet before we have even met a new client, prior to doing a thorough assessment and treatment plan, we decide ahead of time that this will require six 50-minute sessions as mandated by the review authorities. This is only one of the many myths, misconceptions, and invalid assumptions within our profession that are largely unsupported by empirical evidence (Kottler & Balkin, 2020).

Standard and Specialized Assessment Processes

There are some very good reasons that we rely on empirically validated and standardized systems for conducting diagnostic assessments rather than just operating out of impulse or personal preference. We need a common language to communicate with one another. It also seems reasonable that clients receive appropriate, optimal care regardless of their geographic location or resources. Whether treatment is conducted by a psychiatrist, social worker, counselor, psychologist, family therapist, nurse practitioner, or other mental health professional, it is reassuring that everyone operates according to similar rules of engagement. In addition, such systems provide research-informed strategies for targeting interventions to specific diagnostic entities.

Although the *Diagnostic and Statistical Manual of Mental Disorders* (5th edition) developed by the American Psychiatric Association and the *International Classification of Disease* (11th edition) developed by the World Health Organization are considered the standard tomes in the mental health fields by which to conduct assessments, there are also other systems available that rely less on the "medical model" and more on other aspects of human functioning whether developmental processes, behavioral indices, or inner experiences (see Table 11.1). Many of these complementary diagnostic models were developed as a result of input and lessons learned from clients whose experiences were not described very well in the traditional medical vernacular.

We are certainly aware of the limitations and disadvantages of structured diagnostic processes that rely on rigid criteria and formulas. They may help us to sort out complexities, narrow down possibilities, settle on options, and select best practices, but they also rely on relatively narrow models that attempt to reduce certain aspects of behavior to singular discrete labels. We know that the use of such labels often leads to stigmatization and shame. They also are not nearly as useful outside the dominant culture where there are alternative standards for what is considered "normal" versus "deviant."

TABLE 11.1 **Diagnostic Models**

MODEL	PRIMARY STRUCTURE	SOURCE OF INFORMATION	ADVANTAGES	DISADVANTAGES	TREATMENT
Medical	Discrete categories of psychopathology	Quantitative data collection	Symptoms organized into clusters; organization of causes and prognoses	People reduced to labels; categories not as valid as desired	Match treatment (medication, psychotherapy) to specific diagnosis
Developmental	Predictable stages of normal development	Case studies, interviews, observations	Emphasis on healthy functioning and positive growth	Stages overlap and are difficult to assess	Identify current levels of functioning and stimulate progress to next levels
Humanistic	Complex and detailed descriptions of patient's behavior and experiences, as well as the relational connection	Interviews, observations, case studies, personal experience	Focus on capturing essence of a person and the dominant story of what happened and why	Model is subjective, could lead to biases and distortion	Create supportive relationship to explore and understand patient's concerns, issues, and life experience
Behavioral	Identification of problematic behaviors and their reinforcers	Direct observation and careful measurement of effects	Possible to be very specific, descriptive, and focused	Misses complexity of human experience in all its dimensions	Agree on specific goals and plan to reduce or increase target behaviors

Assessment procedures not only take place to settle on a diagnosis but also for purposes of treatment planning. Several clinical decisions are made after an initial meeting with a client to determine not only the best approach but also such things as the type of treatment (cognitive, psychodynamic, feminist, etc.), treatment goals and desired outcomes, treatment modality (individual, couple, group, etc.), length of treatment, and duration and frequency of sessions. In each case, we are attempting to customize, specialize, and personalize the plans in such a way that they best address the difficulties and issues that are in evidence. Such an assessment must not only meet the demands of established professional standards in order to get paid for the work but also the expectations and beliefs of the client who won't stick around very long if progress is not what they anticipated.

Takeaways: Essential Assessment Questions

If we have learned anything from our work, we've learned the importance of choosing our queries very carefully, not only what we ask but also the timing and sequence of the questions. For example, one of the first important lessons learned in clinical skills classes is distinguishing between "closed" versus "open-ended" questions. Closed questions, the sort that most people rely on, can be answered with a single word or gesture ("yes," "no," "maybe," shrug), while the latter requires much more elaboration and detail. Beginners who ask, "Did that work out for you?" would be quickly corrected to try instead, "How did that work out for you?"

There is probably no single nugget you will ever learn in training that is as valuable and instrumental as that one. Hardly anyone seems to notice the difference, even professional journalists and talk show hosts if you ever bother to watch them on media outlets. Because their guests and interviewees have an agenda, book, film, or idea to promote, the interviewers' ineffective, simplistic questions do not seem to matter very much. "So," the host or correspondent begins, "did things work out the way you hoped?" Try asking a surly adolescent, or really anyone else, a question like that, and you will likely get just the answer you were digging for: "Yup." By contrast, you would likely get a quite different reply if that query was framed in a more open structure, such as, "How did what happen compare to what you expected and hoped?"

That may be one obvious example of how our assessment training translates into prompting more interesting conversations and gathering more useful information from others, whether at the dinner table or sitting around with friends. There are many other ways that we have learned to explore people's experiences in more meaningful and productive ways, beginning by inviting someone to tell us a "story" of what occurred. Since we know that the events themselves are much less important than the ways the person experienced them, next on the agenda is to probe for more detail on how the events were interpreted and processed. What does the person think that means? What *seems* to be happening?

Because appearances are often deceiving, we also know how important it is to not necessarily accept what is reported at face value since there are multiple ways such events can be metabolized and described. This might be the point when we are tempted to provide a consensual name for this, whether in the form of a label, description, or even a diagnosis. Someone, for example, admits feeling highly anxious, but from information and details that were gathered from their story, it seems to be a kind of adjustment reaction rather than a global condition of chronic anxiety. This sort of differential decision-making is part of how our brains have been rewired to think logically, analytically, and proactively to make sense of problems and behavior. We follow the procedures and systems that have been researched and validated, but we also go far beyond that at times to include other means to expand the full view of what someone is feeling, thinking, and experiencing.

Questions for Reflection or Discussion

1. What are some ways that your background and training in assessment and diagnosis have been disruptive in the sense that you see evidence of dysfunctional and psychopathological behavior everywhere?

2. If you were meeting an interesting stranger for the first time, what are some of the best "open-ended" questions you could ask to get to know that person in a significant way? If you could only ask three such questions, after which you had to give a talk on what this person is really like, which ones would you select? Try them out on a few classmates or friends.

3. Think of a case in which someone might be experiencing severe symptoms that can be identified and described. Apply several of the diagnostic models in Table 11.1 to conceptualize the problems in different ways beyond the standard medical model.

12

Uncovering Hidden Agendas and Disguised Intentions

It is in the ability to deceive oneself that the greatest talent is shown.

—Anatole France

The Lies We Live By

I once worked with a man for over a year, seeing him every Wednesday morning at 9 a.m., 50 Wednesdays in a row. He had an incredible life story to reveal, one that was so remarkable I often questioned how it could possibly be true. But heck, I am an expert at sorting out truth from lies, having spent tens of thousands of hours in the trenches. I am no fool.

The man had grown up in a part of the Bronx in New York that had been particularly dicey for him during his childhood and adolescence. It was just after the end of World War II and, although Jewish, he lived in a neighborhood adjoining a particularly anti-Semitic area where he was repeatedly subjected to violence and bullying. To fight back against the oppression he experienced, he decided to join the volunteer army that was being assembled in what would eventually become the nation of Israel after the War of Independence. He was trained as a marksman and shared in our sessions the most vivid descriptions of his various missions to assassinate high-ranking political and military leaders. He was the most fascinating man I'd ever met. I had been spellbound by his tales of adventure, horror, disaster, and triumph but also confused by the moral implications of his missions.

It was long after our conversations were over that I really began seriously questioning the extent to which whatever he told me was actually true. Some parts of his narrative just did not make sense, although this could have been related to diminished cognitive functioning in old age. I could not help but wonder, however, if the guy really made up the whole story just to entertain me. We spent a year together in deep conversation about the most intimate, private matters. Surely, we had some degree of trust. But then why was it so hard for me to believe that perhaps many of the things he told me were just fantasies? Honestly, to this day, I cannot tell you if he was genuinely trying to get help or just playing me. It sent me into a quandary, questioning if anything *anyone* ever told me was completely accurate and how I could ever tell the difference. Even more intriguing was how much it really mattered.

Many of the books I end up writing (like this one) are not so much driven by some burning professional curiosity as they are motivated by a personal yearning to make sense of something that confuses me. I once wrote a book about what people do when they are alone, mostly because I was uncomfortable and ashamed about some of the weird things that I do when nobody is around. I wrote another book about managing stress because my own levels were out of control, and standard sources were not helping much at all. I tackled a research project about "the language of tears" because of an episode in which I could not stop crying after a near-death experience. Then there were all the books and articles I have written about failure since that has been a dominant theme in my life. So perhaps it is not much of a surprise that I decided to collect stories of other well-known therapists who were duped and lied to by their clients (Kottler & Carlson, 2011). I wanted to make myself feel better and prove that I was not as guileless and trusting as I presumed.

Sure enough, I heard from dozens of different therapists and counselors who revealed spectacularly embarrassing stories of being tricked, fooled, and manipulated by those they were trying to help. One therapist mentioned seeing a client who had been paralyzed and used a wheelchair—but then one day, he saw her walking around town with no disability whatsoever. Another mentioned a suicidal client who declared he likely would not return because he intended to take his own life. Then he showed up at the appointed time, but only to laugh in the therapist's face and confess he was an acting student who was just messing with him. Still another mentioned a favorite client of his, a man with whom he had enjoyed a fabulous, intimate relationship over the course of a year. One day, the therapist just never turned up for his session, even though he had been so reliable in the past. When the therapist called his house to find out where he was, he learned that all that time, the man had been dying of cancer and never bothered to mention it in sessions. I could reveal scores of other such stories, but the point is that no matter how experienced, perceptive, and skilled we might be, we can never really be certain what is real, what is truth, and what are convenient memories or idealized fantasies.

Some of the seminal stories of our own lives never really happened either—at least the way we remember them. They represent distorted, exaggerated, in some cases manufactured experiences. When we sort through all the various translations, interpretations, and remembrances about any experience, we are often left questioning what really happened. As Spense (1982) has pointed out, among so many others, there is "historical truth" and then there is "narrative truth" which is often quite different, especially when you consider all the levels of translation that take place. First, there is actually what occurred, as if recorded for later playback. Then there is what the client remembers about the events, followed by another loss of accuracy that takes place when the story is shared, often leaving out certain details, distorting others, and sometimes exaggerating quite dramatically. Then there is what the therapist actually hears during the encounter, followed by additional levels of distortion that take place during the interpretations. It is truly a wonder that any conversation or personal disclosure can be considered completely accurate and truthful. So many of the historical events of our lives are more fantasies than objective realities.

I had been told by my parents all my life that I had been born a few months premature, barely surviving the time I'd spent in an incubator. This "fact" about my early existence became a major influence on my life in so many ways. I had even attributed this to be the origin of my extreme impatience—always in a hurry, refusing to ever stand in a line, rushing to get things done or arrive at my destinations as fast as I could. It was only much later in life, after my father had a stroke that destroyed the part of his brain that regulated impulse control, that he confessed to me that I had actually been a full-term baby.

"Wait a minute," I stopped him incredulously. "You told me I was born nine months after you and Mom were married."

My father laughed. "Well, that's what we told you. But your mother was actually pregnant with you before we got married. It was a shotgun wedding, insisted by your grandfather."

"What are you telling me? So I was never premature?"

He shook his head and smiled apologetically. Everyone had lied to me about this my whole life!

Every family has its secrets and deceptions. We have learned to live with them, or at least pretend we do not really know the truth about the family history, or the weird uncle nobody ever mentions, or incidents in the past that have long been covered up. This is not that different from all the lies that practically everyone tells others, or themselves, about their abilities. Nine out of 10 people admit that they lie at least twice each day. Every conversation that lasts more than 10 minutes usually has at least three lies. Actually, I just lied to you since the actual number is *two* times within a conversation. If we add texts and emails to the discussion, that frequency would be significantly higher (Docan-Morgan, 2019; Hart, 2019).

People lie to manage their image, to promote themselves, to minimize their faults, to manipulate and control others. They lie as a joke or prank to play with others. People exaggerate their abilities, claiming they are far more proficient at activities than their performances indicate. Roughly 90% of drivers say they are more skilled than others, about the same as the number of counselors and therapists who claim they are "better than average." It is all about enhancing our appeal to others and ourselves, as well as exaggerating our own abilities as part of the "illusory-superiority" phenomenon or "Lake Wobegon effect" in which everyone believes themselves to be better than everyone else (Hoorens, 1993; Kruger, 1999). It turns out that lying to oneself is an important prerequisite for being able to deceive others.

Truth and Lies

It has been said we live in a "post-truth era," a time when politicians, corporate leaders, and online "influencers" can make up any fictions or tell any lie enough times that it becomes "true" among those who wish it to be so. Yet one way to conceptualize what counselors and psychotherapists actually do is we help people separate denial, distortion, exaggeration, and lies from some semblance of objective reality. In their most extreme forms, we encounter all kinds of variations that qualify as forms of mental disorders. In schizophrenia, for instance, fantasy becomes its own reality. Yet there are many other examples that include memory impairment that leads to fictitious stories (Korsakov syndrome), factitious disorders (Munchausen syndrome), ridiculous exaggerations (histrionic), blatant deceptions (sociopathy), and self-aggrandizing fictions (pseudologia fantastica, narcissism). In less extreme forms, the motives are more likely related to preserving an idealized image and avoiding shame.

For most other creatures on Earth, it is fair game to use various forms of deception like camouflage or disguises to hide their true intentions or change their appearance. Chameleons and octopuses use camouflage to hide in plain sight. Rabbits and foxes change the color of their fur to match the current weather conditions. Insects make themselves appear like sticks to fool predators. Various birds and other animals change their appearance not only to hide from enemies but also to attract mates by ramping up their best qualities, whether tail feathers, coloring, or size of appendages. Humans are inclined to do much the same thing when we color our hair, employ makeup, wigs, scents, surgical procedures, and wardrobe choices to enhance our attractiveness or heighten our perceived status.

In the context of counseling and therapy, we accept the reality that a certain amount of what we hear in sessions is not strictly true. We usually conclude that this is perhaps not so much an attempt at intentional duplicity as much as *self-deception* that permits elevated views of oneself as a defense mechanism. We are almost always astounded, not only during sessions but in the larger culture, by how people can get away with being so clueless about how they are perceived by others and how different those perceptions are from the way that person views him or herself.

Throughout the history of our profession, there have been ongoing debates about the extent to which any of this really matters. Some philosophers and psychologists have argued that "everything is true" if it is believed to be so, while others say that "almost nothing is true" since it can never be verified beyond any doubt. In that sense, we recognize that the parameters between truth and lies are less clear than most people realize, especially when we consider how highly skilled some people are at fooling themselves and others.

It is also the case that some of the fabrications that we might encounter are not necessarily the result of deceptive intentions but rather some underlying mental illness that significantly distorts reality. In other cases, even highly motivated, well-intended clients might engage in falsehoods, manipulation, or a hidden agenda to avoid feelings of shame or disappointing their therapist. When these individuals are asked to confess why they are less than honest with their therapists, they actually provide a number of justifiable reasons:

- "I don't trust my therapist yet, so why should I spill my guts to someone who might judge me critically?"

- "I'm not sure that this therapist is actually competent and skilled enough to handle my problems."

- "I can't really explain that well what's going on with me, but I don't want to disappoint my therapist, so I just make things up."

It is somewhat hypocritical to complain about clients' deceptive behavior when therapists sometimes engage in such actions themselves when the situation requires it. One obvious, universal lie that therapists often tell themselves is that they are quite excellent and highly skilled at recognizing a lie when they hear one. They might mention that they can read nonverbal "tells" that reveal hidden or disguised intentions, just like an expert poker player. Or that they have had a lot of experience working with the so-called criminal element and are thus well aware of any attempts to be deceptive. There are even whole courses that supposedly train professionals to recognize lies by identifying behavioral cues. Nevertheless, in spite of such training and experience, even forensic psychologists, judges, polygraph operators, and law enforcement interrogators only do slightly better than chance during such attempts to seek out the truth (Gelitz, 2021). It would appear that our species is not very good at recognizing lies and deception, especially among those who make a living from such deception and have become quite good at it.

We can readily witness within the larger culture how some political leaders can insist on the most bald-faced lies ("The election was stolen!"), providing no evidence whatsoever, and yet still shrug it off when they are challenged. Even when faced with recordings or multiple witnesses that clearly contradict the exaggerations, denials, or lies, they still find ways to insist they were right after all. Over time, such individuals may even come to believe their own fantasies and fabrications, repeating them so often they actually take on a life of their own. Even more incredible are the legions of followers who know they are being deceived but decide to support the candidate or leader anyway.

Before we become indignant about the state of dishonesty, we would have to acknowledge our own inclinations to lie on occasion, often justified for the client's own good. We will leave the ethical implications of this aside for a bit to admit there are times when it is clearly in someone's best interest if we exaggerate a little, offer hope that is perhaps overly optimistic, or say something that we know is not quite accurate even if it offers some degree of support and encouragement.

"Sure, I *know* I can help you with this." This little lie is mentioned for the most strategic reason: to set up positive expectations for the "cure." It is all part of the placebo effect, in which we program clients to expect satisfactory results by shaping their expectations. Of course, it is actually *way* too early to promise anything definitive, but we know how important it is to come across as enthusiastic and optimistic regarding the prognosis, regardless of any doubts that may linger.

"That's a very good question. What do YOU think? This is the standard stall for those times when we really do not know how to address a concern. We are expected to be all-knowing, to have answers to the questions that plague people the most: "Why do I have this problem?" What's it going to take to make this go away?" "How do I get out of this mess I find myself in?" Since we are not really certain just yet what is actually going on, we find ourselves in situations where we have to just make things up. In the meantime, the most elegant response is to turn the query back onto the client, hoping that this postponement will extricate us from the dilemma, or at least stall long enough until we can settle on an acceptable reply.

"Of _course_ I like you!" Every client wants to feel like they are valued by us. They are often desperate for our approval and validation, frequently trolling for our affection. Sometimes they will even ask directly how much we truly like them. We may have a pat response for that query, but the reality is many of our clients go to such extreme lengths to make themselves as unlikable as possible. They are often referred to us in the first place because they are so annoying and disruptive to others. Although they may engage in all kinds of manipulative games, test us to our limits, and act inappropriately and demanding, we are still expected to _pretend_ that we like them. We may even convince ourselves this is the case, at least until they walk out the door, and we are finally able to take a deep breath after such challenging interactions.

There are other examples of the lies we tell others, and ourselves, but we also recognize this is really the nature of human interactions in which each of us is invested in presenting ourselves in the best possible light. The interesting debate is the extent to which we challenge lies and deception during sessions since they take place within a relational context. Perhaps the person does not feel safe, or feels critically judged, or just has long-standing trust issues that prevent complete openness out of fear of being burned or betrayed once again. So the lesson we learn over time is to consider the particular meaning of the fabrications and untruths: What is the person ultimately trying to do?

Takeaways

What do we do when we believe someone is shading the truth? Even more to the point, what do we do when we catch ourselves in a lie? The answer to both those questions is: It depends. It depends on how safe it feels in that moment to reveal one's doubts and uncertainty. We ask ourselves to consider the consequences of being more open and honest in the relationship versus continuing to play it safe and not stirring things up. Often, we tend to take things far too personally, interpreting a questionable disclosure as a personal affront: "Do you really think I'm _that_ gullible or stupid?"

We know there are always reasons, often legitimate ones, for being less than forthcoming. Often, this is a reflection of underlying feelings of mistrust, whether specific to this relationship or else as a universal policy. We also know there are people in the world, many of whom end up in our care, who make a living out of being dishonest, corrupt, fraudulent, and deceitful. It is not only fun for them, an expression of power, but also highly profitable to play by one's own rules instead of complying with consensual standards of morality. This can make us cynical and suspicious with all the time we spend talking to such people, but it can also help us to appreciate all the different ways that people manage to survive when they feel so insecure and vulnerable.

Questions for Reflection or Discussion

1. What's the most frequent lie you tell about yourself to others that you admit is not actually true?

2. People tend to lie to bolster their image in some way. Since there would be shame and a loss of face associated with a direct confrontation, what do you believe are the most advantageous ways to deal with such deception? What variables and contextual factors might you take into consideration when deciding how to respond?

3. What's an example of a time that someone you were trying to help was less than completely honest with you? What sense did you make out of that situation, and how did you handle it?

13

Exploring and Explaining Mysteries

The most beautiful thing we can experience is the mysterious. It is the source of all true art and all science.

—Albert Einstein

Healing Myself First

I remember after completing my first year of graduate training how curious I had become about why people behaved in certain ways. Never having felt much in control of my life, nor able to manage the unanticipated disappointments that frequently seemed to come my way, I became obsessed with learning to better "read" and make sense of others' intentions. Even more than that, I came to love making predictions about what people might do based on the limited data and cues available. Naturally, I was not very good at these skills quite yet, but I was an enthusiastic student of the process.

I noticed while waiting at the airport some time ago that men and women pulled their suitcases in different ways, whether the hand was positioned forward or backward. Why *was* this, I wondered? It had to be more than just learned behavior or even a fashionable style. After researching this mystery, I discovered that this actually represented one of several clear anatomical sex differences. Women have a larger pelvis to accommodate the birth canal, narrower and angled shoulders, creating a different comfortable position of the wrist when pulling an object. I thought that was fascinating and began to notice other patterns that had previously been invisible to me. Why did young, single women tend to constantly play with and fluff their long hair? Were they drawing attention to their luxurious, healthy hair to display their excellent health status as a potential mate? And why did women color their lips red and cheeks pink? Was this to simulate sexual arousal, or was there something else I was missing? And with respect to males, especially hormonally fueled adolescents, why did they do such stupid, reckless things that seem to make little sense?

I have spent my whole life wrestling with questions like this (so will you). For these first few questions, I later learned tentative hypotheses to explain these mysteries. Long hair is indeed a record of vigor and viability as a mating partner, which also explains why 80% of women color their hair lighter to draw more attention to its features as a record of health. Facial makeup, as well, is similarly used to cover up imperfections and highlight one's most alluring features. As far as adolescent risk-taking, I eventually came to understand that such behavior means something very different in teenage cultures around the world. Whether going on a hunt to kill their first lion or completing a painful initiation rite, young adults in most places are expected to demonstrate their courage, fierceness, and willingness to take risks. These actions are designed to attract prospective mating partners and earn status within their group—and they are actually effective in doing so.

The greatest mystery of all was trying to understand me. Why was I unable to figure out my own propensity to be so hard on myself all the time? How could I become more forgiving of my lapses? What was all this doing for me that made it so difficult to alter this lifelong pattern? I would suggest that these types of questions are our greatest gift of all—the opportunity to turn our valuable knowledge toward ourselves, to apply our useful skills on our own stubbornness and resistance.

Everyday Human Behavior That Still Remains a Mystery

So often we are asked by clients to provide some comprehensible reasons for why they are so miserable. Is it a matter of family configuration, genetic predisposition, environmental factors, attitude, and beliefs, or simply misfortune? Often, we can provide some reassurance and an acceptable explanation, at least one that seems reasonable.

"Why am I so depressed all the time?" a client asks, seemingly more upset about the mystery of it all than the actual annoying symptoms.

"Well, let's see." We try ticking off the options, one finger at a time. "It could be part of your family history, or perhaps a way to protect yourself from further disappointments."

That did not seem to make much sense, so we try again. And again.

"Maybe it's some underlying biological cause, and we should get you checked out for tests? Oh? You've already done that? Well, then, it could very well be a way to get your attention to matters you've been ignoring."

Since this was just a stalling tactic, you would hope the client does not ask *which* "matters," at least until you can find a more suitable explanation.

This ability to uncover meaning, locate possible causes, and make sense of mysteries, is a key part of our jobs. There are many instances when there is no actual "cure" for what ails someone, or when the only option seems to be to grin and bear the suffering with as much equanimity as possible. In such cases, making sense of the experience is the only viable possibility. For many of us, this attraction to mysteries and interest in the unknown is what led us to this profession in the first place.

We are well positioned to also decode the reasons for many other aspects of human behavior that seem peculiar or inexplicable. How do we explain altruism, for example? Why do strangers give away resources, or risk their lives, to help those who are not genetically related? Why do people intentionally jeopardize their safety and health to assist strangers they have never even met previously? Why would anyone give away their money or resources to perfect strangers who will never have the opportunity to repay the favor?

Other mysteries abound, those that you encounter every day. Why do people vote for candidates who do not have their best interests in mind? Why do people leak water out of their eyes when they are feeling emotional? Why do nonverbal "tells" like yawning and blushing give away our internal states of boredom or shame? Why are humans one of the few animals on the planet that are allowed to survive after we can no longer produce offspring? Then there are the really, really big questions: What is the ultimate meaning of life? Is there a God or Higher Power, and if so, what form does He/She/Them/It take? What makes people happy?

Each of the questions that confound us, either in the lives of those we help or in everyday situations, motivates deeper investigations. We are highly skilled at digging into research and literature in order to sort out alluring puzzles. In the case of why older humans still exist, for instance, it has been discovered that the presence of elders provides greater support and care for children, increasing survival rates (Kottler, 2023). When grandparents live nearby, mothers tend to have more children, partially explaining how and why evolution gave us an extra lease on life, adding another handful of decades to our life span (Driscoll, 2009; Gurven & Kaplan, 2020; Hawkes, 2004, 2021).

This sort of deep dive into mysteries and problems has been applied to our field as well, but with mixed results when we accept certain "truths" and standard answers without critical scrutiny. The theories related to "learning styles," "birth order," "stages of grief," and "hemispheric dominance" have been quite popular over the years to explain aspects of human behavior, even though there is actually little valid and reliable evidence to support these theories. They are just some examples of mysteries within the helping professions that have yet to be fully understood and, in many cases, challenged vigorously (Kottler, 2022b). There are also many other mysteries within the work we do that can't be definitively addressed. How does therapy really work, and what are the most universal features of all effective approaches? When is therapy likely to be most and least effective? With whom does therapy work best? What is the best way to do therapy? Each of us has some rather strong beliefs about these questions, but, unfortunately, they are all over the map (Kottler, 2022a).

There are other mysteries that we face on a daily basis, most of which we continue to find bewildering in some ways. Why are some of your colleagues more challenging than your most difficult clients? Why can you never be certain when and if you actually helped anyone? And when you are feeling confident there was a satisfactory outcome, you will likely never know what really made the most difference.

Unsupported and Unchallenged Practices

As mentioned earlier, what other medical practice or health procedure applies the same exact dosage of treatment (50-minute sessions) to everyone, regardless of their age, condition, symptoms, preferences, and resources? Where is the empirical evidence that such a pre-scribed time limit is best for *everyone*, irrespective of their situation? Another example relates to the times we attempt to offer advice about how to manage life. Telling people to exercise regularly, abstain from mind-altering substances, or control their temper may be excellent guidance but hardly anyone ever actually follows such well-intended wisdom—at least not by just telling them to do so. We may well understand that giving advice only makes people more dependent, or else gives people an excuse for blaming the advice-giver when things do not work out as intended, but we still do it because it feels empowering.

Hopefully, one of the lessons we have learned after realizing how futile it is to tell people what to do with their lives is that we refrain from doing so with friends and family. Of course, everyone asks for our advice, given our illustrious position as supposed behavioral experts. "What do you think I should do?" a relative or friend pleads. It is not that we do not have a rather strong opinion on the matter but that we realize that whatever we tell the person is not going to matter very much anyway. One thing for certain, however, is that we surely do not wish to be blamed when whatever we suggest results in outcomes that were not exactly anticipated or preferred. This lesson was finally cemented in my psyche when my son was still in high school. He was walking down the stairs with a shirt in each hand, a blue one and a red one.

"Dad," he asked me, "which one do you like better?"

Now, I just *knew* this was a trap. Whichever one I picked was going to be the wrong choice. But then I noticed that he was wearing jeans, so really any shirt would serve him well.

"Um," I panicked for a moment, really not wanting to annoy him so early in the morning. "How about *that* one?" I said pointing halfway in the middle of the two, hoping that would let me escape unscathed.

"Oh, Dad! Not *that* one!"

I wasn't even sure which one I was pointing to that he disagreed with, but I was already aware that whatever I said would be wrong. Reminder in the future: Just say, "I'm not sure. It's up to you." Of course that would probably have annoyed him as well, but at least I did not make the "wrong" choice. All of this just reminded me of the ways we must live with uncertainty and mysteries in our work and life. We may help people to resolve most of their difficulties, but that is not to say we ever truly understood what was happening at the time. Most often, what we do is hard to explain, and even more difficult to justify why one strategy was necessarily better than others. We may favor one approach above all others, but that does not mean there is overwhelming evidence to support that belief. Living with mysteries is our specialty.

Takeaways

In spite of our doubts, uncertainties, and the mysteries we will never really grasp, there are still several things that we know for certain. It is precisely this confidence, if not faith, in our powers to help and heal people that lends power to our interventions. There are aspects of our work about which we will never fully understand and there are many excellent, justifiable reasons for this. There is a multitude of unknown factors, interactive variables, and complex processes that interfere with any definitive statements about what we are doing. Our own biases and distortions further muddy and confuse the picture.

In spite of such hesitance, there are still a few things about which we can feel reasonably confident. There may be many heated debates and arguments about what it is that is most important in helping efforts, whether to focus on thoughts, feeling, or behavior, whether to operate with couples, individuals, or groups, whether to be highly active or let the client do most of the work, whether to focus on the presenting complaints or underlying issues, whether to concentrate primarily on the present, past, or future. In spite of these variations, most of us conclude there are just a few factors that appear to matter most. First are the client's own characteristics, which include personality style, particular symptoms, and certain traits, like patience, motivation, resilience, optimistic attitude, and support available. All of these contribute to the person's willingness to work hard and cooperatively, as well as to take personal responsibility for progress. Similarly, we would all mostly agree that there are practitioner characteristics that matter quite a bit, especially perceived competence, patience, flexibility, and a "pleasing" personality. Finally, and perhaps most important of all since it accounts for roughly half of all successful therapeutic outcomes, is the quality of the alliance that has been established. Interestingly, this pretty much only matters from the perspective of the client rather than the therapist since there are lots of times we might be pretty pleased with ourselves while the client is sorely disappointed. All that seems to count is the *client's* perception of the relationship, a connection that feels safe, secure, and trusting.

You have heard all of this before since it represents the foundation of almost all helping professions: You cannot help someone if they do not respect and trust what you offer. The important lesson that we have learned is that we may not ever understand all the nuances of relational engagement and psychological growth, but we do recognize that without such a deep connection with another person, there will never be much of an impact.

Questions for Reflection or Discussion

1. What are some of the mysteries of human behavior that interest (and confuse) you the most?

2. What are some of the popular, conventional policies and procedures within our profession that are considered "standard practices," and yet they actually don't make much sense to you in light of the vast diversity of our clients and their particular needs?

3. What is one mystery in your own life that someday you would love to settle on some answers?

14

Interpreting the Past to Explain the Present

One cannot and must not try to erase the past merely because it does not fit the present.

—Golda Meir

Prisoners of the Past?

Like most practitioners of my generation, the first introduction to the study of mental health and disorders began with reading Freud. At the time, there was really only a few major approaches to counseling and therapy, including behavior therapy, humanistic therapy, and various psychodynamic approaches. Freud, Jung, Adler, Kohut, Klein, Winnicott, and others were in their heyday, emphasizing the significance of unconscious processes and how experiences of the past shape our behavior and defensive reactions in the present. While all of these ideas were certainly compelling and interesting, they did not strike me at the time as very practical given that my first jobs involved crisis intervention in which I might have only a single session to make a difference. Nevertheless, I so admired Freud as a writer, especially some of his early works about dream interpretation.

I became fascinated with Freud's life story, far more than his theories that were increasingly becoming obsolete, or at least replaced by more contemporary versions of his ideas. I was so impressed by how he courageously challenged his medical colleagues and then proceeded to challenge himself to dig deeply into his own origins. He always likened himself to an archaeologist who digs up artifacts of the past to explain why things exist as they do in the present. During annual holiday breaks, he would even travel to archaeological sites in Italy and the Middle East to excavate treasures that revealed secrets of ancient human existence. Even the design and furnishings of his office at Berggasse 19 in Vienna actually resembled that of an Egyptian tomb.

One of the foundations of psychoanalytic thought is the notion that our past experiences during early childhood shape our present behavior and choices. Dozens of theorists have since taken this idea and run with it in a variety of different ways, either by exploring family legacies, learning how early memories affect choices, or just grasping the ways that habit formation leads to automatic responses. I had always been looking for reasons to explain many of the difficulties I was experiencing in life. Freud and his followers offered some alternatives but I surely wasn't pleased with the idea that my life was ultimately determined by what occurred in the past, especially aspects that I would rather forget rather than explore further.

If I was to examine any aspect of my self-defeating behavior it made sense, at first, to study how and when this pattern might have first become established. I may not have embraced the most deterministic aspects of Freud's contributions but I was appreciative of any approach that sought to explore and explain why we act the ways we do. One example of this was my attempt to understand why I was so compulsively driven toward achievement and recognition. I found this particularly confusing because, ordinarily, I prefer not to draw attention to myself. Yet, on the other hand, I appeared absolutely desperate to earn accolades for my productivity and accomplishments.

My research and writing projects had taken on ridiculous requirements for time, effort, and commitment as if my life depended on them. My interests were all over the place, as if it did not matter what I studied as long as the subjects were interesting and confusing to me—and truthfully, almost *everything* qualified as a legitimate topic. Although those pursuing an academic career are usually advised to follow a single line of research inquiry, one they can expect to advance throughout their lifetime, I was simultaneously studying a half dozen different subjects, many of which are featured as chapters in this book about ethics, social justice and advocacy, leadership, mistakes and failures, solitary behavior, mysterious behavior, addictions, and transformative travel. Even that was not sufficient to capture my full devotion and commitment since I also delved into the different facets of being a practicing teacher, counselor, or psychotherapist. I was less intrigued at the time by the various theories and techniques circulating and far more interested in what it felt like to be a helping professional, including the uncertainties, doubts, fears, joys, and lessons that we learn along the way.

I am almost embarrassed to admit all the various subjects I have researched and written about, as if I cannot settle on any one thing to maintain prolonged interest. I have written standard textbooks in education, leadership, advocacy, counseling, and psychology, as well as dozens of books for practitioners about relational engagement, working in groups, helping difficult people, developing a professional identity, reviewing popular theories, describing unusual cases, understanding research, and becoming an exceptional practitioner. I have written a best-selling true crime book and others for the general public about solitude and aloneness, creativity, mental illness, relational conflicts, personal changes, spiritual self-discovery, stress management, self-care, and disaster relief. This is hardly an exhaustive list.

Inevitably, this leads to the question I get asked a lot: Why on earth have I been so driven to write so much, about so many subjects, in such abbreviated periods of time? Keep in mind that although many graduate students I've encountered struggle to write a 10-page paper during the course of a 4-month semester, I've written an *average* of four books annually; that is four books every year during the past 4 decades! That's something like 25,000 published pages over my life span, and that does not include hundreds of journal articles. It may seem like I'm bragging about these achievements, but, once again, I have felt as if I must apologize for being so capricious in my interests and so driven to produce so much material.

Back to the original question I posed: *Why* would I do this? Why would I *need* to do this? What is wrong with me that I am so driven to do so much? What fuels this desperate ambition?

Is it recognition I have always been after, the pursuit of fame, wealth, and notoriety? Perhaps there is also a bit of redemption as well, proving to the world that I am not as dumb as everyone once believed. Taking a little assistance from Freud, and a psychodynamic therapist, I tried to uncover the roots of this compulsive drive. I explored how my early childhood experiences shaped me in ways that I would never understand. I uncovered some of the hidden and unconscious motives that helped explain my choices and behavior. Throughout my life, as mentioned in earlier chapters, I have felt so insecure, so inadequate, so wounded that I have been trying to prove to myself—and to others—that I am not nearly as stupid as was originally believed.

In my home office, I have several images framed on the wall, including a few of my best scenic and portrait photographs, a display of the business cards from the 14 jobs I've had during my life (I told you I was flighty), and a framed diploma. The certificate, however, does not attest to my graduation from college, or even my master's or doctoral degrees. Instead, this is my *preschool* diploma from when I was just 3 years old. Added to the bottom of the diploma, declaring that I had completed all the requirements of the curriculum, was also my very first report card displaying my grades in such subjects as "tablework," "outdoor play," "verbal fluency." They were all marked "average." Next to "Intelligence," however, there was just a question mark, as if to indicate that the teacher couldn't quite decide whether I was bright or perhaps intellectually challenged. This became the first indication to my parents that they had best temper any grandiose expectations for what I might accomplish in life. In many ways, it became the template for what would follow me throughout my childhood and adolescence and I had best get used to that.

I still have many of my old school report cards. When I scan the teachers' evaluations of my performance and potential, I can only just shake my head and marvel that I ever managed to graduate from high school. It was bad enough that I could barely attain average grades in academic subjects, but even my "citizenship" marks were barely acceptable. It was clear that my future appeared less than promising.

How does anyone recover from such a dismal prediction of mediocrity? All of my past failures and underachievement limited my choices for the future. Maybe higher education just was not in the cards for me. I suppose my fate was sealed, or at least it felt that way—until a few mentors saw something in me that everyone else (including me) had missed along the way. I eventually learned over time, and with considerable support from a few teachers, that I did indeed have a few special gifts that I might somehow harness in a unique way—if I was willing to devote the effort. Like many clients report after completing their sessions successfully, I came to appreciate that the same struggles, setbacks, and disappointments of the past could very well become sources of strength and resilience if processed differently.

Patterns That Predict the Future

The initial goal of almost any health professional is to collect as much data as possible about a person's family history, previous medical conditions, prior incidents of emotional difficulties, plus whatever background might be useful in order to understand the current circumstances. After all, people tend to follow patterns that became established much earlier in life, often those that continue long after anyone has ever become aware of this original programming. We help clients develop greater insight into those patterns, especially those related to ongoing counterproductive behavior. Depending on the particular approach taken, such insights can be focused far beyond unconscious processes, defense mechanisms, and other traditional psychodynamic priorities to also delve into family dynamics, cognitive interpretations, internalized beliefs, power imbalances, cultural imperatives, and personal meaning making, to mention a few.

Although several decades ago, the primary insights and understandings that were promoted by the most dominant therapeutic models involved learning how past experiences influence, guide, shape, and control current actions, there have since been a number of innovative developments that offer far more diverse and alternative models for helping clients develop insight into their behavior. It is hoped that such awareness might then lead to significant changes, which may or may not follow. Each of the different theoretical orientations thus employs different skills and approaches, depending on the goals they have in mind (see Table 14.1).

Every practitioner has their own preferred ways of promoting deeper understanding of how past influences may impact present behavior and choices. In addition to those signature techniques associated with a particular theoretical model, clinicians have their favorite probing questions that are asked routinely. The responses often reveal important clues about what happened, what went wrong, and what has already been tried and failed previously. Sometimes this is approached directly ("What does this remind you of in the past?") whereas other times access is sought via more subtle inklings: "If you took a wild guess, what do you imagine will ultimately make a difference?" Various approaches offer different strategies for uncovering this buried material, interpreting dreams, employing a "skeleton key," "looking for exceptions," or "curious questioning." The idea is to explore what has worked in the past, what has not worked at all, and what might be useful in the future. In the case of prescribing the optimal antidepressant medication, for instance, the best indicator for producing maximum results with minimum side effects is to begin with a drug that had been tried previously with an older relative. Similarly, one of the most valuable questions to ask someone who shows up for the first time is to ask about previous experiences with a mental health professional in the past or anyone who served in some helping capacity. This is often followed up with the question, "What was most and least helpful to you in that prior experience?"

In addition to exploring the past in order to provide useful clues regarding what happened and why, we are also well aware of how people are inclined to use the past as an excuse

TABLE 14.1 **Models for Promoting Insight Into Past Influences and Present Behavior**

TYPE OF INSIGHT	THEORETICAL FRAMEWORK	SKILL EMPLOYED	EXAMPLE
Awareness of feelings	Person-centered	Reflection of feeling	"You're feeling upset because you don't like giving up control the way you did when you were younger."
Unconscious motives	Psychoanalytic	Interpretation	"The anger you are expressing toward me seems related to feelings toward your mother."
Cognitive distortions	Cognitive	Guided discovery	"Even if you don't get what you want, how does this predict you'll fall apart again?"
Inauthenticity	Gestalt	Confrontation	"You say you are really angry about the ways you were treated in school, but you appear quite calm."
Personal meaning	Existential	Immediacy	"I notice that right now you are withdrawing from our relationship just as you have done with others previously."
Problem redefinition	Strategic	Reframing	"When you say you have a bad temper just like your father, what you really mean is that you are sometimes very passionate."
Family dynamics	Systemic	Restructuring	"Move over there and sit with your wife instead of your children. Talk to one another about what this is like compared to the ways you've communicated in the past."
Power imbalances	Feminist	Exploring gender roles	"How have you limited yourself by the ways you have defined what it means to be a man?"
Sources of influence	Narrative	Outcome questions	"How did you manage to overcome the anger when it tried to control you?"
Social and language influences	Social constructionist	Re-story life circumstances	"Which roles have you adopted from the larger culture that were not of your own choosing?"
Consequences of choices	Reality	Challenge decisions	"Is what you are doing now getting you what you've always said you want most?"
Contingency contracting	Behavioral	Identify reinforcers for target behaviors	"What is it that sustains this behavior?"
Reframing	Strategic	Restructure the problem in a more helpful way	"When you say that you are shy, what you really mean is that you are sometimes quiet when with strangers."

for their present disturbing or annoying behavior. They claim to have "bad genes," a lousy family history, or just some bad breaks: "Let's just say I made some mistakes, and they are my burden to bear." In such instances, a client is absolved of responsibility for their plight since "that's just the way things are; nothing I can do about it now."

We hear things like this all the time, and it drives us a little crazy. Sure, we understand why people would want to blame the past—their parents, their upbringing, the neglect they survived, the lack of resources, a lousy education, toxic influences from their peer group. All of these reasons and excuses are the antithesis of what we believe and practice—that regardless of what has happened previously, it is still entirely possible to alter these patterns if there is sufficient motivation and commitment. But that is a hard sell for most people who are looking for an easy way out.

Takeaways: Opportunities for Reinvention

To what extent does the past really shape, if not determine, how anyone reacts in the present? That depends, of course, on how badly someone wishes to change existing patterns. It is an incredibly powerful insight to realize that at any moment in time, each of us has the capacity to alter long-standing habits and reinvent ourselves. There is a kind of tyranny embedded in the "I'ms" that people sometimes use in their speech, as in "*I'm* lazy," "*I'm* not much of an athlete," "*I'm* lousy at math," "*I'm* not the sort of person that does that sort of thing." We notice the ways that people define themselves in absolute terms, as if because they are sometimes lazy or not very athletic in some activities that somehow captures their essence without exception. The truth is that nobody is lazy, lousy, or inadequate in *every* possible situation; there are always exceptions.

The obvious lesson derived from all these conversations we have with people who define themselves in these singular, denigrating ways is that we can also change the limited ways we view ourselves. That is just one thing that is so remarkable about the work that we do to promote more empowered identities. We also have the option to reinvent ourselves in light of features of our lives that are less than unsatisfactory. I suppose that is why I have changed jobs and moved so often, always hoping that the next opportunity would provide new adventures and significant growth. I am not actually wrong about that, no matter how inconvenient, expensive, and exhausting it is to start over again and again and again.

Questions for Reflection or Discussion

1. What's an example of an event or experience from your past that continues to exert significant influence on your behavior or choices in the present?

2. How have you resisted making needed improvements or changes in your life by falling back on excuses from your past (bad luck, poor genes, lack of resources, lousy education, few opportunities, etc.)?

3. How have you defined yourself in absolute terms ("I'm lazy," "I'm just not good at that") that limit or short-circuit your ability and willingness to learn and grow?

15

Being a Model of Empathy and Compassion

It is my choice to care deeply about others. No kindness is too small to be unimportant— the smile to the bank teller, the sincere "thank you" for all kindnesses received, the reassuring hand on the shoulder of a loved one or friend. There is compassion in selfless generosity, but there is also compassion in heartfelt empathy.

—Jonathan Lockwood Huie

Being an Empath

For most of my life, I have been afraid of my feelings. Perhaps it is more accurate to admit that this fear is more about losing control and falling apart. There once was a time after a devastating breakup in college that I thought I was truly losing my mind. To this day, I cannot decide if I had the flu or a psychotic break, but I felt like I was going crazy and was helpless to stop the uncontrolled spin. I tried everything in my power to regain a semblance of control and clarity, eventually ending up at the counseling center on campus for help.

It is certainly no coincidence that I chose to become a mental health professional. I wanted desperately to protect myself against mental disturbances in the future. Sure I wanted to help others, but that just seemed like an extra bonus compared to the things I would learn during such an endeavor that could be useful in my own life. In that sense, it is also no surprise that I gravitated toward cognitive therapy initially because of the tools it provided to keep extreme emotional responses from taking over.

I once went to the hospital emergency room because I was worried my head was going to explode. It turned out it was only a slight headache, but I had never experienced one before, so the unfamiliar sensations freaked me out. In the same sense, ever since I left adolescence and early adulthood behind, I rarely experienced depression again, even though I spent much of my time talking to people about their own miserable conditions. Depression seemed to be a foreign state of mind that belonged to others.

Things changed for me in later life. I am not sure if it was the result of neurological aging effects, or my greater confidence to manage intense emotional states, but I am no longer so "even-tempered." I mention that in a good way. I feel almost *everything* these days more intensely. I cry during commercials on television. I am moved to tears whenever I am reminded of losses that can never be resolved. My boundaries have either been dismantled or else just worn down over time. I find it interesting that it is not my own direct experiences that hit me so much harder than ever but rather what I sense and feel vicariously in others around me. I have evolved into a kind of "empath," if there is really such a thing given the conflicting evidence. It has been speculated that a small percentage of the population has an enhanced ability to sense the feelings of others, a talent that can be used to increase compassion or else for far darker purposes to manipulate others.

In my case, more often than ever before I feel the suffering of others. I suppose I could turn off the emotional spigot since I do know how to do that pretty easily. But ever since the pandemic, ever since I have seen and felt so much misery around me, learned about so many losses, endured so many disappointments myself, it feels honorable and useful to acknowledge the pervasive despair.

I used to believe that the heightened empathic sensitivity that accompanies the job of a therapist was an awful burden and responsibility. After all, most of us are trained and supervised in such a way that we learn to put aside most of our personal reactions so that we can maintain a degree of detachment and objectivity in the relationship. This perspective allows us to hear and see things more clearly, especially when it is balanced with our capacity for deep empathic resonance. Over time, most practitioners are able to develop and further enhance their empathic sensitivity, especially when they become more skilled at letting disruptive reactions dissipate. That is why I've been so curious about why I have been shifting in the opposite direction, relying far more on my emotional sensitivity rather than only the usual rational analysis. Whereas I used to put clients (and former clients) out of my mind once they left my immediate care, now I seem to enjoy thinking about them in affectionate and constructive ways. I do not mean rehashing conversations simply to process what happened or why but rather to honor the intimacy and trust of our relationship, even when it was relatively brief.

After so many years, I still see, hear, and even *feel* the presence of my former clients and students whose lives I influenced, just as they touched mine. There are many who are just blurred images in my mind but a few others who I think about on occasion and wonder how they are doing. So often we never find out the end of the stories in which we were once included as major characters.

Hurricane Harvey was the most devastating hurricane Houston had survived in a long time, if ever. Tens of thousands of people were left homeless and drenched in the relentless storm. The convention center downtown had been converted into a homeless shelter with people crowded together on cots. Our psychiatric unit had set up a trauma clinic, which was really just a half dozen privacy tents with chairs. Across the aisle, CVS had set up a companion pharmacy where the displaced residents could get their prescriptions filled. There was one woman, in particular, who showed up at my "office" that I will likely never forget, not only because she was so extremely agitated and upset but also because I could so easily identify with her. She was an affluent and successful professional who had just lost almost everything in her life—her home, car, possessions, and mostly her sense of safety.

We strolled around the facility together until we could find an unoccupied private space to talk. We spent several hours just chatting about her life. We showed one another photos of our grandchildren. I tried my best to let her know she was no longer alone. I so envied my psychiatrist colleagues who were prescribing antidepressant and antianxiety medications, whereas I felt so inadequate armed with only my empathy and support. We sat for a while until she was notified that temporary housing had been located for her. We hugged one another. Then she left. And I never saw her again.

It is just so dang frustrating at times that we never find out what happened to people after they depart from our care. Did our conversations provide any relief? Was there really something useful accomplished? How were relapses handled? How will they remember us long after the sessions ended?

I really worried about this woman after we parted and then castigated myself as I recalled the admonishment from a previous supervisor who reminded me that worrying about my clients would never actually help *them*, so it must be doing something for *me*. I generally agreed with that premise, except this time it was less about me hiding from something I was avoiding and more about feeling so incredibly grateful that I was so well positioned to be useful to others.

In this case, I had solicited a promise from the woman that she would reach out to me after she was resettled to let me know she was safe. It was only a few days later that she sent a reassuring message that she was now okay and that her family was rallying to her aid. She thanked me profusely and repeatedly for the help—but here's the thing—it felt like she saved me too!

Empathic Connections

When stories like this are revealed to colleagues or supervisors, we are usually warned about the dangers of losing our composure, putting ourselves at increased risk for compassion fatigue, burnout, vicarious trauma, or "boundary crossings" that could result in breaches of trust. Given how extraordinary the circumstances I often find myself in when working with disaster trauma teams, I have long ago realized that such isolation, lack of resources, and the overwhelming flood of survivors require unusual ways of being helpful. Without an office, operating in the "wilderness" filled with chaos, disruption, dangers, and continued uncertainty, we are often required to do things that would be misguided compared to the usual standards of care.

Anyone who has ever attended the standard, often required disaster training courses may have found it amusing that their strongest recommendation is to do an assessment and then refer victims to the nearest available medical facility for urgent care. That is a fabulous idea—but only if there are such facilities and resources accessible and available—which is often *not* the case when there is upheaval after an earthquake, tsunami, pandemic, war, or mass violence. Although it is certainly great advice to refer trauma victims to expert specialists, that is not exactly possible when the professionals cannot gain access to the territory when travel is restricted.

Working under such close and hazardous conditions, the usual safeguards and boundaries typically enforced in an office, clinic, or screen-based consultation are often set aside for the sake of practical considerations during this altered reality. People are often seriously injured or in the throes of panic. Resources are considerably limited. Lines of communication may be compromised, if available at all. There is even some question about whether one's own safety and health are at considerable risk. For these, and so many other reasons, it is challenging to remain comfortable, calm, and collected when the environment is so tumultuous and those who need help are so desperate and numerous. It is no wonder that the usual dispassionate, procedural processes that we follow do not work very well when the rules of engagement are radically different. It is one thing to remain somewhat detached when sitting in an attractive, comfortable, luxurious office; it is quite another when you are standing at ground zero after a catastrophic avalanche, hurricane, or mass shooting.

Above all else that we might try to do to stabilize and reassure people in such circumstances, so much depends on the empathic connections we are able to create and maintain. This capacity is what distinguishes us from all other creatures in that we have developed the ability to become "mind-readers," or at least the talent to sense and feel with others might be experiencing. Evolution has thus equipped us with the power to reliably and accurately sense what others are feeling and to place ourselves in their shoes (or sandals). This has permitted us to decode others' body language, facial expressions, and verbal subtleties in such a way that we can usually assess whether someone is an ally and friend or a potential threat. This has made it possible for us to function more cooperatively within our social groups and to respond sensitively to members of our "tribe" who need support, reassurance, or assistance (Mafessoni & Lachmann, 2019; Schulz, 2017). The empathic mind is also what makes counseling and psychotherapy work, in all its forms and permutations.

It may very well be the case that empathy is not so much a sensation as a form of hypothesis testing in which we shift back and forth between whatever we think is going on, whatever we are experiencing and feeling, compared to what we imagine is happening for someone else with whom we are engaged. It may be the case that this shared neural circuitry that constructs "social synapses" is similar to cellular physiology in that they create spaces that are conducive to enhanced communication (Cozolino, 2006).

Many of the early humanistic theorists like Carl Rogers, and self-psychologists such as Heinz Kohut, viewed empathy as one of the basic human endowments, along with vision, hearing, touch, smell, and taste: it is the way we *feel* others. Although early psychoanalysts did mention the importance of empathy in any therapeutic relationship, it was Carl Rogers (1957) who brought this feature to the forefront as one of his "core conditions." For Rogers, it was not just about feeling empathy toward clients but also being willing and able to accurately convey this deep understanding in such a way that others feel truly heard and supported. Along with the other core conditions of warmth, genuineness, congruence, respect, acceptance, and immediacy, the counselor's empathy was regarded as the highest therapeutic virtue. It is a component of *every* relational configuration, whether we call it the working alliance, real relationship, corrective emotional experience, or transference.

Counselors and therapists tend to be divided into two camps as far as the types of empathy they value (and practice). *Cognitive empathy* refers to the more analytic style of making sense of others' experiences by entering their frame of reference, whereas *affective empathy* is far more intuitive and focused on experienced emotional reactions. Not surprisingly, the most accomplished masters of empathy employ *both* kinds in order to serve several functions and produce an assortment of different responses (Howe, 2013). This is also at the heart of the main theme of this book—that we learn so many lessons as a result of the work we do, enhancing our empathic sensitivity. It is another reason why clients are often are best teachers.

It is through our close interactions with clients that we are reminded of issues and problems that we have yet to fully address. The deep conversations push us to examine aspects of ourselves that are less than pleasing. They teach us about resilience and courage, but they also test us with regard to setting limits. Most of all, they help us access greater compassion, caring, and yes, a kind of platonic, idealized love.

We are also well aware of how empathy can become a burden as well as a gift, depending on the type employed. There have been four distinct types of empathic responses that are most often employed during therapeutic encounters (Elliot et al., 2011). *Empathic understanding responses* communicate clearly, and reasonably accurately, the client's experience, or at least the facets that were shared in session. This is what we most commonly learned during early training as reflections of content and feeling: "I hear how difficult it is for you to talk about these issues. You are wondering how safe it really is to explore what you are feeling given that others like me have responded so punitively in the past."

Empathic affirmations validate rather than interpret or reflect the client's experience: "It takes a tremendous amount of courage and resolve on your part to continue to push through your ambivalence when you wonder whether the effort is really worth what you will gain. But regardless of the result, you should feel proud of the risks you are willing to take."

Empathic evocations help to probe, invite, facilitate, and draw out deeper explorations of innermost thoughts and feelings: "As difficult as it is for you to talk about your reactions to what happened with your parents, I notice that you seem to feel more relieved getting some of this out and in the open."

Finally, *empathic explorations* dig much deeper to excavate some of the hidden, buried, disguised, disowned aspects of the client's experience: "I notice that although you quickly moved on from talking about the feelings of hurt that have been festering for some time, you seemed to circle back to those issues again and again as if a part of you really wants to heal those wounds and yet you are afraid of the increased pain that may result."

Regardless of how empathy is experienced, labeled, and employed, it is the singular talent that we command that allows us to better function as part of a social group. Other creatures, such as termites or ants, are able to coordinate their extraordinary cooperative actions for trail formation, nest excavation, and food gathering and distribution via chemical reactions. Biologist Lewis Thomas (1978), who spent his life studying the behavior of social insects, noted that rather than functioning as separate individuals, ants and termites are really just a single animal interconnected through their communication system to share a single thought and pursue a common goal. This may sound ridiculous at first, until you consider that these insects work cooperatively to farm their food in the form of fungi, raise their own livestock as aphids, raise and send armies into combat to defeat enemies, employ chemical weapons, confuse enemies through misdirection, even engage in child labor. About the only thing ants don't do, Thomas noted, is watch television.

Takeaways

It's interesting that there is a four-letter word we are *never* allowed to use when talking about our therapeutic relationships. It is a word that never appears in the flagship academic journals, nor even in most of the books that tackle our discipline. It is never heard at a professional conference, except perhaps for shock value.

I know what you're thinking—and you are wrong.

The four-letter word I'm referring to, the one almost never mentioned in the context of our work, is l-o-v-e, love. Naturally, I am not referring to romantic or amorous love, which signifies some form of abuse and professional misconduct in the context of therapeutic relationships. Such inappropriate feelings can lead to dangerous countertransference reactions, resulting in possible exploitation or betrayal.

Instead, I am referring to what the Greeks called *agape*: the type of love characterized by affection, compassion, respect, and deep caring for others, regardless of perceived flaws and annoyances. This type of love almost always includes some kind of personal sacrifice, whether an investment of time, energy, resources, or abilities. Given this commitment, it is no wonder we are compensated for putting others' needs and interests before our own.

I wonder about the extent to which we learn to become better "lovers" in our own personal lives—with friends, family members, a partner—as a result of the compassion, benevolence, and focused attention we devote to our clients Surely in all that time we spend listening so intently to others' stories, giving them the very best we have to offer, there *must* be some carryover to our personal relationships. Of course, this does not occur automatically but rather when we make a commitment to share the best part of our training, experience, and ourselves with those who matter most in our lives.

Questions for Reflection or Discussion

1. What are some ways you try to practice compassion and caring toward others during your daily life? What is a recent example of this that still stick with you?

2. What do you believe is the origin and source of your empathy, as well as the reason why you chose to devote a part of your life to serving others?

3. Think of a time in your life when you were "healed" by empathy—that is, when someone's caring, respect, and support for you ultimately made you feel more whole.

16

Telling Inspirational and Instructive Stories

That's what storytellers do. We restore order with imagination. We instill hope again and again.

—Walt Disney

Storytelling in Therapy—and Everyday Life

Once upon a time, in a land far, far away. . .

I just put you into a hypnotic state. As soon as you read that familiar phrase that sometimes begins a story, your brain likely activated mirror neurons, preparing to take in the narrative that will provide a vicarious experience that will feel almost as real as anything you encounter through direct engagement. Such a capacity allows you to accumulate new learning and significant lessons, all without leaving your chair. You can slay dragons, fight trolls, defeat a zombie hoard, save the world, or launch a noble quest, all without jeopardizing your health and safety. You can travel anywhere in the world, even to planets in distant solar systems, and it only costs a little time.

This capacity for using imagination and cognitive functioning to treat stories as alternative forms of reality is absolutely unique to our species and may very well account for our dominance on the planet. Perhaps even more evolutionary significant than our upright stance and opposable thumbs may very well be the ways our brain developed in order to process stories as a means of transmitting useful information and constructing civilizations. After all, we are the only animals that are able to record our history, store and share critical information for subsequent generations, and imbibe all kinds of important lessons via the experiences of others around us. All of this makes it possible for us to develop greater cognitive flexibility, prepare defensive responses against perceived threats, promote empathy and deeper connections with others, and better interpret motives and the innermost thoughts of adversaries and allies.

With this phenomenon in mind, I would like to tell you a story to highlight the main themes to be explored. It is something I am a little hesitant to share because it reveals my rather peculiar and wild imagination. I have always lived part of my life in an alternative universe. I have been told that as a child I had an imaginary playmate who I would insist have a place set for him at the dinner table, or a seat next to me in the car. Apparently, I kept him around for some time until one evening in the bathtub, I casually mentioned that he had been swirled down the drain with the bathwater. I never spoke of him again.

Perhaps like many young boys of my age and generation, I was profoundly affected by the comic books and other literature I consumed, especially those that featured super-heroes. Being able to fly would be so awesome, a power that I experimented repeatedly to develop with practice. I used to tie a towel around my neck and launch a running start off a table to take off into space—but alas I just ended up with bruises and scolding from my parents. I believed that if only I wished and tried harder, eventually this fantasy might very well come true.

Once I advanced from toddlerhood to adolescence, my priorities definitely changed. I was willing to sacrifice flight for a power that would be even more valuable, considering my particular station in life. I decided to settle on X-ray vision as an alternative for a hor-monally raging adolescent boy. I once saw an advertisement in one of my superhero comic books that featured X-ray glasses that were purported to see through objects, especially clothes. I invested $1 of my hard-earned allowance for this magical device, only to discover that I had been scammed. Nevertheless, ever since then, I became completely enamored by tales of adventure that I would forever be beyond my abilities or opportunities.

Even to this day, I devour a fictional novel every week. My taste is indiscriminate, as I love escape fiction of every genre and type. I find these tales not only entertaining but also instructive in some ways as they help me imagine what I might do in similar scenarios of danger. If you have ever seen a "slasher" movie, the genre where typically scantily clad sorority girls are partying inside the house while a knife-wielding, masked psychopath waits outside for his next victims, then you are already well aware that under no circumstances should you go outside to investigate when you hear a strange noise. There is actually some merit to this advice, although seemingly nobody in the films ever listens to it—except the virgin, who is usually the only person to survive. Given the number of such thriller films and books I've consumed, I am just about as well prepared to defeat a vampire, werewolf, or serial killer as possible.

For some time, I had been thoroughly devoted to a series of books about a zombie apoc-alypse. You know the usual plot. There has been a virus that has transformed most of the human race into the walking dead. The only ones who survive are sufficiently familiar with the literature and films on the subject that they are already well equipped to defend themselves against the ravenous herd (you have to destroy their brains!). These books were delightfully entertaining (and educational!) but also rather haunting since it felt over time that I was truly living in this zombie world. That, of course, is the sign of a well-told story, one that is so immersive, detailed, and vivid that it feels as if it is really happening, and we really are at risk to be eaten. As far as our nervous system is concerned, it really does feel that way.

I did not realize the extent to which this tale had hijacked my brain until I went for a run afterward and found myself highly anxious after another runner passed me and gave me a "high five." I'm sure it was intended as a friendly gesture but my demented mind began to wonder if the guy might have passed along a zombie virus, or something worse, when he touched my hand. Of course, this is utterly ridiculous, if not psychotic, but it still felt like I was occupying this fictional world that had been so thoroughly constructed. I actually turned around and ran home to wash my hands.

I could not decide if I was more ashamed, astounded, or amused by this episode, finally settling on the lesson that it so clearly revealed to me. In all the important jobs I have in my life as a teacher, public speaker, supervisor, therapist, parent, grandparent, and especially as a writer, I am essentially a professional storyteller. I came to realize that what I actually do for a living (and so do *you*) is to honor and "hold" the stories of others, either through conversation, observation, or reading. Second, based on my own experiences, as well as everything I have heard, seen, read, and learned, the other thing that I do most often is to tell inspirational stories to others to influence and impact their behavior.

Features and Functions of Therapeutic Storytelling

There are all kinds of ways that therapists and counselors attempt to help their clients. Among the most common skills and interventions employed are standard practices such as interpreting underlying meanings, reflecting deep feelings, explaining ideas, challenging cognitive distortions, prescribing tasks, and so on. But these are all direct responses, those that are often subject to a certain amount of resistance or denial. As such, we are always looking for ways to bypass this reluctance and defiance through more subtle, indirect methods. When we offer a story to someone who is struggling, especially one that they can identify with and relate to, one that highlights similar themes that are operating in their own experiences, we are much more likely to have an enduring effect.

It is not unreasonable to suggest that perhaps the single most powerful strategy or intervention within a helping professional's repertoire involves the telling of a relevant, personally adapted narrative that reveals themes that might otherwise be ignored. Just consider all the possible features and functions that stories can serve within the context of therapeutic, mentoring, or instructional relationships. Captured within these subtle, often disguised and indirect tales, are lessons that present a kind of "coded" information in an efficient package. They are specifically designed to capture interest and attention through dramatic elements, capitalizing on the natural structural and functional properties of memory retention. It is precisely these novel and surprising features that lead to enduring impact when compared to routine or familiar methods of discourse. So many other advantages and benefits make storytelling one of our most influential options for facilitating new insights and promoting changes.

- ✓ Provides a different form of "direct experience" through vicarious identification

- ✓ Evokes strong emotional reactions that inspire, motivate, or ignite passion

- ✓ Induces altered states of consciousness and hypnotic inductions through immersion in the narrative

- ✓ Resonates with cultural and historical traditions within community, tribal, and social/political/environmental contexts

- ✓ Bypasses resistance and defensiveness through the subtle introduction of concepts and ideas

- ✓ Appeals to multiple dimensions of complexity and cognitive processing

- ✓ Facilitates recognition of patterns across life experiences

- ✓ Introduces overarching, organizing scaffolds to understand phenomena and life experiences

- ✓ Introduces alternative realities (fantasy) that facilitate creative thinking

- ✓ Teaches significant adaptation and problem-solving skills through vicarious experiences

- ✓ Presents alternative pathways and options for viewing problems and their solutions

- ✓ Provides opportunities for rehearsal of new behavior through surrogates

- ✓ Reframes and reconstructs trauma "victim stories" into courageous tales of survival and achievement

- ✓ Promotes restitution, renewal, and redemption when stories are recast in one's own life narrative

- ✓ Provides adjuncts (bibliotherapy) to sessions that support lessons learned or challenge dysfunctional beliefs

- ✓ Leads to critical evaluation of parallel issues that might otherwise feel threatening

- ✓ Promotes wisdom, tolerance, and flexibility in thinking about self, others, and the world

- ✓ Encapsulates the mystery of change, including features and processes that we will never fully understand

Just as the narratives and disclosures we construct and share with clients haunt them in ways that other verbalizations cannot touch, so too do the stories they reveal often stick with us in ways that are unforgettable (Aguilera et al., 2020; Henyon, 2021). It does not even seem to make much difference whether the stories are truthful and accurate or not as to whether they remain indelible memories. In so many ways, fictional stories, whether told in sessions, on the screen, or in a book, are potentially even more impactful because of the ways they capture imagination and attention (Appel, 2008; Shackleford & Vinney, 2020). Just think about all the hours people spend watching television shows, videos, and movies, reading novels, listening to blogs and song lyrics, playing video games, plus all the conversations that take place during the course of the day, most of which involve telling stories about oneself and others. The brain has thus evolved to become essentially a "storied organ" that has the capability of treating vicarious experiences as if they are as real as anything else we might experience (Friskie, 2020; Gottschall, 2012; Hammel, 2018; Kottler, 2015; Spaulding, 2011).

There are so many different forces at work when stories are harnessed for therapeutic purposes. One way to think about trauma, for example, is that it really represents a "disordered" story, one that consists of a bunch of fragmented, incoherent memories that have yet to be placed in long-term storage (Botwin, 2020). Instead, memories become recursive, disturbing, intrusive images that are reexperienced over and over again. What is often required is a professional storyteller in the form of a counselor, therapist, teacher, or even a novelist who can provide an alternative narrative of what transpired but in a far more adaptive, constructive form. One relatively simple example of this is when we "reframe" or "reauthor" a client's disclosure: "When you say you've never really been able to express yourself at home the way you want, what you really mean is that you have not yet worked up the courage to risk changing the pattern of your relationship." Every time we recast client verbalizations, challenge beliefs, reshape attitudes, present alternative interpretations of what happened, we are telling a different, more empowering story instead of one in which the protagonist is presented as a helpless victim.

Mental health professionals most often attempt to reconstruct tales of woe into courageous tales of survival and growth. We emphasize the possibilities for renewal and redemption that can take place, or else highlight the existential search for greater life meaning. The clinician's own judicious use of self-disclosure may reduce the power imbalance and model certain values or attributes that are considered important at the time. Whereas often these personal stories are intended to reveal alternative ways of handling situations, humanizing the therapist, or presenting teaching points, they are also commonly used to provide a sense of immediacy and authenticity to the encounter.

Takeaways

It may not have been part of the standard curriculum, but there is little doubt that a big part of what helping professionals do is offer particular kinds of stories that are intended to highlight core issues and provide alternative ways of processing experiences. A case has been made that one of the unheralded roles of a therapist or counselor is their ability as a consummate storyteller who is able to share both real life and made-up illustrations that are poignant, vivid, and provoke emotional resonance. It is also critical that the examples are perceived by clients as highly relevant and applicable to their own situations.

Among all our talents and capabilities, being an exceptional storyteller should be high on the list, even if it is not typically included in training programs or even mentioned very often in continuing education workshops. Nevertheless, there are few life skills that are more useful, whether as a form of persuasion, influence, instruction, healing, enlightenment, or entertainment. Once it has been decided that this is an important growth edge for future personal and professional development, therapists can become students of this age-old craft that has always been the glue that holds communities together. Throughout history, storytelling has been the primary way to pass along critical information, mark historical events, entertain people, and promote a shared cultural identity. Within most Indigenous communities, the village storyteller, usually an elder, is considered to be among the most important and revered members. The same is true with respect to our own culture where many screenwriters, movie producers, musicians, composers, novelists, and actors are highly respected and extremely well compensated for their contributions.

The most highly skilled storytellers, whether troubadours, playwrights, poets, lyricists, teachers, or therapists, are familiar with the structures and features of stories that are most likely to have enduring and potent effects. First and foremost, a well-told story must grab the listener's/reader's attention—and keep the person riveted throughout the narrative. After all, if the person is disengaged, distracted, or bored, then you are just wasting your time. That is why it is important to give yourself permission to be dramatic, passionate, flamboyant, and highly expressive. Use dialogue and vivid details to make the action come alive. Include something unique, novel, and provocative to catch the person or audience by surprise (heightening attention) and stimulate active curiosity. Access all the senses of sound, smell, sight, and touch, placing the listener *in the story*. The goal, after all, is to move someone emotionally, stimulating *intense* experiences vicariously. In order to do so, the best narrators customize and adapt the story to the specific context to make sure it is personal, relevant, and clearly connected to the themes under discussion.

One final point that is grounded in psychological research, and well-known by any extraordinary professional storyteller, is that the themes and takeaways are best kept somewhat ambiguous and obtuse so that the audience is required to find or create the meaning that is most relevant and applicable to them. Rather than handing them the lesson on a silver platter, it is far better to make them work for it, to own it, to personalize it. They are invited to wander and explore, "Hmmm. That's interesting. What does this have to do with *me*?"

Walt Disney, perhaps one of the greatest storytellers of all time, reminds us in the quote that began this chapter that the most significant and influential stories are those that feature hope and possibilities, especially those that inspire people to take constructive actions. In the immortal words of Dory from the animated Disney film, *Finding Nemo*: "When life gets you down, do you want to know what you've got to do? Just keep swimming."

Questions for Reflection or Discussion

1. What's a story that had a powerful influence or impact on your life? This could have been a fairy tale, myth, or legend you encountered as a child. It could have been sparked by a comic book, puppet show, song lyrics, play, opera, documentary film, movie, television show, short story, novel, or a story told to you by someone else. Regardless of its source, this story continues to haunt you to this day, perhaps in some way responsible for who you have become.

2. What is a story that you frequently find yourself telling clients (or others) to illustrate some favored idea, to inspire, motivate, or support them in some way? This could include a metaphor, teaching tale, self-disclosure, or other anecdote.

3. What are some ways that you might become more sensitive, expressive, and focused on your identity as a holder and teller of stories? What gets in the way of you becoming more creative, flexible, confident, and accomplished as a storyteller?

Doing Less, Not More

I've always been better at caring for and looking after others than I have been caring for myself.

—Carl Rogers

When Less Really Is More

Very little in life has seemed to come very easily to me, even though I enjoyed an extraordinarily privileged life. My parents, although they did not seem to like each other very much and were not around when I most needed them, still provided me with a safe, luxurious lifestyle, an education, and a lot of encouragement, even if it seemed at the time to fall on deaf ears. School was always challenging for me. I had no particular talent as an athlete—or anything else it seemed to me. I did not have much ambition, largely the result of such low expectations from myself and others.

It occurred to me that if I was going to do anything meaningful in life, or accomplish very much, I would have to work *much* harder than anyone else. Given how stupid and inept I believed myself to be, it would have to be determined effort that would become the great equalizer. I quickly internalized the belief that I would always have to do more than anyone else, work faster than anyone else, if I had any hope of personal and career success. It became a habit for me whenever I felt stuck to just push harder and harder until I could break through. I was rejected by dozens of graduate schools and yet kept exploring other options. My first book manuscripts were similarly rejected by every publisher I contacted. The same was true with respect to academic job applications that were limited at the time because of affirmative action and diversity requirements; I spent a decade exiled until such time that opportunities were open once again.

There have been a half dozen different times in my life when this drive to do better, to do more, has led to serious complications and side effects. It helps explain why I've quit so many jobs. The same unrealistic expectations that I have for myself are often projected onto others, often leaving me disappointed and dissatisfied. No wonder I have hit the burnout wall a few times, throwing myself against an immovable object with even greater determination and flailing frustration. Typically, I would just push even harder.

There is a lot of talk these days about the importance of moderating the energy and effort we expend via self-care strategies. It has been apparent for some time that stressors on the job can lead to devastating emotional and behavioral consequences, not to mention reduced productivity. Depression, anxiety, addictions, health complaints can all result from overwhelming pressure. More recently "quiet quitting" is the order of the times, doing the absolute minimum just to get through the days.

I have tried all kinds of things to better metabolize the stress, sleep disruptions, and worries that I hold onto. I exercise every day without fail. I tried tai chi, yoga, meditation, mindfulness exercises, cooking classes, support groups, journaling, taking naps, hiking, going on adventurous trips, reading escape fiction. They are all immensely interesting, entertaining, at times enjoyable, but it also feels like they are just one more burden of responsibility I must take on board. My problem is that I am already overscheduled and have too much to do, so how do I address this? By adding additional burdens I feel obligated to complete? It seems to me that the ultimate in self-care is *not* adding more required things to do but reducing the existing ones to more manageable limits.

Why Self-Care Strategies Often Fail

Although self-care books, media, workshops, and seminars have been the most popular topic for some time; after the accumulative effects of the worldwide pandemic, the need for such efforts became even more dire. One example of the most universal advice offered is that everyone, regardless of age and condition, should become more physically active to increase longevity and improve health functioning. Almost everyone, health professionals and the public alike, agree that this is an excellent idea.

The various media outlets are stacked with simplistic admonishments that we should all take better care of ourselves, offering the kind of advice people love to hear that involves minimum effort and "magic tricks" that will inevitably fail. People are urged to buy scented candles, schedule weekly massages, take hot baths, eat brown rice, practice guided meditation or hot yoga, work out in front of a fitness mirror, repeat verbal affirmations, express gratitude, drink water, stretch, watch funny videos—the list is endless. And they all come with the reassurance that they require only 5 minutes a day to see magical results. There are best-selling books with titles like *Faking It: How to Seem Like a Better Person Without Actually Improving Yourself*, or articles that promise "5 Instant Ways to Counteract Stress When Feeling Overwhelmed." It is not that such literature necessarily offers bad advice, just such simplistic tasks can sometimes create even greater problems over time, leading to increased frustration, disappointment, guilt, and a sense of futility.

Self-care efforts typically involve adding even more tasks, activities, and burdens to an already overstressed lifestyle. Since people often have wildly unrealistic expectations for themselves, especially when it involves launching a new routine, most initial efforts are likely to be less than what was hoped. This sets in motion feelings of discouragement and guilt, further sabotaging future attempts and programming inevitable relapses. When all is said and done, a person may legitimately wonder if it would not have been best to just leave things the way they were in the first place. Interestingly, self-care efforts tend to prove most useful when they are designed to strategically *reduce* involvement in activities rather than adding more things to do (Bressi & Valden, 2017; Havlin, 2019; Lakshmin, 2018).

There are many other reasons why people are unsuccessful in implementing their own mental health and wellness plans. One of the most common mistakes has to do with the failure to recognize and acknowledge the problems that require attention. Like any of our clients, we sometimes engage in wishful thinking that things will likely improve on their own if we just show more patience. When that does not bring relief, next on the agenda is to seek out "instant cures," all the quick-fix solutions that are promised in the media. Drink green smoothies. Take a course on mindfulness. Of course, each of these options does provide some temporary relief that quickly dissipates once the usual commitments and pressures resume.

It is more than a little ironic that the reason self-care is needed in the first place is because of a time crunch in which there just are not enough hours in the day (and night) to complete all the desired tasks. Well over 90% of mental health practitioners report at least some difficulties with stress and compassion fatigue in their lives, a predicament that was considerably exacerbated during and after the pandemic. Besides military personnel, air traffic controllers, or bomb disposal technicians, few other professions are more emotionally draining and overwhelming than our own. This is not because we are subjected to physical dangers as much as an assortment of far more subtle pressures that require us to exercise extraordinary restraint and self-control, operate in isolation, and deal with continuous confusion, complexity, and uncertainty. When intense intimacy and personal triggers are added to the picture, one can easily appreciate the challenges of our strange jobs sitting alone with someone, listening to their worst fears and disturbing secrets.

Stress on the Job

Since therapists are supposed to be superhuman in their ability to manage emotional suffering, there is often shame and reluctance associated with acknowledging our own personal struggles. As mentioned in Chapter 10 on trauma, many of the most distinguished luminaries in our field, those we have been encouraged to emulate, were actually terrible models of excessive workaholism and self-neglect. Because of his bizarre death obsession, Sigmund Freud worked excessively on his various writing projects and practice. As a result, his lack of self-care resulted in blackouts, agoraphobia, and cocaine addiction, plus his self-destructive smoking of cigars even after a cancer diagnosis. Alfred Adler, Carl Rogers, and William James, among so many others, admitted to struggles with lifelong depression. R. D. Laing celebrated mental illness as another form of creativity, all the while he slowly fell apart with mental deterioration. Albert Ellis bragged that he worked close to 18 hours a day, 7 days a week (and he did seem pretty content and lived to be 94 years old). It would appear that emotional disruption may not be a requirement to become a noted figure in our field, but it certainly appears like a common variable among many candidates.

For the rest of us mortals who are trying to earn a living and balance work with family and other interests, we are subjected to different kinds of stressors than the luminaries just mentioned. Administrative oversight may be lacking, or subject to neglect or incompetence. Resources are increasingly diminished. The political climate has led to greater conflict and disagreements. Climate change and global warming are sparking unprecedented fears for the viability of our planet. We are asked to take on even greater responsibilities without commiserate support. The severity of problems we treat is becoming increasingly more commonplace. Once upon a time a half-century ago, the most annoying discipline problems of young people in schools were chewing gum, running in the hallways, or talking out of turn. Compare that to what teachers and counselors must deal with today with verbal (or physical) abuse of teachers and classmates, rampant bullying, sexual harassment, racism, drug addictions, school shootings, and widespread depression and anxiety. How could we even imagine that children would be subjected to "active shooter drills" to prepare for killers with automatic weapons who might at any time burst through the doors?

In addition, the nature of our jobs, sitting in a chair for hours at a time, is at odds with the ways our bodies evolved to be able to run 20 miles each day on hunting expeditions; instead, the average person now walks less than one third of a mile, probably even less so now that so many people are working from home. This only contributes to greater isolation and loneliness, as well as less engagement with other staff for mutual support. There once was a time when meetings, consultations, and supervision only took place face-to-face, creating opportunities to process what happened afterward, commiserating with one another over complaints and frustrations, continuing discussions to find alternative solutions. Nowadays, however, once a distance-based meeting is concluded, the screen goes blank abruptly, leaving us wondering what actually occurred.

Self-care techniques, strategies, and programs often do not make much of a dent in the underlying issues that are really causing most of the difficulty (Kottler, 2021). People complain that they just do not have time to get things done, or they cannot seem to remain motivated to follow through on commitments, or what they tried previously did not work. We hear these excuses all the time from our clients but what they are really saying is that there's something else going on behind the scenes that remains unexamined and addressed. There are always really good reasons that unresolved personal issues continue to plague us, often the result of family problems, interpersonal conflicts, previous trauma, or a lack of meaning in work and life.

Reminders About the Reciprocal Gifts Received

We do indeed receive many "gifts" from our clients in the form of reminders to take better care of ourselves. Sure, there are all sorts of contagious processes going on during our interactions with clients. Just as we are at risk to catch their colds and viruses, we are exposed to their greatest fears, terrors, and shame, and haunted by their traumatic tales of misery and suffering. In addition to these dangers that may affect our own sense of well-being, we are also permitted to bask in the feelings of goodwill that accompany the significant growth that we witness. We are inspired by these improvements in such a way that we can apply them to ourselves. Every session we conduct potentially concludes with a little homework assignment for ourselves to do better in our own lives.

As far as what best anticipates trouble ahead in terms of emotional exhaustion and burnout for practitioners, one of the best predictors is excessive work demands, devoting too many hours serving others without sufficient time for recovery. Next on the list is an incompetent or neglectful supervisor, someone who is clueless but very opinionated and controlling, demanding that you follow instructions that are confusing or inappropriate. Therapists also consistently report a major source of stress related to the toxic organizational culture of their agency, one that includes backbiting, undermining, and competition for limited resources. That is one reason why some practitioners avoid the staff lounge at all costs to avoid hearing the constant whining and complaints that lead to only greater frustration and despair.

When facing struggles, painful and challenging situations, it is much easier to suffer the trials and tribulations when we know they are for some useful purpose. It is worth it to subject oneself to a painful, exhausting exercise routine when it results in improved health and fitness. We may be willing to endure certain annoyances, discomforts, and inconveniences if it is believed that these sacrifices result in new, exciting adventures, or at least some worthwhile benefit for others. It is certainly the case that some of the people we try to help test us in ways that are more than a little frustrating. In addition, some aspects of the job are less than satisfying—the paperwork, administrative oversight, demanding schedule, meager compensation, rude, ungrateful clients, meddling family members, to mention a few of the stressors. But we can put up with the aggravation when we can see clearly the desired results and outcomes. And indeed there are few other lines of work anywhere that offer more gifts and growth.

Much of our effort to make a difference in people's lives becomes considerably eroded when we do not also take better care of ourselves. This is not about adding additional requirements to our daily schedule but rather acknowledging the ways that our lifestyles are less than optimal. By the time self-care programs are actually needed, it may be too late—it just feels like there's no discretionary time to add another thing that will only increase the levels of stress. The nature of our contemporary lives with 24-hour access to our mobile devices is that we are never really off duty any longer. The average person now physically touches their phone over 3,000 times a day! Three quarters of young people actually *sleep* with their phones, leading to a new phenomenon of "sleep texting" in which a person will receive a message in the middle of the night and then reply to it without ever remembering that occurred.

Just as we spend considerable time and effort helping clients examine their lifestyle choices in order to improve the quality of their daily lives, we are encouraged to do much the same. We not only know well what it takes to keep the mind and body in the best shape, but we teach this to others on a regular basis. It is worth mentioning once again how important it is to listen to the advice we tell clients about what most likely leads to well-being and a satisfied life—a healthy diet, regular exercise, meaningful work, and a few close friends. In addition, there are a few personality traits that are most associated with such life satisfaction and success:

1. *Conscientiousness* is essential to get stuff done. Such individuals are both responsible and responsive. They look both ways when they cross the street. They listen to their doctor's advice. They always show up on time and do what they say they'll do. As such, they tend to be respected and valued by others.

2. *Hardiness* is that quality of maintaining control during times of upheaval, as well as being able to recover quickly after disappointments or setbacks. This trait immunizes people against extreme mood swings and encourages successful relapse prevention.

3. *Resilience* is also a strong component of any self-care process, one that increases confidence, resourcefulness, and the ability to deal with any unforeseen situation.

These are some of the characteristics that most immunize anyone against stress, as well as increase life expectancy. We help others to strengthen these traits and abilities, all the while internalizing some of the lessons in our own lives. Most important of all is one of our most valuable skills of cognitive restructuring that we teach on a daily basis, helping others to convert *distress* into *eustress*, the type of positive arousal that actually improves performance. Instead of seeing novel situations as frightening and disturbing, we think of them as stimulating and exciting. What is initially viewed as annoying or inconvenient can be seen instead as challenging and opportunistic. What may have felt discouraging can be changed into hope. This is precisely what we teach to others that can so easily be turned toward ourselves.

Takeaways

The single most popular posts on social media include the 20 million messages declaring the intention to take better care of oneself. Millions of people each day promise they are going to practice self-soothing, self-enhancing strategies to improve their well-being. This explains why three quarters of people who have gym or fitness memberships never, *ever* use the facilities. Each month they dutifully pay their fees (averaging $60) believing that *eventually* they will manage to walk through the doors—but they never do. It is like paying insurance premiums to make oneself feel better but never actually following through on one's intentions. This is not unlike the reality that people make the same New Year's resolutions every year, often 10 times in a row, vowing to lose weight, start an exercise program, end a relationship, catch up with neglected tasks, but "forget" to follow through.

There is no greater hypocrisy than mental health professionals who neglect their own mental health. A majority of professionals admit that they continue to see clients even though they are experiencing their own symptoms of depression or anxiety. It is a mystery how certain colleagues seem to barely manage their own lives, and yet they attempt to assist others with the same problems. This is just absolutely unacceptable and completely ignores the potential benefits of learning significant lessons from our clients about the importance of facing the stressors in our lives.

It is worthwhile to do an honest assessment of one's own daily functioning and lifestyle choices prior to making a plan regarding which cutbacks might be appropriate and wise. If aspects of your life feel a bit out of control, if you are starting to feel weighed down or discouraged, then the best solution may not very well include additional self-care tasks but instead may involve reducing stressors to more manageable limits.

Questions for Reflection or Discussion

1. What are some of the sources of stress that you could reduce or eliminate in your life?

2. What are some other examples of how the rule of "less is more" could be applied, besides the obvious ones like diet and consumption?

3. What is a self-care strategy you've tried repeatedly without much success over time? What could you do instead of that option that might actually involve less effort rather than an additional burden?

18

Improving Patience and Composure

If the person you are talking to doesn't appear to be listening, be patient. It may simply be that he has a small piece of fluff in his ear.

—A. A. Milne

This Is Who I Am

Let's acknowledge that I am not the most patient person. I became a therapist in the first place under the misguided notion that I could fix other people's problems because I felt so helpless to deal with some of my own difficulties. I suppose impatience is one of those at the top of the list.

Under the best of circumstances, I am in a hurry to get things done. My inbox is usually empty. I respond to correspondence or messages within hours, if not minutes. Sometimes I think that those "close door" buttons on elevators or switches on crosswalks were invented just for me—even though they rarely seem to work (I've wondered if they are not really just decoys to give us something to do while waiting).

I have always felt that life is short and that anything worth doing can be done more quickly and efficiently. I suppose many others must agree with me considering that we now have options like speed dating, 7-minute workout apps, and even speed yoga.

As a life philosophy, I do not believe in standing in line—for almost *anything*. There is no movie, restaurant, or shop, no object of desire that is worthy of my time to wait endlessly for people to take their turn. I would prefer to go somewhere else or just do without. Yet in spite of that policy, it feels like I have spent half my life waiting for people to get moving, to do what they say they are going to do. After all, it seems like I have spent too much time waiting for clients to get into gear and achieve all the goals they *say* are so important to them. But instead, they stall. They equivocate. They make excuses. They blame everyone else. They often seem to move at a glacial pace. And the more I try to hurry things along, the worse things seem to become.

Over time, I have learned to moderate myself, to proceed at the often measured pace of some of my clients who want to take their time thinking about all kinds of things before they ever move into action mode. "That's okay," I repeatedly reassure myself. "They will move forward when they're ready." I say that sort of thing all the time, but I must not believe it very convincingly considering how often my impatience takes over. I remember one example of this quite well, mostly because it could have ended in such a disaster. I suppose my best defense was that in those days there were so few effective strategies for countering cocaine addiction.

I agreed to see a new referral when he told me on the phone he was having some family issues. That sounded both familiar and relatively benign, the sort of thing I could "fix" within a relatively short period of time. I already had a full caseload, mostly of relatively long-term clients, so I was eager to work with someone who might show immediate improvement. I would feel so much better about myself if I could actually definitively help someone in a relatively short period of time.

Graham seemed like the embodiment of a successful business executive. Expensive suit. Tie loosened at the collar. Rolex watch. Gucci loafers. Haughty attitude. As soon as he walked in the door, I found that I did not like him very much.

"How can I help you?" I began right away. He seemed like the type of guy who would say something like, "Time is money."

"Well, as I mentioned on the phone, I'm sort of having some family problems."

"Family problems?" I prompted, settling into the familiar routine.

"Yeah," he shrugged. "Mostly my wife."

He then went on to explain that his wife was the one who urged him to seek help because she believed he had some sort of drug problem. When I looked at him quizzically, he just shrugged and said, "I do a little cocaine from time to time. Nothing too excessive. Just a few lines when I need it. I have a very stressful job. Lots of responsibility. Lots of pressure. People depend on me."

Graham could tell I was not exactly buying his version of the story. It turned out, after pressing for details, he admitted that he was going through a gram of cocaine each day, hitting lines every few hours to fuel his energy and confidence in the face of unremitting pressures. For the first time, I felt some degree of compassion for the guy, realizing just what his world must be like, the appearances that must be kept up, the difficulties he was facing. I was also struck by his desperate image management; appearances were so important to him. I kept looking at him and wondering what I could possibly say or do that would make any real difference. Whereas Graham seemed to be putting on a good show of confidence and optimism, actually believing I had some answer for him, all I could feel was despair and helplessness.

When I asked Graham what I could do for him, or what he wanted from me, he just kind of shrugged again. He had made it clear the only reason he showed up in the first place was because his wife insisted he see someone to talk about this. I looked at my watch and noticed that only 20 minutes of the session had elapsed. Yet I knew, I just *knew*, that talking to him further was a colossal waste of time for both of us. I was not only feeling impatient, but I was also bored by this interaction because I could see where it was going and where we would end up. And it was not pretty. I had already been through this with so many others during the previous months, and the outcome was always hopeless: Clients would make promises they would never honor, always ready with a convenient excuse.

Maybe I was just tired, or in a bad mood. Certainly, I was feeling impatient. (These are the best reasons I can muster after the fact.) I just looked at Graham and shook my head. "I'm sorry, Graham, but I don't think I can help you."

He looked shocked. I do not think he was used to anyone telling him "no" about anything in his life; he was used to getting his way. He started to argue with me until I held up my hand for him to stop. "Please let me finish," I said to him. "You asked me what I think, so now I'm going to tell you. And you aren't going to like it."

Graham reluctantly nodded his head, waiting for what came next. I could tell that he was already preparing his next argument.

"Look," I said in a shrill voice, trying to command his attention, "the nature of your addiction to this drug, the amount you are consuming on a daily basis, qualifies as having a rather serious addiction, both physiologically and psychologically. You are spending thousands of dollars each month just to maintain your habit. You are hiding your behavior from everyone, lying to your family, friends, and colleagues, and mostly to yourself. I just can't help you. Your prognosis is terrible." After this rant, I just crossed my arms and looked at the door, waiting for him to depart in a huff.

The man just refused to believe that I could not, or would not, help him. He insisted that I do something on his behalf, whatever the cure might require.

"You want to know what the cure is for your condition?" I said to him in an almost angry voice. "You want to know what will fix this? Okay, here's the solution. You will continue to increase your drug use over time. Then you'll start to act out in even more extreme ways—sexually, risk-taking, decision-making, impulsive behavior. The cost of your habit will skyrocket out of control until you can no longer afford to hide the extent of what you're doing. You will be so far in debt, you'll probably end up in bankruptcy. You'll lose your job. Your marriage will end. Your kids will blame you for everything and it will take you the rest of your life to repair the damage. When, or *if*, you ever recover after you've lost everything you'll still have some chronic health problems that will take years off your life span—that is—if you don't die of abuse or an overdose sooner rather than later. I'm so sorry but there's just nothing I can do for you."

Graham stood up with dignity, shook my hand, and thanked me for my trouble. Then he calmly walked out the door. I still had 15 minutes left in the session to consider how inappropriate, unprofessional, and wildly shocking my behavior had been. I wondered if it might be time to take a break from this work since my impatience was so out of control.

This interaction was actually part of a pattern that emerged during this time in my life and career when I had lost some of my passion. I was tired of working with the relatively affluent, "worried well" in private practice. I was tired of listening to the complaints of people who were mostly bored with the routines and emptiness of their lives. Of course, there was a parallel process going on in which that was *exactly* what *I* was feeling in my own predicament. This led to considerable soul-searching and a decision to quit what I was doing and rededicate myself to public service and working with indigent clients. In some small way, Graham helped push me in this direction.

The Pace of Change

If there's one consistent area of my work that I have long needed to improve it is my patience, my willingness to allow clients, students, and interns to proceed at their own pace. Sometimes I just cannot help myself: I push and push and push, ignoring all the signals that announce pretty clearly, "I'm just not ready. Yet."

I have studied all the likely reasons for the pressure I put on others to proceed a little (or a lot) more quickly. I get bored easily, and I am ready to move on to something else, *anything* else, after sufficient time. I feel helpless and frustrated that we are not making faster progress, reflecting poorly on my ability to be helpful. There are aspects of my own behavior, and the larger world, that I cannot seem to do much about, so it feels even more urgent to push things along where I have some semblance of power and control. Sometimes I just feel the suffering of others too intensely and I just want those feelings to go away by changing the other person instead of myself.

There is a darker side to my lack of patience and tolerance as well in that I prefer to push—or ruin—things on my own terms. When I sense that progress isn't forthcoming at the rate and pace that I prefer, I am inclined to accelerate rather than reduce the pressure so at least I feel like I am doing something, even when it is making things far worse. If I become frustrated waiting for something that is taking too long, regardless of the opportunity, I sometimes decide to just pout, walk away, and tell myself I did not want it anyway.

It is easy to appreciate how I most frequently get in trouble with people I am trying to help. If I do not respect their preferences and priorities, it is obvious that one or both of us is going to be disappointed and frustrated. There is usually a running commentary inside my head all the while I'm pretending to listen compassionately (and patiently): "Come on already! Aren't you tired of this crap? We've been talking about this same stuff over and over again. When are you going to stop all this whining and complaining and finally *do* something about your situation?"

Every person moves forward at a pace at which they are capable and ready to proceed further. Run too swiftly and a fall is likely. Crawl too slowly and it may be too late. One of the major insights that we learn from helping others is that each such transformative journey has its own unique velocity, pace, and process. Client readiness levels vary considerably, depending on several factors, the first of which relates to previous attempts to fix things that resulted in success or failure. People become either discouraged or invigorated based on their past performance.

Other factors that may determine the pace of change that is possible for an individual at any point in time include the following:

Specific nature and seriousness of the symptoms. It only makes sense that the pace of progress depends on the severity of the problems confronted. A client can make relatively rapid headway with a common adjustment reaction as compared to a chronic personality disorder or psychotic process.

Intensity and duration of discomfort. In addition to the gravity of the problems confronted, it also matters how well the person is handling the situation. Motivation is significantly increased when the suffering seems intolerable.

Available time and energy to devote to the task. People are known to move just as fast as the situation requires to get the job done within the time parameters. If there is some urgency, then complacency can be overcome by necessity.

Realistic and attainable nature of the desired goals. When the objectives are out of reach, then the results are preordained to end in disappointment. When the declared goals are too optimistic, given the client's abilities and readiness, then futility may sabotage consistent progress.

Core beliefs and attitudes about future possibilities. People tend to be limited by their own vision of what can be achieved. When clients believe that they are not really capable of accomplishing very much, then they just stick with those minimal efforts. Likewise, when clients have optimistic and hopeful expectations for what the sessions can do for them, they are more likely to get the most from the experience.

Abilities and relevant skills that would be useful. Those who are particularly well-suited to complete a task are more likely to complete it in a timely way as opposed to those who don't have the requisite abilities. One's pace would be considerably accelerated if the person feels confident and effortless in applying new learning.

Health functioning. If someone is cognitively impaired or physically disabled, it may very well slow down the pace of growth and learning in some regard. This would especially be the case if energy levels are compromised by wear and tear on the body.

Planning for what lies ahead. Whether conceived as relapse prevention, rehearsal, or homework assignments, people are willing to accelerate their pace if they feel adequately prepared. The prospect of failure is much less concerning when you believe you can easily recover and continue onward.

Disruptive influences among family and peers. Most of the setbacks that people experience often result directly or indirectly from friends and relatives who actively or unconsciously sabotage their efforts. The pace of change may have to be significantly slowed down to accommodate the adjustments that others are required to make.

Supportive resources that are available. In addition to having friends and family members who are generally on board with the changes that are being initiated, it also helps to have access to other resources besides a counselor. This might include participation in social groups, membership in organizations, financial reserves, job flexibility, all of which may affect continued progress.

All these factors, plus so many other influences, do indeed affect a person's willingness to make needed changes. The particular speed and pace of this progress, however, depends as much on the quality of the therapeutic alliance as any of the factors just mentioned. It is that security that makes it feel safer to experiment, take risks, try novel strategies, test limits, and likely repeatedly fail prior to a successful result. When clients sense our own patience (or impatience) with their progress, it can either lead to renewed support or feelings of discouragement. It is certainly understandable that we would feel frustrated at times, not just because we want so badly for clients to feel better but also because our own healing powers are coming up short, reflecting poorly on our sense of competence.

A recent experience comes to mind when I found myself arguing with a client.

"I'm curious," I began haltingly, wanting to get the phrasing right, "why exactly it seems so difficult for you to follow through on the tasks that you said you wanted to complete." Good job, I said to myself. Level, neutral voice.

"Well," the client replied, shaking her head. "I never said I was going to do ..."

I take a deep breath. "Actually, you did. Last time you said ..."

"Well, what I *really* meant was that I was working myself up to it, but I wasn't actually ..."

"I see." Now I *did* see. Why was I quarreling with this woman? I was putting her in a position to defend herself, and now we were stuck in this senseless debate. Deep breath and a reminder to back off.

It is precisely that deep breath that helps us at times to stop imposing our own agenda and time line on people when it does not fit *their* current priorities. We have to remind ourselves who is really in charge of the proceedings. As discussed earlier, people have very good reasons for postponing action. There are certainly benefits for remaining stuck and all kinds of hard work associated with taking steps to rectify things. It makes perfect sense to wait as long as possible until there's no longer a choice in the matter.

Takeaways

Counseling people sometimes feels like we are operating on a battlefield, arguing different perspectives, selling new and different ideas, overcoming resistance to change. Clients bring to the table the most disturbing, catastrophic, often bizarre behavior that they often work hard to protect in spite of the deleterious consequences. If there is one attribute that we gain in strength, it is composure under these challenging circumstances. Sometimes the most useful therapeutic strategy within our repertoire is simply remaining calm, patient, and unruffled during high tension. It is as if our manner and style are communicating consistently, "No worries. I've got this. *We've* got this. It may not seem like it but things really are under control."

This, of course, isn't quite true. We may *tell* clients that all is going to be well. We may even pretend to believe it for the sake of veracity. Maybe in some ways exhibiting patience really means just tolerating and hiding our own impatience. Ultimately, however, we realize that it is often important for us to appear and sound perfectly capable and optimistic, even when we have considerable doubts. In spite of any lingering concerns, uncertainties, and reservations, it is through our own calmness, composure, and seemingly endless patience that we allow people to proceed at whatever pace they can reasonably manage.

We learn important lessons from our clients who teach us that there is nothing that sabotages a relationship faster than being oblivious to the other person's willingness and ability to comply with tasks that we believe are important. We also learn that so-called resistance is in the eye of the beholder. What feels to us like someone is being obstructive or uncooperative may very well be an example of a clear message that our expectations are out of line with reality. If we take this feedback to heart, it enables us to sensitively respect the needs and interests of others in all our relationships.

End of the Story

I hesitate to mention the end of this story with my client, Graham, for fear that it will dilute the main message that impatience gets us into trouble. But here goes. Perhaps I would not have had the courage to share this if the outcome were unknown or uncertain. I have thought about Graham for over 30 years, always wondering about the fallout from my impatient and misguided choices. I worried that I had done him serious harm when he was so desperate to reach out for a lifeline. Instead, I had left him to drown. I even wondered anxiously whether I pushed him over the edge and should be held accountable for the damage I inflicted.

It is apparent I learned a lot from my brief interaction with Graham, enough so that I spent so many years trying to make sense of what happened and why. I used that experience as a powerful reminder to monitor carefully my impatience and frustration, and to access greater compassion, even when my own sense of helplessness is triggered. Full disclosure on that mission: I am still very much a work in progress.

Nevertheless, I have an update on what transpired after Graham left my office that day, a report that took so much time to find its way back to me. A few years ago, one of my brothers who still resides in the same city where I used to have a practice, literally ran into Graham on a nature trail. Since my youngest brother and I look very much alike, it is not that unusual that former friends or clients see the resemblance or recognize my last name.

"Hey, I ran into another one of your ex-clients again," my brother told me with a laugh. He always seemed to get a kick out of this.

Silence from me. He knows I will not acknowledge whether someone was ever my client or not, and he thinks that is pretty amusing as well.

"He wanted me to say hello to you. He told me this amazing story about you."

"Oh yeah?" I answered, partly apprehensive but also quite curious. It is so rare that I ever find out what happened to some of my clients after they left my care.

"Apparently, this guy came to see you one time. You didn't even let him finish the session. You told him he was a hopeless case."

"Oh crap," I thought. NOW I'm in trouble. I immediately thought of Graham and figured he must have tracked me down through my brother, and now there will be hell to pay. Heck, I probably deserve it. I held my breath waiting for the rest.

"Anyway, you scared him to death. You told him he was going to lose everything in his life, and there was nothing he could do about it until he lost it all." My brother was laughing as he said this. "Did you *really* tell him that?"

I just shrugged.

"So, anyway, he said that after he left your office, he just crawled inside his car and started crying. He was absolutely terrified. He had a vial of coke in his glove compartment, and he reached inside for it."

Okay, now I was *really* worried. I drove the guy into greater despair and a deeper addiction! At least he didn't take his own life since, apparently, he was still sufficiently alive and kicking that he could tell my brother what happened. Oh, the humiliation!

"But, apparently," my brother continued, "you scared the crap out of him so badly that he opened the window of his car and threw the coke vial away. He told me from that moment on he never touched the stuff again. Went cold turkey. Anyway, he wanted me to thank you for what you did for him."

You just never know.

Questions for Reflection or Discussion

1. How are you most likely to become impatient and aggravated when things don't proceed at your preferred pace and speed?

2. What are some exceptions to the rule that we should go only at the client's pace? When are times when it's advisable to take over to accelerate progress, regardless of the client's deliberate balking?

3. How have you noticed that the patience and composure you've mastered when in session are also sublimely useful in other aspects of your life?

19

Taking Constructive Risks

Twenty years from now you will be more disappointed by the things you didn't do than by the ones you did. So throw off the bowlines, sail away from the safe harbor, catch the trade winds in your sails. Explore. Dream. Discover.

—Mark Twain

Almost all changes in life are accompanied by a certain amount of risk. When people are asked about the times when they underwent some major transformation, it was usually associated with doing something that they had never tried before, some novel or experimental option that likely had a high likelihood of failure. It is not only inevitable but also an important part of the journey that trying out new behaviors often results in confusion, awkwardness, and discomfort. Whenever possible, we prefer to stick with whatever is most familiar, even if it has annoying side effects.

I have described previously how growing up I did not believe I had much going for me. I did not consider myself very smart or capable, believing that most of the advancements I ever made were just the result of luck or persistence. I was pretty good at refusing to accept "no" for an answer when my initial efforts failed or were rejected. Since I did not feel like I could rely on any superior intellectual ability, athletic talent, or academic skills to succeed in school, I instead preferred coloring outside the lines, so to speak. When it felt like the usual or traditional ways to get things done were unavailable to me, I tried pathways that others might not consider. Naturally, I might get in trouble a lot but I came to expect that as just part of the price paid for doing things differently.

I used to love reading biographies of famous people who broke with the established traditions of the day (Charles Darwin, Mahatma Gandhi, Franklin Roosevelt, Frida Kahlo) in order to invent some new procedure or way of doing things. Sigmund Freud's life captivated me, not because of his particular theories, which did not particularly appeal to me over time, but rather because of his courage and creativity to challenge the orthodoxy of his times. Like other figures who inspired me, their intrepid efforts didn't necessarily work out the way they had hoped, but I still admired their chutzpah. During times when I felt stymied and out of options, I took inspiration from their unusual choices and felt encouraged to think way outside of the box.

While in college there was one assignment in a Psychology of Learning class in which we were expected to answer several rather challenging questions on a take-home exam.

I could fake my way through a few of the options, inserting boilerplate descriptions from the text or my notes, but there was one question that continuously troubled me: "What was B. F. Skinner's theory of forgetting?" My first reaction was wondering if he even proposed such an idea.

After reviewing my resources and checking for clues (this was before the internet!), as well as the course materials, I concluded that there was actually no direct reference to a "theory of forgetting" in Skinner's writing. He talked a lot about reinforcement principles, but I could find nothing about failing memory processes. I searched everywhere, determined to unravel this puzzle. Maybe it was a trick question, I wondered.

Time was running out, and the deadline was approaching the next day to submit the assignment. Desperation often leads to options and risks that would normally never be considered. But what the heck, what did I have to lose? I had the glimmer of a crazy idea.

Surprisingly, when I searched for "B. F. Skinner's" name and personal information, I discovered that he was actually listed in the Cambridge, Massachusetts, directory (I knew he taught at Harvard and had once heard him lecture there). Could I really just call the dude on the phone and ask him about this theory of forgetting? Would he really just tell me the answer? I thought it was worth a try.

After I dialed the number listed, I waited nervously until I heard a woman's voice answer the phone. "Skinner residence."

"May I speak to Dr. Skinner please," I said.

"Sorry," the voice said. "He's not home." I could hear a loud noise in the background that sounded suspiciously like a vacuum cleaner.

"And," I replied impudently, "who might I ask are you?"

"Just the housekeeper."

Hmmm. That caught me unprepared. *Now* what could I do? I was running out of time. "Um. I have a question for you," I persisted. "By any chance, do you know what Dr. Skinner's theory of forgetting might be?" I knew this was ridiculous and hopeless but now I was committed.

"No, sorry," she answered and then hung up on me.

You might imagine that I was rather disappointed and frustrated after the call, but I was actually feeling quite elated. This felt like a turning point for me, a door that opened into a world I did not know existed. I might have had (or believed I had) all kinds of handicaps, limitations, and personal difficulties at the time, but I realized that I was willing to do things that others might not think of, or even consider. It seemed to me, in that moment, that it was entirely possible to at least try to reach out to almost *anyone*. The worst they could do is decline, or not respond at all. I did not care about that very much since at that point I was only aware that taking risks like this could result in so many unexpected benefits, regardless of whether the original outcome was ever achieved. I felt so proud of myself for pushing limits beyond what I imagined were possible.

I turned in my exam the next day. Under the question about Skinner's theory of forgetting, I wrote something like, "I don't believe that Skinner had a specific theory of forgetting since instead he talked about "extinction" when behavior isn't reinforced. In order to confirm this conclusion, I called Dr. Skinner's house directly to ask him what he might say, but he was not home. Or at least that's what his housekeeper told me."

The instructor was greatly amused and impressed with my effort, although he did not give me full credit for that one response. But I learned an important lesson that has served me well ever since. I realized that doing things differently, experimenting with alternative options, trying out new and novel behaviors, most likely will not work out well during initial efforts. After all, first attempts at *anything* are usually awkward and inefficient. Once I increased my tolerance for such disappointing performances, I felt so much freer to engage in actions that others might not consider.

I learned to become immune, or at least resilient, in the face of rejection. My first single-authored book proposal was rejected by over 30 different publishers. I was rejected by about the same number of graduate schools because of my poor GRE scores and mediocre grades. The only program that would give me a chance was in Sweden so I decided to give *that* a try until I could find my way into a more traditional school. Nothing seemed to come very easy to me. And I came to expect that I would get a lot of pushback whenever I inevitably tried options that were not listed on the original menu.

I read somewhere that it usually takes an average of 17 *years* for a new innovation, invention, or breakthrough to find itself finally accepted by practitioners. Just consider all the novel advances that were scandalously ridiculed before they were eventually endorsed as useful—vaccines, light bulbs, umbrellas, bicycles, automobiles, really *anything* that renders previous devices obsolete. There is a lesson in this for the rest of us, whether we prefer to remain within the safe confines of conventional practices, or whether we like to push the boundaries of what's considered acceptable.

What Leads to Change—Inside and Outside Therapy

No matter the context, situation, or behavior, change usually is not very pretty. It tends to be chaotic and unpredictable. In the environment we inhabit, for instance, changes occur as a result of earthquakes, tsunamis, floods, and tornadoes. In the case of our species, changes also most likely occur during times of turmoil or uncertainty. It is during circumstances of disruption that people are most likely to risk doing some of the difficult things they have been avoiding previously. Often it feels like there is little choice in the matter, especially after crises, separations, threats, or losses.

Whether walking around in daily life, or attending counseling sessions, there are particular times when people are most likely to consider making major transformations. Such decisive actions rarely occur based on a whim or a random opportunity; when changes do take place in such circumstances they rarely last very long. It is only during extremely novel situations that so-called quantum changes usually occur, resulting in major alterations in personality, attitudes, values, and conduct (Kottler, 2014; Miller & C'de Baca, 2001).

When are people most typically motivated to change some aspect of themselves? Most common on the list is when they "hit bottom." This can occur in a variety of situations, during those times when (1) addictions run out of control; (2) depression and anxiety seem untreatable; (3) trauma hijacks decision-making; (4) unresolved abuse, neglect, or losses take their toll; (5) developmental life transitions spark crises; (6) medical issues jeopardize health; (7) close brushes with mortality lead to crises of faith; (8) chronic self-deception and denial fall apart; (9) novel situations require inventing new coping methods. In each of these cases mentioned, the favored, comfortable, familiar habits must be abandoned, requiring new and different actions that have uncertain and risky outcomes.

Every practitioner has some favorite best practices, those that have worked in the past or feel effortless to employ as needed. These are the standard interventions that are relied upon most often; they tend to work consistently because of the skill and ability that's been developed over time with practice. It is when everything in that bag of tricks has already been tried and failed that it becomes necessary to experiment with novel strategies that are unfamiliar.

Generally speaking, beginners would much prefer to avoid doing anything that is especially risky or untested, given the fear of hurting someone or getting in trouble with a supervisor or administrator. Yet risk and fear are inseparable. It is the primary reason why clients resist doing things differently even when they are certain that present options just will not do the job. It is also the reason why mental health professionals may feel reluctant to break loose from their own comfortable routines. We have been warned repeatedly that even if we do not help anyone to be careful about doing harm. There is little doubt that risking some new strategy or novel approach increases the risk of things going wrong.

The first few times you try something, whether some supposed new breakthrough cure or just some adaptation of a technique observed in action, it is to be expected that it will feel awkward and uncomfortable. In any sport, after altering your grip, stance, or method, the results initially may not show much improvement. Mistakes are made. Miscalculations occur until new pathways are formed that guide responses. Because the process is temporarily unscripted and improvised, the results are less certain. It takes considerable time before a new strategy or procedure or habit becomes sufficiently internalized to feel natural.

We spend our days talking with people who are actively demonstrating courage in their lives. They are facing their demons, trying to take charge of their lives even with the likely setbacks. The very choice to seek help in the first place took considerable effort given the pushback that people often receive from significant others in their lives who may feel threatened by the changes they are undergoing and will require others to make adjustments.

Sometimes clients tell us they have no choice other than to risk reaching beyond their comfort levels, but of course, there are always other options that they have been ignoring for some time. This persistence and courage we witness are contagious in some ways. We feel inspired to examine aspects of our own lives that have been neglected or have lapsed into complacency. In addition, there are so many risks just associated with the job, not necessarily the same sort of physical jeopardy faced by law enforcement or military personnel but all sorts of psychological risks as a result of the horrifying stories we hear, the tales of abuse and suffering, the ways we are manipulated, the toxic energy of some of our most disturbed clients. Sometimes it is hard *not* to take the negative energy, distressing interactions, or haunting stories on board when they seem to penetrate our souls. The same can also be said for the fearlessness we witness in those we help who, in spite of the dangers, risks, and difficulties, still persist in their efforts to remake their lives.

Takeaways

Therapists and counselors are more than mere technicians and applied scientists. We are explorers who delve into new and unknown territory that others fear to tread. We have been trained in experimental methodologies, testing hypotheses, sorting through empirical evidence, applying logic, and analytic problem-solving, all of which make us well prepared to assess risk and reward scenarios. After all, the secret of innovation—in *any* discipline or context—is experimentation, taking risks, and trying things that perhaps have never been attempted previously. As such, initial failure is likely, mistakes are inevitable, and criticism is a certainty, especially by those whose personal interests may be jeopardized by some advancement that renders what they are already doing irrelevant, unnecessary, or simply obsolete. It takes courage and tenacity, even in the face of unrelenting attacks, to continue moving forward with ideas or innovations that are not exactly embraced by others.

Emotional upheaval comes with the territory we are expected to survey and explore. For those who do couples work, practitioners are exposed to brutal arguments and senseless quarrels, sometimes with people even coming to blows, with us stuck in the middle of the skirmish. We also have to deal with some very miserable and disagreeable people during times when they are at their worst. This puts us in vulnerable positions at times, but there are also those situations when we are most likely to consider corresponding changes in our own lives as a result of what was triggered in sessions. "If things seem under control," observed race car driver Mario Andretti, "you are just not going fast enough."

Questions for Reflection or Discussion

1. Think of a time you took a major risk that ended with disastrous results. What did you learn from that experience that has since helped you during subsequent attempts at experimentation?

2. The point is repeatedly made in this chapter that change usually occurs during desperate times when it feels like there's no other choice. What's an exception to this "rule" when change was initiated even though things were already going quite well?

3. What's an example of something risky you tried that resulted in a major shift in the ways you behave in the future?

20

Becoming a Curious Truth Seeker

All truths are easy to understand once they are discovered; the point is to discover them.

—Galileo Galilei

A book reviewer once called me the "conscience of the profession" because of my tendency to talk about subjects that others have mostly ignored. I wrote the first ethics book in the field almost 50 years ago, after which I found myself in a bit of trouble because I suggested that therapists should not have romantic or sexual relationships with their clients while they were still seeing them in treatment. I recommended instead that at *least* they should wait until after termination. This was considered controversial at the time to restrict therapists in this way.

Ever since then, I have chosen to write and talk about topics that others have chosen to neglect or avoid. I have always been mostly interested in what it *feels* like to be a therapist, our inner world, the things that we experience but almost never mention aloud. As you have certainly noticed, I have found the things we learn on the job fascinating, the ways the work has such a profound influence on our own development. I have been curious about the endless debates and arguments we have with one another about which approach is superior to all the rest. I have been intrigued by all the self-promotion that takes place in the field in which each side fights for dominance. It has also been interesting to explore the ways that we shade the truth about what we do and how we do it. One such claim that I mention frequently is that we do not really know what we are doing some of the time, just improvising until we can figure out a small part of what might be going on. Another truth is the reality of how little we truly understand about the changes that take place. Heck, the whole foundation of our field is built on lies if you remember the extent to which any memories or recollections shared are so subject to distortion, exaggeration, or fabrication. In the beginning of his investigations, Freud believed *everything* his clients told him. Eventually, he shifted to much greater skepticism, wondering if most of what he'd been told were actually fabrications and fantasies.

I have often thought that what I do for a living is point out to stubborn people that they are lying to themselves (and often to others) about how well their chosen actions were resulting in their ultimate articulated goals. How many times do we hear people confess their honest assessment of their situation: "Hey, I'm not the one who really has a problem; it's just that other people won't get off my case." Once they admit that what they are doing is not working very well, then they have to do something about it.

As much as I stand for truth telling and honest self-assessment, I also have to admit that I am as prone as anyone else to deny that I have a problem when it is just as easy to pretend that everything is just fine. After surviving the stream of successive traumatic incidents that were described previously (forced retirement, earthquake, fire, hurricane, freeze, pandemic, fractured leg and ACL, *really* bad COVID symptoms) I insisted to anyone who asked that I was just fine, although perhaps a little uneasy at times. But I hid the truth for many months—the sleep disruption, depression, disturbing images, fantasies of escape, sometimes of just disappearing. "Hey," I heard myself say more than a few times echoing my clients, "I don't really have a problem." But of course I did. And still do.

I tried to hide the extent of my disruptive symptoms. Once I managed to regain some modicum of stability, it felt like I took another major hit once all the crazy political shenanigans dominated media coverage every day. With too much time on my hands, I got sucked down the rabbit hole of despair hearing about the resurgence of deceit, racism, oppression, lies, corruption, and more lies that were being accepted as an approximation of reality. The whole notion of a "post-truth era" in which political leaders could declare election results fraudulent, or make up any fictitious story they want, made my head explode. While I was working on this chapter, I came across a story (now quite familiar) about a recently elected congressperson who lied about *everything* in his official biographical profile. He never graduated from the university he claimed, never worked at the company he said he founded, was never employed in the places listed on his résumé, never held positions mentioned, never contributed to the charities he claimed, never lived where he said he did—and when confronted with this deceit, he said he was a victim of a conspiracy. Even more remarkable, he won the majority of votes in his district! Even after all his numerous deceptions and lies were revealed, many of his colleagues in Congress *still* supported him!

Whatever has the world become that truth and honesty no longer seem to matter very much? How is it that so many elected officials not only ignore but actively undermine the rights of oppressed and marginalized people? It has felt like all that I valued most was being discarded to "make America great again." Of course, that is just a coded declaration to make America the way it "used to be" with fewer immigrants.

If I am truly honest, I have to admit that in spite of my best efforts and claims otherwise, I just cannot let go of my disappointment, frustration, rage, and yes, my despair, about the state of this country and the larger world. Maybe that is just the rant of another old guy, just like all the previous generations that complain that "things ain't like they used to be." But things really *aren't* like they used to be. The world seems like, and feels like, a very different place. Since the aftermath of the political chaos, the pandemic, the ways that work life and even leisure time have become irrevocably transformed, we are all struggling to make sense of this new world order and how we fit into it. I have not been doing a very good job with that, and it feels good to finally admit it.

Diagnoses and Motives for Lying

As mentioned in an earlier chapter on "hidden agendas," nature equips most creatures with the means by which to hide, disguise, or trick potential adversaries. Frogs, lizards, moths, butterflies, and other insects use camouflage to hide in plain sight from predators. Chameleons and octopuses can change their appearance to blend into their environment. The fur coats of tigers, leopards, lions, and other big cats are designed to fool potential prey until it is too late. Some animals can exaggerate or minimize certain traits to discourage enemies or attract potential mates. The goal is to highlight and broadcast strength while hiding vulnerabilities, all without having to engage in active conflict. Almost every living being has been provided with the mechanisms to hide their intentions, take advantage of opportunities to deceive others, or change their appearance for some advantage in love or war.

Within our own species, there are all kinds of ways that humans alter their appearance in order to attract the attention of suiters or warn off possible competitors. People color their hair, wear makeup, create bulging muscles or a sleek physique, cultivate a special wardrobe, and even undergo surgery in order to enhance their perceived attractiveness. Additional verbal exaggerations and deceptions are also just part of the attempt at managing one's image and heightening status within one's identified group.

We discussed previously in Chapter 12 on hidden agendas that people are most likely to lie in situations where there would be a loss of face or shame from admitting some mistake. In other cases, people attempt to deceive themselves so they can better fool others. "I don't have a problem." "I meant to actually do that." "Of course I like you." "I swear I'm telling the truth!" Each of these statements can be presented with convincing enthusiasm, especially if you believe them yourself. Unfortunately, such denial and self-deception are the antitheses of what is required to make much progress in counseling sessions. Clients lie to themselves—and to us—frequently and unabashedly. It is our job to help them to face some semblance of truth and self-honesty. Of course, there is an assortment of reasons why people might be less than honest with themselves—and their therapist.

One of the most extreme reasons why people appear divorced from reality, living in their own fantasy world, is that they are experiencing the most florid symptoms of psychotic processes. Their paranoid beliefs, delusions, and visual and auditory hallucinations all create an alternative universe in which "truth" has a quite different meaning. Other very bizarre and interesting forms of mental dysfunction alter the perceptions of what is actually true or false. Also explored previously are conditions like Korsakov syndrome when severe memory impairments lead people to make up wild stories that they absolutely believe really happened. Still other pathological lying we might encounter, such as *pseudologia fantastica*, leads people to absolutely believe the fictional, self-aggrandizing stories that are told to others.

In a much milder form, almost all clients tend to first test the waters, so to speak, before they might blurt out what is really bothering them. Who in their right mind would immediately open up and spill their guts to someone before they know it is safe and trustworthy to do so? Naturally, they also fear humiliation and disappointing their therapist in some way. When questioned directly as to the reasons why they held back what was really going on or shaded the truth in significant ways, they might offer the same dishonest response to their dentist, "Of course I floss every day!"

Then there is the confusion about what actually qualifies as a lie since quite often people do not even realize they are being less than open. Is someone being dishonest if they have convinced themselves that what they are saying is really true? In addition, there are so many different versions of what actually occurred in any situation. Ask any three people to tell the story of what transpired between them, and you will likely hear very different reports about what occurred, each reflecting their own unique, self-serving perceptions.

Everyone Lies—to Both Themselves and Others

If it is the therapist's job to help people to become more clearheaded and honest with themselves, then we certainly have a number of challenges to overcome. This not only involves confronting others who are self-deceptive but also confronting our own fibs and lies. Of course, any research on truth telling that relies on self-reports is always going to be a bit suspect because of the tendency of respondents to engage in bolstering their self-image. That might explain why three quarters of people say they hardly ever lie (Serota et al., 2022).

One additional compelling reason that lying is rewarded is that there is a big difference between highly skilled "good" liars (representing less than 5%) and those who are clumsy: the good ones are rarely caught (Verigin et al., 2019). Once particular individuals learn that lying can be highly advantageous to manipulate and control others (if you can get away with it consistently), it becomes a favored strategy that only improves with practice.

Many of the people we are required to help are among the most successful avoiders of truth, those who have made a living trying (and often succeeding) to fool others. They seek our services, or more likely are mandated to do so, because their strategies are no longer working for them. In other words, they have been caught repeatedly in their attempts at deceit and manipulation and are now in trouble because of their ineptness.

Although therapists might self-deceptively view themselves as experts at closing in on truths, the reality is that we can be fooled just as easily as anyone else. In one collection of such cases described earlier, a number of prominent, highly experienced therapists admitted dramatic instances when they had been played by clients who led them on a merry chase running around in circles. The inescapable conclusion is that although we might worship honesty and truthfulness as the ultimate goals for growth, learning, and recovery, our clients may have very different ideas about the risks and rewards that might occur as a result.

Takeaways

There are two primary issues related to applying the ideas embedded in this discussion. The first has to do with practical concerns: How do we handle situations when we *know* someone is being less than honest? Do we confront and challenge the deception or just ignore it? Whether in the context of helping relationships or any daily interaction, much depends on the reasons for the lies. Is this an attempt at manipulation and control, or else just a matter of being oblivious to the behavior because it's so habitual? It is always interesting and revealing to discover the meaning of this behavior before deciding how to handle it.

Clients lie to their therapists—and to themselves—for all kinds of reasons that make sense at the time. They often feel pressured to reveal secrets or disclosures before they are ready to do so. They feel vulnerable and exposed and so seek to protect themselves from potential harm. They do not much like the one-sided nature of the therapeutic relationship in which *they* are the ones who are required to take all the risks. They sense that even if they were fully and completely honest, they would still be disappointed because they realize we can't actually "fix" them. It, therefore, makes perfect sense to hold back, exaggerate, or deny certain "facts" when you can get away with it.

Just like everything else we encounter in our work, truth telling and truth seeking occur in the context of the relationship, especially the levels of trust and caring that have been fostered and maintained over time. It is hard not to take things personally when we discover that things are not as they appeared, that what a client told us was actually pretty distorted and deceptive. We cannot help but ask ourselves about the meaning of this behavior in such a way that we don't overreact and overpersonalize the interaction as a kind of betrayal (which in a sense it really feels like that). Do we confront and challenge the client or let it go? Do we just pretend that we are on board with the deceptions or rather wait patiently until the actual motives can be revealed? Regardless of how such interactions and predicaments are processed in sessions, one of the possible gifts that we learn along the way is to take a more forceful stand for our own curious truth seeking, someone who is consistently committed to fidelity, integrity, and honesty in our relationships with colleagues, friends, and loved ones—except perhaps when others around are us are not quite ready to hear what we are prepared to say. During this time when the very concept of "truth" is being degraded and diluted, it has never been more important for us to model what we expect and want most from others.

Questions for Reflection or Discussion

1. Think of a time recently in which you intentionally and strategically lied to others for some personal gain. What do you conclude from that experience?

2. Bring to mind an instance when someone lied to you, which led to feelings of betrayal.

3. Under which circumstances do you believe it is perfectly okay to lie to others?

4. Which would best represent your position: (a) almost nothing is completely true, or (b) everything is true?

21

Embracing Life's Adventures

Life should not be a journey to the grave with the intention of arriving safely in a pretty and well-preserved body, but rather to skid in broadside in a cloud of smoke, thoroughly used up, totally worn out, and loudly proclaiming "Wow! What a Ride!"

—Hunter S. Thompson

When Travel Becomes Transformative

I was surprised to find that after I exited the plane that the only shuttle service available to my lodging was a dogsled with a dozen barking, growling huskies. We had just landed in a small seal-hunting village on the east coast of Greenland where I would be spending a few weeks doing research for a project. There had been reports of child abuse in the village, as well as people who had suddenly gone missing, whether they had fallen through the ice or were the victims of some nefarious plot.

I had already spent several months working in nearby Iceland, teaching at the national university. After so much time away from home, I was aware that some of the experiences I already had, and was about to have in this desolate part of the Arctic, had changed me in profound ways. I was more than a little familiar with how travel experiences like this could be so powerful. Based on prior similar adventures, I concluded that I might be far more effective in my work as a promoter and facilitator of behavioral change if I was a travel agent instead of a psychologist. As many times as I had been in therapy as a client, nothing had quite the same impact as certain kinds of excursions that tested me in ways I never could have imagined.

As much as I enjoyed teaching in the classroom and conducting sessions in my office, I believed that nothing came close to having as much enduring impact as taking people on trips to places that would test their mettle. Over the years, I had brought hundreds of students, friends, and colleagues with me on service trips to Nepal and elsewhere in the world. It never ceased to amaze me how much these adventures changed the participants in profound and lasting ways. I just returned from such a trip a few months ago, and, once again, when some members of our group returned home, a few of them quit their jobs, relocated their homes, divorced their partners, and rededicated their lives to another mission. I have found this is not the exception but the usual rule.

I learned to plan and structure such adventures to maximize influential effects. There would be no tourist activities, eating familiar foods, and living in the lap of luxury. Members of our team were subjected to all kinds of adversity and challenges. Because it was Nepal, there were almost always delays, strikes, protests, earthquakes, floods, political upheaval, and even a civil war. Most of the activities involved working in schools and conducting home visits with children who were at greatest risk to be neglected, abused, or even trafficked. There was just no way anyone could encounter this level of poverty and deprivation while maintaining their equanimity. The most disturbing thing of all was to see how incredibly happy and satisfied most villagers were in spite of their lack of resources or even reliable food and shelter. In our world, we have almost everything we could ever want, and it is still never enough.

It is precisely the kind of high emotional arousal that accompanies travel adventures that most often results in important life lessons. Many of these experiences we would never intentionally choose, yet we are forced to deal with them anyway. It may seem wildly exciting and interesting to spend time in a remote Greenland Inuit village, but trust me when I tell you that this land of floating icebergs, treacherous weather, and hidden violence was often very uncomfortable, and sometimes quite terrifying. I would also suggest that it was precisely these dangers that softened me up for the traumatic adventures that would soon follow.

I had hired a mountain guide to escort me to the largest, most remote glacier in Europe to complete a photographic book to be called *Icelandic Winter*. Thus far I had captured exploding volcanoes, white-out blizzards, spectacular waterfalls, turquoise glacial lakes, and all the beauty of this unique region. A specialized vehicle designed for the terrain dropped us off at a mountain hut located a 3-hour drive across the glacier. The moment after we arrived, the weather turned treacherous, making visibility impossible. It snowed so much and the wind howled so hard that we could not even leave the tiny hut. To stay warm, we marched around in circles much of the day and took turns leading aerobic classes inside our tiny prison. What little food we had, froze solid. We tried to call for help, but the radio did seem to be functioning, or at least we could not get any reception. We were stranded. Isolated and alone. Day after day, we waited for rescue, watching our supplies of food and fuel grow perilously short. After we got acute cabin fever, we forced ourselves to go outside on ski expeditions to find higher ground and perhaps get a signal to radio for a rescue. We lapsed into despair when the weather finally broke, yet nobody came back to retrieve us, even though it was 3 days beyond our scheduled pickup.

We eventually came to accept that we were stranded, likely our last day or two before the end was near. We decided to confess to one another our most shameful secrets and our worst mistakes in life since it seemed we would not survive much longer anyway. After waiting anxiously one more day for rescue, the weather finally broke, and we considered trying to ski back to civilization even though that option was pretty hopeless. I cannot recall ever feeling so lost and miserable. We had been reduced to eating uncooked, dry pasta. We were frustrated, angry, despondent, and quite scared.

Eventually, the vehicle did show up later that day, just as we were about to set off on our own to save ourselves. Apparently, they could not arrive any sooner because of the inclement weather; they offered no explanation or apology for the broken radio. As miserable as I had been, I found it interesting that a few weeks later, I would not have traded this experience for *anything*. The world appeared different to me after that near-death experience. It would have taken me years of therapy to get to the same point.

For the past several years, I've been interviewing people who, like me, have experienced major transformations as a result of their travels (Kottler, 1997, 2014; Kottler & Safari, 2019). I have been particularly interested in what it was about their journeys that produced life-altering experiences, as well as what change processes might have been involved that resembled what we do in therapy. Almost everyone had a seminal story to tell, and interestingly, most of these experiences were not altogether pleasant at the time. In fact, it appears that the most constructive life-altering trips were those that involved some sort of awful, traumatic, or uncomfortable events that forced the person to develop new resources, increase confidence, and solve problems in new ways. Oh, the stories afterward may sound very amusing and quite fun, but actually, they were not nearly as enjoyable at the time. Quite often, they involved being hopelessly lost, miserable, or frightened. In other words, there was some type of emotional activation that made the person ripe for altered perceptions and new learning.

The implication of this premise is interesting because it means that the best stuff that happens on adventures are those events that were unforeseen. As long as people stay on tour buses, sleep in comfortable hotels, eat familiar foods, and stick with guides and planned itineraries, they may have a lovely time but they will probably not experience any major personal transformations. They will return rested and relaxed, but the effects will often not last very long. That might be perfectly fine for most people who are not expecting anything other than what is on the planned agenda. But once people stray from what is predictable, force themselves to take constructive risks, embrace unstructured time, or allow themselves to experiment with new behaviors, the benefits increase a hundredfold beyond what can be learned in any classroom, book, or therapy session.

Transformative Travel

Experiences and adventures like those just described only solidify the belief that what we do in counseling and therapy (plus teaching and supervision) is really to escort people on adventures. They might take place in an office or during a screen session but they are still conversations that are designed to shake things up and introduce new skills and abilities to deal with life's challenges. They often involve "tours" of interesting places, even if they are not so much physical locations, as they are options for behaving differently. Just like any other adventure, they tend to be rather emotionally evocative, sometimes quite stressful endeavors.

It is interesting to examine the features of travel and adventure that make these experiences so potentially influential and memorable. It helps to begin the study by first looking at the kinds of travel adventures that do not have many *enduring* effects. These are the type of sojourns that are not intended to produce any sort of transformation but rather are designed for fun, relaxation, and recovery from life's demands. Unfortunately, besides the credit card bill that will arrive precisely 30 days after returning from the trip, there is not much to hold onto except perhaps a few souvenirs that will gather dust on the shelf.

If sticking to the tried and true, the most familiar and comfortable aspects of normal life do not appreciably change very much, then going in the opposite direction produces very different results. Once you are separated from daily routines, normal habits, familiar friends and family, and predictable patterns, there is a much greater opportunity to reinvent yourself. It is mostly exposure to new ideas, novel environments, unfamiliar sights and smells, and different experiences, that tend to shake things up. Once you are forced to decode the rules of a new environment, figure out new ways to get your needs met, find your way around without ending up completely lost, plus make sense of people's behavior in a strange locale, flexibility becomes the order of the day. When you are surrounded by strangers who do not know how you typically behave, you are freed up to play with alternatives you might not have previously considered.

Instead of sitting still in a chair, there is something both unnerving and unusually exciting about moving through time and space. Our brains and senses have been designed to pay extra close attention to every novel smell, sound, and sight in a new environment. This is how we anticipate potential dangers and learn how to find our way but also locate nutritional sources, shelter, and safe spaces. It is when we are in transit that we are hyper-focused on *everything* around us, continuously assessing anything that might be of concern or interest. It was discovered, for example, that during the worldwide pandemic, one restorative action that helped to immunize people against psychological difficulties and maintain their well-being was engagement in adventures, especially those that involved some kind of physical activity or immersion in nature that ramped up both situational and internal awareness (Boudreau et al., 2022).

It is in this state of intense arousal that we often occupy a kind of altered state of consciousness. This is the sensory condition activated during therapy when clients are potentially far more suggestible than they would be during normal consciousness. It is as if during optimal engagement the person is in a trance state that makes them more amenable to change. I sometimes marvel at how clients might dwell enthusiastically on every word I utter, but once out on the street again, hardly anyone cares what I have to say about anything. We occupy this elevated position that allows us to speak in that soft, soothing voice that puts people into a kind of daze such that they are far more likely to hear and act on what is said to them. It sometimes seems like magic.

Once placed in a new, unfamiliar environment, it always seems as if it is enriched with all the fresh features that we may have not encountered before. The air feels different. Everything just seems so fascinating precisely because it is so new. The nervous system kicks into high gear just to process all the stimuli flowing through the senses. This makes people far more ripe and amenable to "teaching moments" or insights that can result from novel stimulation. It is certainly ironic that during these times when you feel most unsettled and lost, there are actually more opportunities to find something that you have always been looking for. Time and time again, once people recover from some adversity they have faced, they cannot help but apply the lessons learned to future challenges.

What Has the Most Potential Enduring Impact?

It would appear that almost everyone these days is searching for ways to explore novel experiences and different territories during their discretionary leisure time. That explains why the travel industry has jumped on the bandwagon to meet the increasing demand for interesting adventures. When surveys were conducted of prospective consumers, people expressed a deep craving for trips that involve hiking, backpacking, climbing, rafting, kayaking, and similar activities that appear to awaken their joy, passion, and excitement, as well as provide opportunities to reflect on meaning in their lives. Researchers found that people most frequently mention motivations that include learning new things, making deep connections with others, stabilizing their mental health, improving their physical conditioning, and enjoying stimulating novel experiences (Beckmann, 2017). Of course, this is the foundation of organizations like Outward Bound, Wilderness Adventure Program, and National Outdoor Leadership School that seek to help people learn new skills and more fully engage with nature. When there is a suitable match between people's abilities and the challenges they face, there is increasing evidence of significant improvement in subjective well-being and resilience (Kelly, 2019).

How do we translate what we know and understand about personal change processes to the pursuit of adventures in our daily lives? It turns out that similar principles that operate in therapeutic relationships are also embedded in memorable adventures, at least the kind that produce lasting changes.

Create a mindset for change. The initial stage of a helping relationship always involves establishing hope and optimism. Whether capitalizing on placebo effects or simply stoking up enthusiasm for a cure, it is important to set things up for success. It is all about expectations for what you want most to occur. If it is just a holiday or a bit of relaxation that is desired, then that is what you will likely get.

Insulate yourself from usual influences. It is only when someone is fully immersed in a novel environment that it's possible to look at things differently and solve problems in new ways. In therapy, we isolate clients temporarily to command their attention and prevent interruptions; the problems arrive once they resume their normal activities surrounded by the same toxic influences. One of the factors that makes travel adventures so powerful is that they require people to deal with situations without the usual resources at their disposal, many of which can become a source of dependence (or codependence).

Get lost. One of the reasons that counseling can be so helpful is that the sessions happen to occur during a time when clients are most vulnerable and lost. They feel desperate and insecure. It is because of this window of temporary fragility that they are willing to listen and do the tough stuff they would much prefer to avoid. The most enduring memories and impactful experiences tend to be those that are unexpected and occur as the result of unforeseen circumstances. It is when you lose your luggage, miss the bus, get left behind, or simply become hopelessly adrift that most of the action takes place. There is seemingly no other choice except to figure out the best option, regardless of where it may eventually lead.

Face fears. Instead of avoiding the things that are uncomfortable, most growth and learning take place when confronting the tasks that are potentially the most challenging and stressful. In therapy, we may discuss such issues in depth, but during actual adventures, the person is required to act decisively. It is during travel experiences, especially to new locales, that one is required to deal with all kinds of surprises, inconveniences, and annoyances that might ordinarily be fearful and avoided at all costs. Sometimes there is no other choice except to rise to the occasion.

Experiment with new ways of being. People get used to their conveniences and comforts, ordering food deliveries, and visiting favorite spots, all navigated in a language and within customs that are familiar. Once we find ourselves in a different culture and location, we cannot always get what we want, when we want it, exactly like we prefer. Instead, we must settle for alternatives and develop new options that may be acceptable. This often helps to promote greater flexibility, innovation, and creativity.

Process the experience with others. While this could be with a therapist or supervisor, anyone with whom you are intimate might be an option to talk about what happened and the influence it had on you. It is important to announce to others that you are different so that you aren't continuously pressured to revert back to what you once were. In addition, if the ongoing effects of the experience are to last over time, it is critical to find ways to apply the lessons learned to other aspects of daily life.

Generalize to other aspects of life. Plan for reentry in such a way that you retain and build on what was learned. What distinguishes a truly transformative adventure from one that is time limited is related to the extent to which the themes have been fully explored and personalized. There are limits to what solitary self-reflection can do without having the chance to talk to others about what happened and how it fits within the spectrum of one's life. Counseling happens to be an ideal forum for this sort of exploration, but the important point is to have (or create) opportunities to apply what was learned to other situations.

Plan boosters. Momentum wanes over time. Once you reenter the demands of work and life, whatever commitments that were made become drowned out by all the responsibilities and obligations that have been waiting for attention. Excuses proliferate: "I don't have time." "I forgot." "I'll get to it later."

From this review of features of travel that tend to be most impactful, it is readily apparent that there are many similarities to what we attempt to accomplish during sessions. All day long, we listen to tales of adventure and catastrophe, disclosures that may at times be difficult to hear and process but also inspire us to create more exciting quests in our own lives.

Takeaways

Among all the subjects we have covered, this one has perhaps the most potential takeaways that apply to daily life. As Helen Keller once observed, "life is either a daring adventure, or nothing at all!" There could not be a statement any more inspiring from someone who was already both deaf and blind. And it is certainly true that during this one shot we have at life on Earth, it is up to each one of us to make the most of the experience. It is always hard, and definitely hypocritical, for us to persuade clients to try out new adventures when we have been reluctant to do so ourselves, remaining safe and secure ensconced in our comfortable chairs.

Let's end with a quote from one of the most intrepid, passionate travelers of all, an adventurer such as Anthony Bourdain (2007): "Travel isn't always pretty. It isn't always comfortable. Sometimes it hurts, it even breaks your heart. But that's okay. The journey changes you; it should change you. It leaves marks on your memory, on your consciousness, on your heart, and on your body. You take something with you. Hopefully, you leave something good behind."

There is little doubt that Bourdain, the most well regarded of all food and travel writers, struggled with his own demons, eventually taking his own life. Only he could say whether his suffering and sacrifices were indeed worth the good he left behind. There is indeed sometimes a steep price to be paid when anyone pushes themselves beyond the limits of what is comfortable and manageable.

Adventures come in so many different flavors, depending on interests, abilities, resources, and opportunities. Some people in search of enlightenment or personal transformation favor physical challenges like climbing mountains or challenging their capabilities in sports, competitions, or quests. Others prefer to delve deeper into the mind, pursuing meditation, psychotherapy, or other means to come to terms with the past or open new possibilities for the future. After all, according to expedition leader, John Amatt, among so many others, "Adventure isn't [only] hanging on a rope off the side of a mountain. Adventure is an attitude that we must apply to the day to day obstacles in life."

Questions for Reflection or Discussion

1. Describe a travel adventure in your life (however you wish to define it) in which you felt completely lost and disoriented, and yet the experience resulted in major growth for you.

2. If you were going to plan a trip and adventure that was intentionally designed for one specific purpose—to support making significant changes in your life—how would

you structure such an experience to maximize the effects? *Where* would you go? *How* would you arrange things differently than usual? *What* would you do, or not do, that could program greater opportunities for growth and learning?

3. There is a quote by writer Hunter Thompson that begins the chapter, urging people to treat their lives as wild adventures rather than safe and cautious journeys. Where do you fit on this continuum?

22

Capitalizing on Signature Strengths

The good life is using your signature strengths every day to produce authentic happiness and abundant gratification.

—Martin Seligman

How Is This Possible?

I was in the middle of a supervision session with a student intern when I accidentally dropped my pen on the floor. As I reached down to retrieve the object near the intern's chair, she began shaking and making strange sounds. I looked up from the floor and noticed her arms were wrapped closely around her chest as if she was holding herself together.

"What's wrong?" I asked, immediately concerned about the woman's condition. She seemed to be having a panic attack.

The intern's mouth had opened, but she was having trouble making any sound whatsoever. Her lips just opened and closed. Then she ran out of the room.

I did not quite know what to make of this interaction, much less what to do about it. This woman obviously had some serious emotional problems that I had somehow triggered. I wondered if she had been abused in the past, but even so, her reaction seemed rather extreme, so much so that it seemed like a clear cry for help, or at least attention.

Although I was concerned about the student's condition, I was also responsible for protecting her clients' welfare. I had already been warned that she was rather fragile and told to be especially careful around her. Although I certainly wanted to be sensitive to this beginning therapist, I wondered how I could possibly support her continuing participation in the program given how unstable she appeared to be. Not everyone is cut out for this sort of work, and she seemed far worse than most candidates about whom I had serious concerns. In a staff meeting, I even brought up the possibility of dismissing her from further study, or at least referring her for treatment until she could maintain better emotional control.

Here is the thing that was most strange of all about this case. I had heard through the grapevine from several other people that this woman was highly regarded by her clients:

they absolutely loved her! I wondered how someone so extremely anxious and wounded could possibly be helpful to anyone else. Her clients had to be exaggerating just to make her feel better about herself. Maybe they sensed she was so fragile that they had to pretend to be satisfied with her service or else she might totally fall apart. I was trying desperately to make sense of this.

Such an explanation might support my dominant preferred theory since I believed this intern was not really capable of maintaining professional competence because of her own unresolved personal issues. It seemed apparent to me that her clients must have felt sorry for her and needed to reassure her they were feeling much better as a result of her efforts. Upon further reflection, and a lot more feedback from her former and current clients, I eventually came to realize that in spite of her own difficulties, there was something about her that clients seemed to respond to. I found it hard to believe she could somehow put her own problems aside and focus exclusively on others' welfare, but it seemed that she really did have some hidden strengths that were not immediately apparent or obvious. Somehow she was able to access hidden inner reserves that were highly valued by those she helped. I had to accept that there was something going on that was beyond my ability to explain or defend.

What this experience highlighted for me are the many different ways that any of us capitalize on what we do best in our jobs. This particular intern seemed to be more fragile and disabled than almost any client I had ever seen, and yet she still managed to be somewhat effective at helping others. Even more than that, there was something about her manner and style that actually appeared to make it easier for many clients to relate to her. She had somehow found a way to harness her insecurities into signature strengths. In spite of this rather remarkable phenomenon that seemed to contradict everything I believe about the power of personal presence, I still had my doubts about what might really be going on. But perhaps that reflected my own rigidity and stubbornness.

Reflecting on this supervision session so many years later, I could not help but consider my own limitations, disabilities, blind spots, and weaknesses and how I managed to minimize them over time, focusing instead to the few things I do well. In my own way, I was almost as "impaired" as this intern had been; I was just much better at hiding it. This eventual realization is what led me to begin a more intensive study of my own failures, mistakes, and lapses as opportunities for learning rather than experiences of shame and regret. Don't get me wrong, however: I'm still pretty hard on myself when I screw up or fall back into old dysfunctional patterns. During such times, I sometimes clearly and vividly recall those moments I spent with the student intern who somehow, some way, discovered ways to compensate for her many faults with extraordinary adaptation and resilience.

Playing to Strengths

Mental health professionals are hardly a homogeneous group. We were trained in a variety of different professions (social work, psychology, counseling, family therapy, medicine, nursing, pastoral care) that introduced us to an assortment of varied philosophies, strategies, and options. Each practitioner has a unique personality and style, one that has hopefully been crafted to best feature one's own abilities. Some clinicians emphasize their compassionate, gentle nature, while others prefer a far more confrontive, challenging approach. Some like to home in on cognitive processes and others prefer to work primarily within the domain of unexpressed emotional responses. That explains why there are so many different theoretical orientations and specialties within the field, each of which reflects the particular interests and skills of an individual practitioner.

During training years, most students and interns are pressured to adopt a therapeutic style that is congruent (or identical) to that of one's supervisor or instructor. You are certainly aware of how our field has developed cult followings that tread carefully in the same footsteps of the leaders, authors, or presenters who are selling their ideology and persuading others to join their exclusive club. There are journals, books, organizations, conferences, workshops, and certified training programs that focus solely on one approach often identified solely by initials (CBT, MBT, EFT, CFT, DBT, EMDR, FAP). True believers are expected to honor the carefully curated "party line" with respect to approved methods.

In all fairness, there is a tradition in most health professions, or for that matter almost any sport or discipline, that beginners are expected to follow the template established for them by their elders and authority figures. They are not permitted to go their own way until such time that they have established a certain reputation. The problem with this, of course, is that although there is a body of empirically supported research and evidence-based therapeutic approaches, these methods are not necessarily applied in the same exact way by everyone, with every particular client and presenting complaint. Each of us has a unique perspective and voice. People respond to us in vastly different ways, depending on age, gender, size, ethnicity, appearance, personality, as well as our favored strengths.

There are few universal formulas or standard protocols that would work equally well with everyone in every situation. Just as each client requires an individualized treatment plan that best addresses their concerns, preferences, expectations, and personality, so too must practitioners adapt what they do, and how they do it, to empower what it is that they do best. It is hardly luck or a coincidence that some professionals end up working in private practice and others in the prison system or inpatient unit. Although we often end up in certain jobs because of opportunities that came our way, more often than not the way we choose to operate in these positions reflects personal preferences to a certain degree.

We emphasize to our clients how important it is to find or create space that allows them to express themselves most authentically. We stress how life satisfaction is often the result of personal agency rather than simply following scripts written by others. We tell them how critical it is to find their own way in life instead of the futile search for approval from others. We urge them to explore their own core values, clarify their priorities, honor their cultural identity, and assess their unique strengths, all in service to a personally developed pathway to life and work. The same could be said for how we operate as professionals, that our optimal functioning would be best empowered when we play to our own unique strengths, whatever those might be.

We Are Mostly in Agreement

Regardless of one's theoretical affiliation, spanning the range from the most orthodox psychodynamic practitioner to the most radical critical race or feminist clinician, almost everyone these days incorporates the contributions and borrows ideas from other models. It is virtually impossible to be a "purist" any longer because of the importance of integrating the latest research and developments into our work. Recent investigations into neurotechnological approaches, digital interventions, gender-affirming care, posttraumatic stress, treatment-resistant depression, psychedelics, microprocesses, and mindfulness techniques are just a few examples of research innovations that mostly transcend any particular theoretical orientation.

Another groundbreaking innovation from a few decades ago that has received a lot of attention from varied perspectives are the ideas from positive psychology that focused on people's "signature strengths" (Peterson & Seligman, 2004; Seligman & Csikszentmihalyi, 2000). Many other schools of thought such as solution-focused therapy, brief therapy, narrative therapy, and constructivist therapy have introduced their own versions of this approach exploring the positive aspects of a client's experience or looking for exceptions to the presenting problem. The main universal idea is to not dwell continuously on what is always going wrong and instead to celebrate those times when the problem was "defeated." For most of us, this was a valuable reminder to balance our discussions of life challenges with some attention to successes and achievements in spite of the difficulties involved.

We are well aware of how homing in on signature strengths can assist people to reduce their emotional distress, increase well-being, bolster confidence, and improve performance. There is even some research that the most abbreviated single sessions devoted to strength assessments can still have a significant impact on life satisfaction (Dolev-Amit et al., 2021; Schutte & Malouf, 2019). It is during such strength-based conversations that we attempt to help people to more clearly and carefully identify their major assets, especially as they relate to core traits that relate to wisdom (curiosity, flexibility), courage (honesty, bravery), temperance (forgiveness, modesty), justice (collaborative, compassion), and transcendence (gratitude, spirituality). It is clearly the case that our own best qualities of fairness, honesty, kindness, compassion, and emotional regulation are especially appreciated by those we attempt to assist (Huber et al., 2020).

There is thus a consensus that, in spite of our many differences of opinion and varied therapeutic styles, we all favor some attention to the small, incremental successes and achievements that people attain along their path toward further recovery and growth. Whether this takes place as a casual inquiry ("I wonder if you could mention a time when you were actually feeling some improvement this week?") or as a systematic and comprehensive assessment process employing a character survey, the intention is to improve morale and motivation by encouraging people to celebrate their small but significant victories. We would be well advised to do the same.

Takeaways

Before one can increase influencing power, it is first necessary to truly know and understand what you have to offer that is most potent. Each of us has a skill set that hopefully highlights the things we do best. Some practitioners really love the drama of family conflict, belligerent adolescents, and emotional breakthroughs that sometimes take place. Each of us also has favorite techniques and strategies that we most prefer to employ, either because of their consistent potency or the comfort we feel with their familiarity.

As one example, I love using the technique of "immediacy" whenever I can get away with it. I find it to be the most fun, interesting, dramatic, and revealing way to bring a client's attention to something they are doing (or not doing) *as it is taking place in the moment*. Now, I am not saying that my tendency to do this as often as I can is necessarily a "good" thing, or even a wise choice in all situations, especially because I may very well be doing this as much for my own entertainment instead of for the client's welfare. I mention this mostly to prompt some self-reflection about your own signature strengths and preferences, as well as weak spots you tend to ignore.

- What are your favorite techniques or interventions—those that energize you the most? What do these particular choices say about you in terms of your signature strengths?

- What would you describe as your "secret weapon" (if you have one)? This is your almost foolproof favorite strategy for dealing with someone's resistance.

- Which sorts of clients, or presenting issues, engage you the most? These are the concerns that have you rubbing your hands together with delight.

- What would it take for you to incorporate into other areas of your work and life more of the pleasure and satisfaction you feel when using these particular strategies with clients?

- What are some specific ways you could better personalize and customize your methods to better fit your own style? How might you declare greater independence from a regimented approach that limits that potential?

We teach others that there is altogether too much attention devoted to what is *wrong* with them, what they *don't* have, and what they *can't* do, instead of what they are already doing quite well. We also get sucked down this same rabbit hole because of the emphasis we place on assessing difficulties, recognizing patterns of dysfunction, exploring self-defeating behaviors, diagnosing disorders, and identifying psychopathology, all of which lead us to focus on the worst aspects of human functioning. It is hard not to overpersonalize all of this in our own lives when things don't proceed as we expect or desire. Yet it is another one of those gifts we receive from our conversations with clients that we could also become far more committed to recognizing and celebrating our own strengths more often instead of commiserating about what we've done wrong.

Ending With a Reluctant Confession

I will fully acknowledge and own that after almost every single class or workshop that I teach, counseling or supervision session that I conduct, my head (and heart) immediately home in on the mistakes I made, the things I may have missed, the expectations that were not met, and mostly all the things I wished I had said or done instead. Every time I read the participant or student evaluations after a class, speech, or workshop is over, I ignore most of them who thought I did pretty well and immediately focus on the few that thought I was awful. Then I replay my own voice regarding something I said recently to a client or student: "In spite of all the things you wished you had done differently, tell me about all the other things that turned out quite well, especially those about which you feel especially proud."

I wish I could admit that I am usually relatively compliant and cooperative in this endeavor, rattling off a list of my particular strengths and achievements, but alas, I habitually lapse back into the mistakes and failures. After a surge of regret and shame over my inability to practice what I preach, I tend to justify the habit by telling myself that I'm only being honest and dedicated to improving my performance.

Questions for Reflection or Discussion

1. Here's the obvious first question: So, what are *your* unique signature strengths and abilities that could best be harnessed in your therapeutic style? What do you do best?

2. What are some of the weaknesses in the ways you engage with others that could limit your ability to help others?

3. What are some of the obstacles that you face that make it difficult for you to become more creative in your work and life?

23

Challenging Oppression and Injustice

When you get these jobs you have been so brilliantly trained for, just remember that your real job is that if you are free, you need to free somebody else. If you have some power, then your job is to empower somebody else.

—Toni Morrison

Why Would Anyone Do This?

We were standing on the roof of a homeless shelter on Skid Row in downtown Los Angeles. It was close to midnight, but it looked like we had been invaded by a zombie hoard down below. The streetlights that were not already destroyed cast long shadows of stumbling, jerking walkers who were either shuffling along the sidewalks or leaning against walls to avoid falling over. I noticed one guy who was stooped over at an almost impossible angle with a syringe still hanging from his arm. When he eventually collapsed on the ground, I seriously wondered if he had died from an overdose.

Every semester, I would take a group of students to spend the weekend sleeping at a homeless shelter, hosting an ice cream social on the street, serving food in the dining room, and spending time with the residents to hear their stories. There is all this endless talk by professional organizations about social justice and advocacy, but it is so challenging to encourage others to truly remain committed to a cause over time. Scolding and admonishments do not work. Mandating continuing education or required courses just encourages people to go through the motions without true commitment. So I was always looking for ways to instill some sense of enduring passion for this sort of work since there is often little follow-through after graduation with a focus devoted to paying off student loans and establishing a professional identity.

The experiences that we had during the weekend were both very disturbing and incredibly revealing. While walking through the neighborhood, escorted by a police sergeant, we had come across a dead body hidden in a tent, women providing oral sex for a hit of crack, and a park where the Crips and Bloods negotiated a truce to coordinate their illicit drug deliveries. Everyone walking around seemed to be either in a drug-induced stupor or a psychotic haze. Understandably, I noticed some of the students shutting down, even joking about the insane chaos around us, which was so alarming.

We settled ourselves into a circle to chat further with a few of the homeless residents. There was one older man who confessed that he had stopped drinking because he was afraid of what he might do next. A man had raped and murdered his daughter, and he had been impatiently waiting for years for the guy to be released from prison so he could exact revenge. But now he said he was willing to forgive the man and was trying to remain clean and sober for their eventual meeting. Each of the residents had a comparable story of trauma or crushing disappointment that left them destitute. Some of them had been living on the street because they had nowhere to go, but others actually chose this lifestyle, either because they enjoyed the freedom from obligation and responsibilities or else they were intentionally punishing themselves for some transgression. One man admitted to us that he had done some terrible things while serving in the military, perhaps at one of those secret torture prisons, and he felt it necessary to subject himself to suffering and deprivations until the price was paid. Others related similar stories of being (or feeling) discarded by their families, losing their jobs, becoming addicts, and engaging in criminal acts.

I looked around the circle at the students and noticed a few were yawning, exhausted after such a stressful day, now close to the early morning hours. Others I could tell were totally blown away by everything they had seen, heard, and experienced. You just cannot come away from something like this and remain the same afterward. I have since kept in touch with many of these students over the years, even more than a decade later, and I am delighted (and still a little surprised) that the effects seemed to have endured. Several of them have chosen to work in jobs with the most indigent, neglected populations.

As for me? I try to dig deeply as to why I (or anyone) would be so invested in helping perfect strangers. On some level, it makes little sense to expend time, money, resources, and energy to assist others who are not directly part of your gene pool or tribal affiliation. Maybe on some level, all of us who donate money to causes, volunteer for some service project, or serve others in some capacity for no financial remuneration, do so for profoundly personal reasons—to make amends for past failings or faults, redeem a life of suffering, pass along wisdom to others who might find it useful, or find greater meaning in one's life. If I am honest, I know that I do so because of the kick I get out of feeling useful, even important in others' lives. But there are also other benefits in terms of gaining respect, status, and kudos in others' eyes. Being viewed as generous, altruistic, compassionate, and giving improves one's image, as well as leads to other benefits and opportunities as a result of perceived trustworthiness and generosity. It's maybe something we do to help others in need, but it pays off to us as well in reciprocal rewards at a later time.

It has been said that the human inclination to protect others who are not genetically related is the single most significant evolutionary advance within our species, more so than opposable thumbs, an upright stance, or the power of storytelling. It is what permits our extraordinary level of cooperation to create communities, cultures, reciprocal exchanges of resources, and mutual care. It is also the impetus for our species' relatively unique pair bonding and collective responsibility for offspring, patterns that have improved both survival rates and quadrupled our life span.

Plenty to Do Already

You have already heard plenty about social justice and advocacy subjects since they are pervasive throughout every aspect of the curriculum and professional identity. They are even an integral part of our ethical codes to advocate on behalf of marginalized people who are not able to protect themselves against oppression, injustice, neglect, and abuse. Alfred Adler was among the first to emphasize the commitment to "social interest," but every school of thought now includes components that are focused on addressing issues of poverty, racism, homophobia, oppression of women and minorities, as well as the plight of refugees and immigrants.

Most of us just give lip service to this supposed obligation, or at least try to balance the commitment with so many other burdens and responsibilities. First of all, we attempt to manage all the nuances, details, and tasks related to actually helping our clients improve. The successive hours are exhausting and challenging, even if fulfilling, but then there are all the intake forms, treatment plans, progress notes, quarterly summaries, assessment instruments, and diagnostic forms that must be completed in a timely way. Since there are only a few minutes in between each session to use the toilet, grab a beverage or a snack, return a message or call, and chat with a friend or colleague, the paperwork pileup can easily get out of control. Then there is the pressure we feel related to managing our own lives, earning a decent living, supporting a family, and taking care of our own needs. So who has much spare time to fix the rest of the world?

This helps explain why most advocacy efforts are not really sustained over time or why efforts to change human systems often collapse and regress if not consistently supported. I have made some impulsive decisions in my life, reaching out to someone as a gesture of kindness, after which I found myself trapped in a situation that I never really intended. As I have mentioned previously, my first major effort to extend myself way beyond clinical practice and apply my skills to address a major problem never felt like a choice at all.

It was while doing research in a remote part of Nepal near the Indian border that I first learned that girls were "disappearing" from their villages, likely trafficked to Mumbai where they would end up in brothels as sex slaves. This was just the sort of cause that almost anyone would donate money to or offer to volunteer to offer a bit of help during convenient, spare time. But then imagine you were introduced to an emaciated 12-year-old girl who you have been told is a likely candidate to "disappear" since her family could no longer afford to send her to school. After learning that it would take only a pittance to keep this child alive, fed, and supported in school, almost anyone would have followed the impulse to hand the school principal 3,000 rupees ($50), which was sufficient to keep the girl safe for the next year. I clearly remember in that instant that although I have spent most of my life serving others, this felt like the single greatest thing I had ever done, saving a girl's life for the cost of a meal.

I was exhilarated beyond measure, that is until my Nepali colleague explained to me that the principal would likely keep the money, and the girl's situation was hopeless unless I agreed to return to this place to check on her again. I mention this not as a heroic story, one in which I enjoy considerable adulation for my supposed unselfish efforts. But the thing that nobody really understands is that I never wanted to do this. I never aspired to become involved in a human trafficking project. I already had plenty to do, books to write, classes to teach, mountains to climb. In that sense, this was truly not so much an intentional devotion to social justice but rather a situation that I felt trapped in. It felt like I had no other choice but to return and continue the efforts, not just for one girl but as many as we could find. Well, that's the real truth, not so much an act of generosity as impulsivity.

If we walk through life with our eyes, ears, and hearts wide open, it feels impossible to ignore Toni Morrison's admonishment in the quote that began this chapter: if we are free we have an obligation to help others attain greater freedom, whether that is liberation from oppression or the internal prisons of their own creation.

It is fascinating to explore the multitude of ways that our therapeutic knowledge and skills can be adapted and applied to a much larger scale. What we understand about family dynamics, cultural identity, gender equality, and education inequities are all instrumental when advocating on behalf of the dispossessed, marginalized, or oppressed.

Options for Making a Difference

Although there may be great passion and enthusiasm to become more actively involved in some advocacy effort or social justice project, there are practical considerations that must be acknowledged. The reality is that most of us are already overscheduled and overwhelmed with personal responsibilities and professional commitments that demand considerable time, resources, and effort. Although it is a nice gesture to volunteer or provide assistance as a token, one-time offer, it is *sustained* effort that is most needed to address inequities. With that in mind, it is important—and most helpful—if we are truly honest and realistic with ourselves about what can truly be taken on board without significantly increasing the burden and stress. Fortunately, there are so many different kinds of help that might be offered, depending on interests, abilities, and time availability.

1. *Challenging* systemic inequities within an organization or community. This involves first *recognizing* that some individuals or groups are marginalized in some way and then *doing something* to change the status quo.

2. *Transforming* social institutions. Once inequities are identified, steps are taken to change the ways that schools, agencies, government departments, and other organizations operate.

3. *Inviting* fuller access to resources and full participation on the part of excluded people. Again, this involves constructive *action* (rather than mere talk) to advocate on behalf of those without equal rights because of their race, age, religion, gender, disability, sexual orientation, education, socioeconomic status, or group membership.

4. *Bringing attention* to issues of oppression, prejudice, and social inequities within an organization or community.

5. *Combating* racism, prejudice, homophobia, ageism, and sexism as it is witnessed. Speaking out and taking action in the face of injustices and oppression.

6. *Advocating* on behalf of human rights, especially among those who have minority status or who have been historically denied privileges afforded to those of the majority. For example, this could refer to Native Americans, African Americans, and other minorities within the United States, or those of the "untouchable" caste in India, the Kurds of Iraq, hill tribes of Cambodia, Palestinians in the Middle East, and so on.

7. *Empowering* those who have historically been without a voice. This may involve personal self-sacrifice, as well as surrendering some of your own privileges and advantages.

8. *Volunteering time and devoting personal resources* to make a difference among those most in need. Whether this is with the homeless in your own community or with those most at-risk across the nation or abroad, you develop and implement strategies to make a difference.

In each of these cases, professionals, as well as anyone else involved in altruistic pursuits or prosocial behavior, report a number of benefits they experienced along the way (Baumsteiger, 2019; Haller et al., 2022; Lazar & Eisenberger, 2021). This has resulted not only in significantly improved well-being and happiness but also other health benefits that are highlighted in Table 23.1.

Sometimes, practitioners are simply bored or burned out with individual sessions and want to make a difference on a larger scale. That was likely true in my case. In other instances, clinicians wish to expand the scope and breadth of their helping efforts or pay good deeds forward after the help they once received during a time of need. They are developing new areas of expertise and gaining valuable experience. This can range from beefing up one's resume to developing skills that will be useful in the future. For some individuals, it feels to them like they are following a spiritual path. This can be either self-serving (a ticket to heaven) or following some divine inspiration. Some professionals may be well compensated for their jobs but still feel the need to expand their reach to those who could never afford or access the services.

TABLE 23.1   Benefits That Accrue to Those Involved in Selfless Service

Greater life satisfaction
Improved mood and emotional regulation
Reduced loneliness and isolation
Sense of affiliation, belongingness, and social support
Status and prestige
Spiritual transcendence
"Helper's high" (surge of hormonal arousal)
Renewed faith in self and others
Greater life meaning
Redemption and use of one's own suffering
Sense of wonder in people's courage and resilience
Immunity to diseases
Increased life span (as many as 7 extra years of life!)

Benefits and Burdens

Those involved in advocacy enjoy some personal benefits perhaps best exemplified by the so-called "helper's high", the surge of oxytocin, serotonin, and dopamine that often accompanies altruistic behavior and results in a boost of goodwill (Dossey, 2018). This is Nature's way of rewarding our generosity on behalf of others within the tribe or community, better ensuring that we all take better care of one another.

Altruistic efforts are often overromanticized and made to appear as if it is all great fun and tremendously satisfying—which of course it can be at times. But what is often downplayed, if not swept under the rug altogether, is just how disturbing, exhausting, and soul-draining involvement in these projects can become. When operating in a novel culture or "foreign" environment (which is a virtual certainty) the experience is almost always confusing and chaotic. Often, the norms and languages spoken are incomprehensible. Tremendous sacrifices must be made in terms of time pressures, neglect of other responsibilities, and especially functioning in less-than-ideal circumstances that may involve discomforts, emotional upheaval, or physical dangers. Sometimes there is considerable resentment, resistance, or even obstructiveness in response to one's best intentions. Vicarious trauma, compassion fatigue, and contagious despair are common reactions among those exposed to such tragic circumstances of people's lives (Branson, 2019).

The gifts from such efforts often arrive in the form of our own post-traumatic growth. Just as many of our clients enjoy tremendous benefits when they process their disturbing life experiences in more constructive ways, so too do we potentially benefit from processing the upsetting things we witness or encounter. Some of those most common benefits include becoming more appreciative of all our intimate relationships, acknowledging greater personal responsibility in our lives, developing greater resilience and hardiness, and facilitating a cascade of other small changes that might take place in our lives as a result (Deaton et al., 2022; Tedeschi et al., 2018), including the neuroplasticity of our brains as a result of the empathic attunement that takes place (Desautels, 2023).

There can also be a dark side to this in cases where the overinvolvement in "causes" becomes a way to hide from other things that professionals may wish to avoid. Helping others is a good distraction from dealing with unresolved difficulties that may be painful, or avoiding problems that feel overwhelming. Some therapists also enjoy feeling like a martyr, making sacrifices, and suffering deprivations, all for the greater good. I plead guilty to this one!

Takeaways

Ultimately, the most important question to ask oneself when involved in advocacy efforts is whether the actions are really about *doing* good for others versus *feeling* good about oneself. So often the results that were initiated are not sustained over time, leading to greater despair rather than hope and relief. In other cases, professionals may rush to action prior to truly understanding the circumstances and context of others' lives. That's why improving cultural knowledge, multicultural sensitivity, and the range of one's therapeutic options is so critical in such programs.

The same themes that are evident in cases of post-traumatic growth with clients are also effects that are experienced by their helpers and advocates. Lessons learned from such work encourage us to be far more flexible and open about possibilities that we may not have considered previously. Spending time in "foreign" cultures and novel environments makes us more psychologically minded and sensitive to the sort of reciprocal changes that take place in helping relationships. The extent of that impact is intensified once it is decided to make this personal growth more of a priority, looking for the changes that may occur, talking about them to family, colleagues, and friends, and processing and honoring those experiences in such a way that they become internalized.

The role and responsibilities of a counselor or therapist have expanded beyond what we do during client sessions. One ideal of our profession, at least codified into our ethical mandates, envision us walking through life as advocates for the marginalized and oppressed. We do this, of course, to help change the world to make it somehow better in some small way, even if just to break up a fight, help someone who is indigent, or offer kind words to someone we see who is suffering. But we also do this to save ourselves.

Questions for Reflection or Discussion

1. Think about a time you were involved in some service or advocacy project. What were some of your greatest joys as well as those experiences that were most frustrating and disappointing?

2. If you were going to pick a target population that speaks to your heart, what sort of social justice effort would you someday like to begin?

3. What commitment are you willing to make to become more actively involved in a project locally or on a global scale? How will you sustain your efforts over time by recruiting friends and colleagues for support?

24

Facing One's Own Family Drama and Legacies

Like all the best families, we have our share of eccentricities, of impetuous and wayward youngsters, and of family disagreements.

—Queen Elizabeth II

Families of Origin

There are many different reasons why someone would choose to become a mental health professional. I remember a conversation I once had with an Indigenous healer in the Amazon basin who was quite puzzled by my claim that it was my own choice to become a healer. He found that astounding given how demanding, challenging, and even dangerous this sort of work can be. Because we spend so much time in the world of suffering, he believed that the negative energy of our clients is potentially contagious if we are not careful. In his culture, nobody would ever willingly heed the call of service unless there was no other choice.

There are some within the profession who selected mental health services as a career because their sole acknowledged motive was to be helpful to others. I suppose I have trouble believing that. I accept that this can be partially true for some people, maybe even *mostly* the case for a small segment of our guild, but I am convinced that almost all of us do this work because of some underlying unresolved issues in our own families of origin. Okay, for those of you who are pushing back against this premise, maybe I am overgeneralizing a bit because of my own personal experience. I admit that maybe I never really had much of a choice about what I was going to do with my life given how I was "trained" in my family. Let's just say there was a lot of drama, and I often found myself in the middle of the chaos.

I noticed that I am reluctant to provide many of the details about what it was like to grow up in my family. I do not want to reveal all my family secrets and shameful events, but let's just agree that there was a fair amount of dysfunction, emotional disorders, addictions, conflict, and scandals. You know, the usual stuff.

As I was the eldest child, there were exalted expectations for my capabilities and life path. We were the first generation to attain some degree of respectability, and I was programmed to lead the charge into a position of affluence and privilege. Once I managed to find a university that would accept me with such a mediocre academic record, I was forcibly enrolled in business administration so that I might someday take over the family printing business where I had worked part time throughout high school. I remember showing up for the first orientation of those within my business major and scanning the room thinking, "These are definitely *not* my people." Everyone present was male—and wearing a suit and tie. There was no way I was going to spend the next 4 years hanging out with these straightlaced folks. Besides, I had already attended my first finance class and was totally lost.

I excused myself from the orientation session to wander the halls for a bit, peering through the windows of doorways that led to other majors. I could tell immediately there was a room set aside for music majors because all their favored instruments were visible on the floor. There was another room, in particular, that caught my attention for a couple of reasons. For one, I heard people laughing inside—that was a good sign for sure. Second, I noticed the gender balance was more advantageous for my interests. And third, the students were dressed informally. I was not sure what they would be studying in there, but I decided that this was a much closer match to my preferred peer group. It turned out these were psychology majors, and the promise of this discipline was that we would get to learn about all the ways our own families, early childhood experiences, and environmental influences shaped our choices and behavior. Once armed with advanced knowledge about interpersonal dynamics, change processes, and other psychological principles, we could free ourselves from toxic family effects and finally establish our own personal identity. This had long been a personal priority because I had so many unanswered questions that plagued me. Why did my parents divorce? Even more surprising, I wondered why they ever got married in the first place because they did not seem to have much in common. In an earlier chapter, I revealed they had a "shotgun wedding" because they had gotten accidentally pregnant (with me). You may recall that I did not learn this until just a few years ago after my father had a stroke. In addition, I had a lot of questions regarding the ways that our family environment impacted each of us.

Families are, of course, the foundational unit of our civilization. We learn from our clients that although they are usually the result of genetic linkage, they can also become configured via all sorts of voluntary recruitment as marital partners, roommates, friends, and even pets. If familial dysfunction often produces the outcomes that lead people to seek our services, we are also aware of the ways that people can construct their own families and support systems through intentional choices.

Perhaps like many other members of our profession, the struggles within my family of origin certainly handicapped me to some extent, but the experiences also provided me with deep insights into the nature of toxic interactions. In one sense, I learned some valuable coping skills that still serve me well to this day, not only managing my inner life but also better understanding what others are going through. I would like to think the origins of my deep compassion and empathy for others were forged through the trials and tribulations of my childhood and adolescence.

The Families of Family Therapists

There are so many ways that our own family of origin experiences affect the ways that we work with our clients. After all, we carry our parents and siblings with us wherever we go and whatever we do. As Albert Einstein once observed about the nature of quantum physics, applying equally to human relationships, "The distinction between the past, present, and future is only a stubbornly persistent illusion."

While it is certainly true that our own family experiences can lead to blind spots and distortions in our work, they can just as often provide opportunities for us to examine more closely the impact of early childhood events. One therapist of my acquaintance, who lost her mother to cancer as a child, found ways to include discussions of maternal deprivation in all her cases. Another practitioner who was sexually abused earlier in life, and who chose to specialize in working with survivors of neglect or abuse, consistently helped her clients express their rage toward the perpetrators, an act that she had not yet been able to complete. A third clinician who had been smothered and overprotected earlier in life as the youngest child of many siblings, tended to help all her clients develop greater autonomy and independence from their families, regardless of their cultural background. Still another who grew up in a highly emotionally restrictive environment liked to help all his clients more fluently express their feelings toward their parents. In each of these examples, the professionals' clinical choices were influenced, in part, by their own personal experiences, just as their current lives were shaped, to some degree, by their interactions in sessions. This is not just about countertransference reactions that may have some negative impact but also the gifts we receive from our clients that open up new avenues to make sense of our own early upbringing and its ongoing effects. Such new personal insights learned during sessions can become the impetus for improved and sustained self-care (Kottler, 2021; Norcross & VandenBos, 2018). This is especially true when practitioners are able to neutralize the shame they may feel regarding their previous suffering and are able to leverage these lived experiences into significant insights that assist them in their work (Victor et al., 2022).

Many well-known therapists and counselors have revealed that the primary source for their interest in psychological phenomena was firmly lodged in their own childhood experiences. Whether they were exposed to abuse, neglect, violence, disabilities, poverty, or just incompetent parenting, these individuals sought to heal themselves by studying ways to better immunize themselves against future problems. While this has been a time-honored way to deal with unresolved issues, there is also a greater risk that clinicians who are recovering from divorce, family conflicts, or tragedies are more likely to act out or engage in unprofessional conduct than those who are operating at optimal personal functioning (Kooperman, 2018).

There's an extensive list of well-known and influential theorists in our field who have struggled with their own mental demons as a result of early childhood experiences that predisposed their interest and devotion to psychological healing. Examples include Marsha Linehan (borderline personality disorder), Kay Redfield Jamison (bipolar disorder), and

Elyn Saks (schizophrenia), to mention just a few. So many other groundbreaking thinkers like Sigmund Freud, Alfred Adler, Milton Erickson, and Victor Frankl, were influenced profoundly in their ideas by the ordeals of their lives. Freud, after all, became obsessed with death in later life and was convinced he would die at age 62. William James, credited as the first psychologist, struggled with debilitating depression for much of his life. Alfred Adler almost died of pneumonia as a child and struggled afterward with being frail and sickly and believing he was inferior; he later developed a theory about compensating for disabilities. Lawrence Kohberg, an influential developmental theorist, became obsessed with moral choices, eventually choosing to take his own life. Likewise, some of the early family systems theorists developed their concepts of codependence, enmeshment, circular causality, and triangulation not only from observing their clients in action but also as memories of dynamics within their own families.

In various studies conducted over the years, somewhere close to half of all mental health providers admitted that they have experienced severe symptoms of depression, anxiety, or burnout while on the job; one third disclosed that they had contemplated suicide at one time or another (Tay et al., 2018; Yasgur, 2018). In one survey of close to 2,000 faculty members who teach psychotherapy or counseling, as well as their students, 80% of them admitted that they had experienced mental health difficulties in their lives and half had at one time been diagnosed with a specific mental disorder (Victor et al., 2021). Of course, there is no reason to believe that we would be any more likely to escape such conditions as anyone we have treated previously. It surely can't be a coincidence that we ended up in this field as opposed to, say, economics, engineering, or computer programming.

The Challenges of Difficult Family Members

For worse, and sometimes for the better, our families of origin were the proving grounds for becoming a healer in the future. For some people who were fortunate to grow up in a loving, supportive, permissive environment, this created a model of what might be possible for others. Those who survived a somewhat less stable and peaceful childhood learned other important lessons that have been just as instrumental and revealing. This would be particularly useful when dealing with so-called difficult clients, those who appear resistant, reluctant, critical, demanding, or just plain ornery and uncooperative.

Each of us may have a very different opinion on the matter of who actually qualifies as challenging to deal with, often depending on what we encountered within our own families. Because my parents argued and fought so much, resulting in a prolonged and messy divorce, I have shied away from doing the kind of couples work when partners are volatile and abusive toward one another. I just find it hard being in a room with people who are not being nice to one another. I recognize this is a clear limitation but I get triggered easily when I hear and see people yelling at one another so disrespectfully.

On the other hand, because my adolescent years were filled with so much anguish and disappointments, I absolutely love working with teenagers who act out dramatically. Rather than becoming frustrated by their belligerence and obstructiveness, I find it all familiar and even amusing. That is why it is so interesting to think about which types of clients and problems any clinician finds most difficult to treat since we do not necessarily all agree about that. Some therapists absolutely adore the chaos and drama of group, couple, and family sessions, perhaps even selecting a therapeutic approach that allows them to become forceful, intense, and melodramatic. Other practitioners much prefer clients who are far more controlled, cooperative, and obedient so that they can follow their familiar templates for treatment plans.

With that said, there is still pretty much a consensus about the types of clients who are experienced as most challenging, not only because of their behavior but also because of the family legacies we carry around within us. If you were going to nominate the cases that are considered most challenging, what immediately floats to the surface?

Surely first on the list, mentioned so often in the literature and in complaints to supervisors, is borderline personality disorder and other such toxic manipulative traits. Also added to the list would be clients who do not so much present a specific diagnosis as hold exaggerated unrealistic expectations or have poor motivation to really change anything about themselves. Some have a limited capacity for insight. Some say they are too set in their ways to make any adjustments. Some just have negative attitudes about everything, complaining that things never go their way so there is really no hope to even try.

As a result of our own early experiences, unresolved issues, and family upbringing, we might actually be the ones who are making some clients difficult because of our own rigidity and the ways that we are triggered by these interactions. We might have wildly unrealistic goals for what is possible because of our own need to demonstrate consistent progress. Countertransference reactions can lead us astray, especially during those times when we project onto others distorted reactions based on people we have known from the past. Other times, we may complete all the necessary work and preparation but still bungle the relationship because of something important that we are neglecting or missing. I will never forget the example of how during the 7th century BC, Imperial China spent centuries constructing the Great Wall to keep out the Mongol hordes from invading their territory. Determined to construct an impenetrable barrier that could never be breached, they erected the structure to not only stretch 4,000 miles across the Northern border but also to reach 20 feet high and constructed 16 feet thick. It does indeed appear impenetrable. So, what did they forget?

The door! Spaced throughout the wall were a series of entrance gates that permitted people to pass through for commercial or military purposes, carefully defended by guards, the weak link in the plan. The Mongols simply bribed a guard to sneak them through the secret entrances, making the wall itself superfluous. I'm reminded of this story during times when I am feeling overconfident that I have everything under control. It is often inattention and neglect that collapse all the best-laid plans. As General Eisenhauer, supreme commander during World War II, once admitted, planning for engagements (or anything) is absolutely indispensable; however, during battles, these plans are mostly useless. The same could be said for any certainty we might feel about any case, given all the variables that are beyond our awareness or comprehension.

The inescapable conclusion is that perhaps there is really no such thing as "difficult" clients but rather *we* are the ones who are the problem because of our own rigidity and blind spots (Kottler, 1992). When one or both partners in the therapeutic process are not satisfied with the progress, it is often because there is an inadequate alliance, resulting in diminished trust. This can compromise potential outcome gains along with ongoing unresolved issues of the past that reduce family and peer support.

Takeaways

It is fairly obvious that we are products of the families and home environments in which we were raised. One's sense of identity, capacity for trust, core values, habits, attitudes, and life mission have all been shaped by these early influences. When we are privileged to peer into the intimate relationships and interpersonal dynamics of other families, we cannot help but reflect on our own experiences growing up. This sort of self-scrutiny provides a structure for processing and working through difficult or challenging cases by asking ourselves several key questions:

- What assumptions of mine are getting in the way of seeing things more clearly?
- What am I doing—or *not* doing—that is making things worse?
- What needs of mine are not being met in this relationship?
- How am I acting out my impatience?
- What am I missing?

Instead of blaming the client for being uncooperative, or blaming the client's family and friends for sabotaging progress, it is far more empowering and personally revealing for us to accept partial responsibility for any breach in the alliance or difficulties making solid progress. The pattern most children follow when things go awry is to look for someone else to blame, whether a sibling, a mean teacher, or the dog who ate the homework. It is ironic that therapists, as well, typically blame their clients for being resistant and uncooperative when progress does not occur. Yet these are also the gifts that keep on giving, teaching us lessons we couldn't learn any other way.

A quarter century ago, I explored the ways that a therapist's early family experiences provide both the foundation for patterns of interpersonal dynamics and invaluable intelligence about the nature of what occurs in families that are falling apart. "This is both the plague and gift of our work," I concluded. "We have the opportunity, every day, with every family we see, not only to help them heal their wounds but also to help ourselves heal our own" (Kottler & Parr, 2000, p. 147).

Questions for Reflection or Discussion

1. What do you see as the most significant influences and events that occurred within your family growing up, several of which led to your career choice?

2. Based on your early experiences, what are some of the issues that might arise in a session that could "trigger" or distract you?

3. What "gifts" did you receive from your family upbringing that helps to immunize and protect you against stressors that you face?

25

Promoting Creative Breakthroughs

Around here we don't look backwards for very long. We keep moving forward, opening up new doors and doing new things, because we're curious ... and curiosity keeps leading us down new paths.

—Walt Disney

A Workshop About Nothing—and Everything

I was waiting to appear on stage, prepared to deliver a keynote speech at an international conference. I was restless with nervous energy, ready to do my thing so I could relax and enjoy some unscheduled time and explore the area. But I still had a few hours to go.

I looked up from a couch where I had been reviewing my notes and organizing slides. I did not really need to rehearse what I was going to say, but I wanted to be as organized as possible because I knew it was going to be a tough audience: They'd be tired after lunch.

I glanced up from my comfortable couch and noticed the coordinator of the conference pacing back and forth, talking animatedly into her phone. She looked panic-stricken. How did I know this? Based on my superior therapeutic skills, I deduced many symptoms of extreme anxiety. Besides, she was screaming loudly enough for me to hear: "What the hell do you *mean* you're not coming!? There's a hundred people waiting for you!"

After she completed the call, she seemed about ready to burst into tears. My hunch was confirmed after she muttered to herself, loud enough for me to hear: "I just want to cry."

"Something the matter?" I said to her with real concern. I liked this person a lot and appreciated all she had done to bring this conference together.

She just shook her head, unable to speak, so I just waited.

"I've heard 'em all," she said, shaking her head in disbelief, "this takes the cake."

"What's the matter?" I asked again.

"Oh, no big deal. It's just that there's a program set to start in fifteen minutes—just over there." She gestured with her arm in the direction of a room where people were filing in.

"Yeah? So what's the problem? Looks like a good crowd to me." She nodded her head. "Would you believe that the presenter just called me?" She looked down at the phone she was still holding in her hand, squeezing it tightly, practically strangling it for bringing her unwanted news. "She said she won't be able to make it here."

"You mean the person who's supposed to be doing this program isn't showing up?"

"Exactly. So I've got a room full of people sitting in there waiting for a workshop, and the person they came to see is a no-show."

"What's it called?" I asked her, not sure what else to say.

"Art therapy. It's a workshop on art therapy. Now what the hell am I going to do? These people are going to be bloody upset, and I don't blame them."

I still do not know what made me do it. Arrogance? Unbridled confidence? Maybe it was because I was feeling pretty pleased with myself, reflecting on the success of the previous speech I had already delivered. But before I could stop myself, I heard a voice come out of my mouth, as if someone else was inside my body: "Well, if you need someone to bail you out, I can do the workshop for you." As soon as I said the words, I had this sickly smile on my face, feeling both amused and horrified at what I had just volunteered to do.

The woman looked at me with stunned surprise. "You mean you can do a workshop on art therapy? I didn't know you knew anything about that topic."

As a matter of fact, I hadn't a clue what the topic was about. I can honestly say that in my whole life, I had never even done a single minute of art therapy, unless I count the time I stopped a kid from drawing on the wall of my waiting room.

"Well, sure, I can take the group for you. I'm sure we can come up with something that we could do together, but. ..."

Before I could finish the thought, the coordinator had raced off to the room and was making an announcement that they were going to have a special treat. She was telling them that the keynote speaker was going to do a special session for them, and he would be right in.

I took a deep breath and started walking toward the room. Immediately, I had a flashback to another time in my life, at the very beginning of my career. I had been added as the fifth presenter to a program at my very first national conference. I was a lowly master's student at the time, just beginning my first semester of classes. My advisor, who was quite well-known, decided to add me to his program as an afterthought. Along with a friend of his, who had just authored a best-selling book, and two doctoral students, we were going to present the program together. This was to be my very first public presentation, although my role was going to be fairly limited with all these famous dudes carrying most of the weight.

As it turned out, the best-selling author never showed up at the conference, nor did he bother to mention that he would not be attending. My advisor had been out drinking all night, so when I went to his room to get him out of bed, he refused to answer the door. So that left me and the two doctoral students. Since they were both experienced counselors and supervisors, and one of them was even a champion athlete who had won a gold medal in the Olympics, I still was not particularly worried: I would just follow their lead since they had presumably done this sort of thing before.

When we showed up at the room, there was a huge crowd packed into the space. It was not just standing room only, but people were literally sitting in the aisles—hundreds of them who had come to catch a glimpse of the famous author and my advisor. I peeked into the room, feeling my heart pounding, wondering what the heck we were going to do. I skipped over a few bodies blocking the door, nudged my way through the crowd, and fought my way to the front of the room. There were dirty looks all along the way since nobody could imagine that someone as young and innocent looking as me (I was only 23 but looked like a teenager) could possibly be one of the presenters.

When I turned around to face the audience, I saw only one of my partners standing next to me. It seems that one of the doctoral students, the Olympic champion, absolutely freaked out when he saw the huge audience: he fled, leaving just the two of us to handle things on our own. We stood before these hundreds of people, all of whom were expecting someone and something quite different, and looked at one another with a shrug. Somehow we would get through this. Surprisingly, the program went incredibly well—and we got a standing ovation—at least from the people already standing.

I had exactly this same feeling as I now approached the room full of expectant people at this international conference 25 years later. They wanted a program on art therapy, and I did not have a clue about what that involved; I couldn't even begin to fake it. I reviewed every option within my extensive repertoire and still came up utterly blank. So instead, I asked the group, now growing restless, what it would be like to participate in a workshop without a name. "What if you could be part of an experience that addressed something you had always wanted to explore in greater depth?"

"I thought we were here to do art therapy," someone called out from the audience.

"I already explained that to you," I said as patiently as I could. Damn, I knew this wouldn't work! Then I said, a little more forcefully than I intended, "I know that is what you came for, but that is *not* what is going to happen. After all, being a therapist is about being flexible, isn't it? It is about going with whatever clients bring to us, no matter what we have prepared ahead of time. It is about improvisation and creativity—that is, devising solutions to problems that had previously seemed unsolvable. It is about letting go of things outside of your control and going with the flow. And that is what we are going to do today."

"You mean we aren't doing art therapy?" another voice called out.

I counted slowly to myself. "That's right. No art therapy. So, what do you want to do instead?"

We spent the next few hours talking to one another about what we needed most and what was getting in the way of reaching those goals. I had no idea where things were going, or where we would proceed next. I just listened carefully, not only to the people speaking but to the wayward voice inside my head that had landed me in this predicament. Or perhaps to say that differently: this was the voice helping me to find my way in a situation without markers or signs, without even a trail. But then that is often what it feels like to me when I do therapy in the beginning stages, especially when the client and I are venturing into new territory. That is what makes the process so exciting and such an adventure. We may have encountered what appears to be a familiar situation, and yet the best work we do takes place during creative breakthroughs when we go far beyond the boundaries of where we have tread before.

I would not claim that this program was the best one I had ever done. How could it be without a minute's preparation, no structure, and an audience that had some rather highly defined expectations for what they had come for? But still, I think it was one of the most satisfying workshops I've done. I do not think many of the participants left disappointed, at least those who were willing to surrender their initial expectations and go with what unfolded.

In many ways, I did the perfect "anti-workshop" workshop. It was a program completely without structure, without an agenda, without handouts or slides, without any defined goals or outcomes. It was just an opportunity for a group of professionals to let go of their expectations and embrace whatever was available and present. This led to some very interesting interactions among those who were present.

This experience was a major breakthrough for me, not only as a presenter but also as a therapist, supervisor, and author. I had finally found my voice and had learned to trust my own ability to be helpful without needing to plan so intentionally what I was going to do next. Just as I somehow managed to take care of business in my very first professional presentation decades earlier, this time I was able to do a workshop on art therapy without knowing anything about what the subject was about. Instead, we examined how we could all be more creative in our work and what was holding us back from being even more innovative.

Facilitating Creative Breakthroughs

There has been a lot of attention directed toward the historical legacy of rather eccentric, wild figures in the field who engaged in all kinds of crazy, unconventional, provocative behavior to assist their clients. Some of our field's most creative mavericks like Fritz Perls, Carl Whitaker, Salvador Minuchin, Virginia Satir, Jacques Lacan, or Milton Erickson could just as easily have been viewed as crazy or foolish. There are hundreds of stories circulating about some of the rather unusual things they did with their clients. Many of these cases have attained legendary status, not so much because we wish to emulate them but because they have such entertainment or shock value.

Virginia Satir routinely "sculpted" family members into pretzel-like positions to exaggerate their power dynamics. Salvador Minuchin asked a mother to arm wrestle her adolescent son to demonstrate who was more dominant. Carl Whitaker fell asleep while a client was talking to highlight how boring the guy was. When someone once complained to Fritz Perls that he could not feel anything, Perls slapped him in the face, asking if he could feel *that*. William Glasser went for long runs with his client to teach her to stop eating from garbage cans. Arnold Lazarus escorted his shy client to a bar to teach him how to approach women. Ralph Greenson, founder of the Los Angeles Psychoanalytic Society, psychiatrist to Hollywood celebrities, and therapist to Marilyn Monroe, demanded that his famous patient move into a house around the block from him so she would have easier access for twice-daily sessions (as well as to run errands for his wife). Albert Ellis conducted weekly public therapy sessions on stage at his institute for many decades, challenging his audience: "I'll cure any fucking nut in this city for five bucks!" He would frequently attempt to do so by singing songs with them, including the standards, "Whine! Whine! Whine!" or "Maybe I'll Move My Ass."

I mention these examples not as legacies we should follow but rather as reminders of how many of the shakers and movers in our profession went to great lengths to test the limits of what might be helpful in extraordinary situations when the usual methods have already been tried and failed. After all, one of the most frustrating, as well as exhilarating, aspects of our work occurs when we are left with no other option except to improvise or make something up that may have never been tried before.

We are not discussing creativity in situations in which the practitioner might be feeling bored of the usual routines, employing some strategy for entertainment purposes, but rather those instances when some desperate measure is required because there is nothing else left to do. Such experiments often result in major breakthroughs in a variety of different fields when failure ultimately led to new developments or inventions such as the microwave, Viagra, and penicillin. In one sense "the talking cure" was even invented in the first place when Freud found that hypnosis alone was insufficient to make much of a difference in his patients.

It is precisely the experience of being (or feeling) lost, when all previous efforts have utterly failed, that one is best positioned to experiment with alternatives that have never been considered previously. As such, creative experiments sometimes represent acts of desperation when it becomes necessary to challenge conventional wisdom. Under such circumstances, the usual norms and standards may be discarded (safely) to increase one's cognitive flexibility so that one can discover novel solutions. Often, this involves broadening one's perspective in such a way that new and different details make themselves more readily accessible. New ideas may be tested, leading to significant conceptual leaps into new domains. More often than not, our most ordinary personal experiences may help connect disparate elements in order to make a useful breakthrough.

As a representative example of this phenomenon that leads to new creative insights, a half-century ago biopsychologist Gordon Gallup was shaving in the mirror when he accidentally cut himself. He immediately reached out with a tissue to blot the blood on his face, instead of the reflected image in the mirror (most humans have learned to distinguish between the two). This provided him with an instant revelation since, at the time, he was researching chimpanzees' sense of personal identity. He realized in that moment that he could test their ability to differentiate their likeness in the mirror from their actual self. He found they can!

It is not that difficult for any of us to recall a similar instance of creative revelation when we were able to develop or invent something new, or at least different from anything we have encountered previously. This process, involving both inductive and deductive reasoning, intuition as well as analytic thinking, personal experience as well as professional training, is what had led to breakthroughs throughout the history of our species.

Although it may appear as if such innovations and advancements occur serendipitously, such creative efforts usually involve considerable courage and strategic risk-taking, especially if realizing that most such advances are often criticized, ridiculed, and rejected. Consider the ways the likes of Copernicus, Galileo, Van Gogh, Monet, Stravinsky, Beethoven, and Freud were treated by their colleagues. Sometimes it was not their scientific or creative innovations that led to their attacks as much as their perceived beliefs. English philosopher, cryptologist, and mathematician Alan Turing had a huge impact on the war effort, not only for inventing the first computer but designing algorithms to break Nazi codes. Yet he was forcibly chemically castrated once it was discovered he was a homosexual. An even more familiar story is that of Robert Oppenheimer, head of the Manhattan Project that ended the war. Yet afterward, his reputation was destroyed during the McCarthy Era when he was accused of collaborating with Communist Russia because of his concerns about nuclear proliferation.

And then there was poor Ignaz Semmelweis, the Hungarian physician who was the first to recommend that surgeons sterilize their hands before performing operations to prevent bacterial infections. The poor guy was hounded out of the profession for accusing doctors of killing their patients through neglect. He was confined to a mental institution, where he was eventually beaten to death by the guards. It was only years later when Louis Pasteur confirmed the existence of bacteria and the critical need for hygienic medical procedures that Semmelweis's reputation was restored. According to a review of scientific and research developments (Morris et al., 2011) this is really not all that surprising considering that the average length of time it takes for a scientific or creative breakthrough to become accepted is an average of 17 years!

Takeaways

What does it take to become more creative in daily life, whether at home or in session? First of all, it requires the intense desire to reach beyond current functioning, knowing that efforts to do so will likely feel awkward and uncomfortable, and most likely fail during the first few attempts. We are talking about challenging the conventional wisdom and standard practices that have been drilled into one's psyche. It is about demonstrating the courage to try something new and being willing to deal with the consequences, all of which must be undertaken without risking client safety. Sometimes we just feel so lost and confused that we have little choice except to create novel or unusual options.

One of the outcomes of interviewing two dozen famous therapists about the most creative breakthroughs they have ever tried with their clients is that these examples might inspire us to experiment with alternative ways of helping people (Kottler & Carlson, 2009). At one time in their careers, most of the luminaries we admire felt stuck in the conventional methods they found so limiting. Given that we may be somewhat cautious and traditional in our selection of methods, it is important when pushing limits and testing boundaries that we still remain within our own comfort levels. This has become even more challenging since the pandemic because practitioners are now employing all kinds of different ways of reaching and influencing their clients beyond face-to-face, hour-long meetings. This opens up so many new possibilities for treatment, many of which are still quite novel—and untested.

Each of us must decide what is best for our clients' welfare, as well as which approaches are best suited to our personal style, values, and priorities. Some clinicians have learned, for instance, that in spite of their initial enthusiasm and excitement related to surrendering their offices and switching to doing online sessions exclusively, this option is just not suited to their style and clinical priorities (face-to-face relational engagement). Yes, it is convenient, cost-effective, and minimizes transportation and parking issues (did I mention it was so convenient?) but it is just not suitable for everyone—unless there is no other choice. Some therapists just need to be in the room with people. They need to see the pupils of their eyes and what their hands and feet are doing. They need to smell their clients' breath. At times, they need to offer a reassuring gesture or even a hug. They need to be able to control the space; in fact, they need to *share* the same space as their clients so that they can more closely monitor their reactions to whatever is happening.

The thinking on this matter may be old-fashioned, perhaps even obsolete given the way so much has changed in recent years, yet one important takeaway from this discussion on creativity is that each of us must find our *own* way to operate best, not only when handling familiar issues and the usual challenges but especially when we find ourselves required to employ something we have never tried before.

Questions for Reflection or Discussion

1. Even if you don't consider yourself a particularly creative person, what are some instances when you experimented with something novel and new and struggled with the awkwardness of the situation, yet learned something really significant as a result?

2. What do you believe are the biggest obstacles and impediments for you to become more creative in your work and life?

3. Get together with a few other people and share examples of when you did something wildly creative to help someone else. If you are doing this on your own, then generate a list of at least a handful of such instances. Review these incidents and identify some of the most common features that they all share.

26

Explaining Feelings, Behavior, and Other Mysteries

The most beautiful experience we can have is the mysterious. It is the fundamental emotion that stands at the cradle of true art and true science. ... The important thing is not to stop questioning.

—Albert Einstein

Playing Detective

I have been a mountaineer most of my life, having climbed or trekked up some of the highest peaks in the world, perhaps not to the scale of Everest heights but well over 19,000 feet a few times. It is not the altitude or the grueling vertical march that gets to me. It is certainly exhausting to begin the summit attempt walking all through the night, blinded by ice storms, hoping not to fall through a hidden crevasse. But none of those things are dealbreakers for me. In fact, I love the challenge of pushing myself beyond the limits of what I believe I am capable of doing. I thrive on training for these adventures and testing myself in new and different ways. But what worries me most on these expeditions is my fear of heights, or at least, that is what I have called this reaction most of my life. You see, I almost never go on balconies or allow myself to get too close to the edge of a cliff or a building. The thing is—it is not that I am afraid of falling; I'm afraid I might jump. I think to myself I could just impulsively decide (it would be so quick it would not even be a decision) to just leap off the edge and, before I would realize it, I would be flailing in space, thinking to myself, "Holy crap! I didn't mean to do that." But it would be too late.

I have carried around a lot of shame about that inclination to suddenly take my own life. Or at least that is what I *thought* was going on. Even though my life was proceeding spectacularly well, everything just humming along, no particular dissatisfactions, I would still occasionally feel this strong urge to just do something utterly crazy and self-destructive. I remember once sitting in the audience of a play when I had this compulsive urge to stand up and walk on stage. I knew if I did that, it would not only ruin the performance but also destroy my reputation. Still, it felt irresistible, so much so that I gripped the armrests of the seat to keep myself in place. Once again, I assumed this was irrefutable evidence of my essential mental instability, proving that I never had any business pretending I was in control.

Over the years, I adapted to my presumed "disability," doing my best to avoid open spaces where I might suddenly fling myself into the abyss. I would joke about it to others in such situations, once again assuming it was just a fear of potential danger (which of course it was). I reassured myself that in other contexts of my life, I had no inclination to do myself harm. I attempted to test myself over and over again that I could manage this anxiety by forcing myself to complete difficult climbs. I developed a routine when crossing high ridges, elevated bridges, or narrow cliffs to just stare at my feet one step at a time. There might be a 2,000-foot drop on both sides of the narrow ridge on a glacier, but I would focus only on what was right in front of me. Once again, I was not so much concerned that I would fall but rather that I might suddenly just jump. Crazy stuff, I admit.

The story does not end here. I thought it did. I believed that the meaning and under-standing of my behavior were altogether clear and settled. It was best to keep this under wraps and just keep myself away from open balconies. At least when climbing, I was firmly attached to the mountain with ropes and carabiners.

Because I am a therapist, I frequently read stuff about human behavior and all its nuances. I have long since moved on from psychotherapy books to those that explore evolutionary, psychobiological, and neurological aspects of functioning. I do this for research projects like this one but also for fun to learn about various subjects that intrigue me. I also read a lot of escape fiction, and while deciding what to write for this chapter about explaining confusing feelings, I happened to finish a novel about a retiring assassin who described this exact same impulse I have been describing. And the character gave it a name, casually mentioning it in French, *l'appel du vide*, "the call of the void." I looked it up and discovered that what I previously believed were indications of my suicidal tendency or fear of heights were actually conceived in the research literature ("high place phenomenon") as the exact opposite: It really signals an affirmation of the will to live and how much someone wants to survive (Hames et al., 2012). The sensation is a relatively common impulse shared by half the population. It is the rush of exhilaration of realizing how fragile and time-limited our life span is, appreciating the reality that it could end any second, whether from impulse, accident, or fate. There is a complex and compelling surge of instantaneous and unnerving terror but also a momentary sense of being totally alive, aware, and fully present. In this teasing of possible annihilation, there are corresponding feelings of shame, disgust, and self-loathing. It is actually the misinterpretation of what the impulse signifies that is more of a problem than the disturbing thoughts themselves.

I mention this one chronic terror of my existence as an example of the sort of mysteries we are often required to interpret and explain to others—and ourselves. We are frequently called upon to make sense of behavior that appears inscrutable or to uncover buried feelings that have long been denied. We operate as sleuths on occasion, solving mysteries that plague those who seek our help. Again and again, we search for clues, paying attention to seemingly insignificant details that reveal hidden or disguised information. We record detailed notes, attempting to make connections between events of the past and current actions. We apply logic and test hypotheses to rule out factors that may be irrelevant or distracting and home in on what we believe may be the essence of an issue or problem. Based on our observations, suspicions, research, experience, and deductions, we offer possible explanations that may, or may not, be accepted by our clients, but still represent one stage in the ongoing experimental journey. And it is in so doing that we stimulate curiosity and greater wisdom, not only about our craft but also the mysteries that most confound us in daily life.

A License to Learn

The excitement over discovering a new idea or concept that further illuminates the meaning of behavior and our deepest feelings is just one of the gifts we receive almost every day or at least each week. We are continuously adding to our bank of valuable knowledge that we draw upon to help others better understand their choices. We operate as investigators, decoding the meaning behind a person's actions and solving mysteries that interfere with making constructive choices. After a lifetime of studying such puzzles, we will still never fully grasp why people do some of the things they do or why certain peculiar behavior still persists.

Absolute truths are both elusive and always evolving. Those of my generation can certainly remember sitting around the pool on a hot summer day, dangling our feet in the water because we had just finished lunch. Everyone believed at the time that if you jumped in the water after eating you would probably die of a stomach cramp, likely within minutes. If that was not bad enough, we were also warned about eating chocolate, which would most certainly lead to acne, or we were forbidden from chewing gum in case it was swallowed and would remain in the intestines for at least 7 years. It is a wonder that we ever survived.

There are so many mysteries that circulate throughout daily life, and we are in the privileged position to investigate and better understand what they mean and how they affect quality of life (Kottler, 2022b). Why do teenagers appear to take such stupid, ill-advised risks like jumping off buildings, driving recklessly, drinking excessively, or having unprotected sex? (They earn status and kudos among their peers.) Consider all the common emotional reactions we witness every day that seem downright bizarre: Why does water leak out of the eyes when someone is upset or joyful (crying), or make unintelligible "yip yip" sounds when amused (laughter), or open one's mouth wide and exhale breath when bored (yawning)? So many other questions come to mind—the origins of racism, the enduring evolutionary purposes of homosexuality, and the reasons for widespread racism.

One perplexing mystery among all of them is why people over 50 are still alive at all when it is known that almost every other animal and plant that exists expires when it can no longer produce offspring. There are only a few species on the planet that survive beyond menopause (humans and orca whales among the lucky few). Every other creature dies after it can no longer procreate, vacating the premises to provide more space and resources for those that are still fertile and "productive." By the way, in case you are wondering, the suspected reason for this last puzzle is revealed in a proposition called "the grandmother hypothesis" in which it was discovered that if there is a grandparent who lives within commuting distance of the family, the parents will likely have more children who have a better chance of surviving until adulthood (Hawkes, 2004; 2021). As supporting evidence, it has been observed that when orca whales are on the hunt for food, the parents must dive deep into the ocean to locate their most delectable meals (squid). While the parents are taking care of business, the orca grandmother remains on the surface to babysit the kids, just like in extended human families (Driscoll, 2009).

Another mystery dear to our hearts explains the persistence of altruism. Once again, it appears to make little sense that anyone, in any circumstances, would willingly surrender their money, resources, time, or effort, much less risk their lives, to help a perfect stranger with no genetic connection. Remember, it used to be the case long ago during ancient times that everyone within one's tribal group was direct kin. It seemed perfectly reasonable that individuals would make sacrifices, share resources, and even risk their safety and security to benefit others with whom they share genetic material. But as human civilization expanded into larger communities consisting of allied groups, immigrants, refugees, visitors, and guests, evolution pivoted to "reward" those who would behave selflessly to safeguard others. Within many species of birds and mammals, for instance, a scout is posted to watch for predators and will choose to sacrifice her own life to alert her mates. This might not be in the best interests of her own survival, but it is absolutely functional and necessary for her herd or flock to flourish, much less survive.

These few examples are mentioned to highlight some of the mysteries that we seek to uncover every day. Does depression have some functional purpose? In what ways are emotional disorders designed to be helpful in some way? Why do some people engage in such obviously self-destructive behavior that is virtually guaranteed to get them in trouble? Even more perplexing are those questions that relate directly to the practice of counseling and psychotherapy.

There are so many things we take for granted and never really question, even within our own professional practices (Kottler & Balkin, 2020). Take the supposed 50-minute hour, for instance: How did *that* ever become the inviolate standard regardless of the client, issues, preferences, and resources available? Does everyone need the exact same treatment dosage all the time? Even more peculiar and inexplicable is the phenomenon that clinicians appear to do such different things in their work, focusing on cognition or emotion or behavior, exploring the past versus the present versus the future, being gentle and supportive or challenging and confrontive, taking on the role of a teacher, parent, mentor, guide, or healer. How do we account for the reality that a dozen different therapeutic approaches, all of which *seem* to be doing such different things, still produce desirable outcomes?

While you are attempting to address that conundrum (and it *is* a struggle) consider some of the other enduring questions that we still cannot answer definitively: (1) How does therapy *really* work and what are the most universal features of all effective approaches? (2) *When* is therapy likely to be most and least effective? (3) With *whom* does therapy work best? (4) What is the best way to do therapy? Every practitioner may have rather strong opinions already about each of these questions but how do we truly explain how and why they manage to be completely contradictory with one another?

There will be controversies, debates, and arguments for some time, dueling research agendas, each of which may claim to have cornered some semblance of truth. Yet we are already well aware of how certain "best practices" and "standard protocols" that are considered the "gold standard" may not, in fact, have overwhelming evidence to support these practices. Since we are "explainers" for a living, uncovering the reasons why things exist as they do, we have also been naive and negligent when challenging some of the "sacred cows" of our profession that actually have little empirical support. We have covered many of these already like the belief that one's choice of theory matters most or that we truly understand perfectly how and why symptoms persist and how to make them go away. In so many cases, we are operating not only as scientists but also as faith healers.

Takeaways

It is hardly much of a revelation to find that so much of what you study in classes and learn on the job relate directly to your own life struggles. It is virtually impossible to avoid personalizing the content or asking oneself, "I wonder how this applies to *me*?" Each and every class taken, every workshop attended, and any supervision session not only highlights useful ideas to improve professional effectiveness but also personal functioning in a multitude of ways.

We are continuously called upon to explain things, to provide definitive answers to the question, "Why?" Clients badger us with such queries: "Why did this problem arise now?" "Why am I stuck in this situation?" "Why are others so mean to me?" "Why does this therapy stuff seem to take such a long time?" Always, why, why, why. And as if that is not enough pressure, supervisors and mentors pester us with still more questions: "Why do you believe your client is behaving in this way?" "Why did you choose to respond in that manner?" "What sense do you make of that situation?" "What diagnosis would you assign to this case?" They are all mysteries that we are expected to unravel, or at the very least, invent some fairly reasonable explanation that will be accepted temporarily.

We are constantly questioning the meaning of almost everything a client says and does: "What is he *really* saying right now?" "I wonder why she chose *not* to talk about that subject?" "There must be some reason why this person is consistently late." "It looks like her posture and nonverbals are saying something quite different than her words." We are always analyzing *everything* that occurs in session to decode their hidden, disguised, or latent meanings. Once the meter is turned off, we cannot help but continue this scrutiny and meaning making with our own internal reactions.

In the story that began this chapter, I shared just one example of a phenomenon that occurs almost every single day in our lives—when we learn something profoundly applicable to our own lives while we are preparing to help someone in our care. Every time we speak to clients to reflect on their underlying feelings, clarify the content of their verbalizations, and interpret disguised meanings in their behavior, we are also potentially talking to ourselves as well.

There is nobody better equipped to explore the mysteries of human experience, or at least learn to live with them, than a counselor or therapist. We are trained specifically in how to deal with the inexplicable, as well as how to live with uncertainty. We *thrive* on this stuff: It defines us!

Questions for Reflection or Discussion

1. What's a recent example in your studies in which you discovered some principle, concept, theory, or insight that clarified something significant for you in your own life?

2. What is a mystery in human behavior that absolutely fascinates you, a particular choice or action that people consistently make that doesn't appear to make much sense or have much functional value?

3. What would you say is the greatest mystery of your own life and existence?

27

Counteracting Boredom, Burnout, and Fatigue

The cure for boredom is curiosity. There is no cure for curiosity.

—Dorothy Parker

Between Boredom and Anxiety

Life is short; then you die. That has been the motto of my life, a time line that is now quite limited and abbreviated. I once calculated how many heartbeats the average human organ can manage prior to wearing out. After all, the heart is simply a muscle that contracts thousands of times each day and night to pump blood, nutrients, and oxygen throughout the system. Sometimes, especially when I was feeling bored or distracted, or wanted to escape my current predicament, I would place my hand on my chest and feel the regular thumps in my chest, reminding myself that I was slowly dying with each pump of blood. Any time I hesitated before doing something difficult that really needed to be done, or was avoiding some adventure or new challenge because of anxiety and fear, I would once again feel my heart beating away. Each breath could very well be my last.

This thought is never far from my mind, a prospect that might seem rather distressing and unnerving, but I have always thought of it as one of my greatest gifts—the urgency to seize the day, so to speak. One of my burdens in life has been to try and manage my constant desire (need?) for stimulation, excitement, new adventures, and movement. I have tried and failed with medication, mindfulness, yoga, and tai chi, all of which seem to trigger more restlessness. Others have tried to "fix" me, or at least persuade me to slow down a little, but I just do not want to miss anything with so little time left. Since I was like that when I was 30, you can well imagine how that urgency has accelerated now that I'm in my 70s.

Perhaps an example would help. I remember sitting in a staff meeting a few years ago about to explode in frustration. There were some people present who just love to hear themselves talk, as if there is nothing else that we have to do. There was one person in the room who felt the need to speak constantly, as if everything that anyone said was directed specifically to her, requiring her extensive opinion and take on the matter. This was a complete waste of time. I put my hand on my heart, feeling the beats wasting away, and I wanted to scream. There was absolutely nothing being accomplished; we were just occupying time when there were so many tasks waiting for completion—papers to grade, lectures to prepare, appointments to keep, and other infernal meetings to attend. I kept repeating to myself a quote I remembered from comedy writer, Dave Barry: "If you had to identify in one word the reason why the human race has not achieved and never will achieve its full potential, that word would be *meetings*." I could not agree more.

I tried checking out for a while, but that seemed rude unless I reminded myself to continuously nod my head when someone was talking to pretend I was actually listening. Then I settled on a fun game to play: I started counting the number of times the annoying person spoke up in the meeting, just to collect data to support my cause. The tally was going quite well until I lost count somewhere over 220 distinct verbalizations within the first 80 minutes (20 minutes left to go!). By the way, this is *not* an exaggeration; this really did happen.

I scanned the room to see if others were as annoyed and bored as I was. I noticed one guy playing with the phone on his lap, another seemed to be reviewing notes for some project. A few others were pretending to take notes, but when I peeked at their computer or tablet screens I clearly observed that they were checking sports scores, social media, and the news. One person was shopping on Amazon. The only two people in the room who actually seemed fully present were the verbose person and the department head—and even she looked incredibly bored as well, even if she refused to acknowledge it. It was as if we were all trapped in an alternative universe where there was only verbal blather but nothing was really ever accomplished. I put my hand on my heart again, and I stifled another scream of frustration.

I would like to admit that this is an unusual experience in my life, but that is clearly not the case. This is actually my default reaction when I feel stuck in situations that appear to be going nowhere, or else when it seems like we are just doing the same things we always do, over and over again. That is why some of my clients begin to sound the same. I become annoyed with all the complaining that does not seem to lead anywhere meaningful or useful. I became bored with myself, tired of hearing my voice repeat the same stories over and over. I do have some really great stories, but I have told them so often, I sometimes feel like I'm just in a play reciting my lines as scripted. I wondered if I was just wasting my life.

I know that I sound burned out, an experience that has been familiar to me several different times throughout my career whenever it felt like I was not learning anything new. This awareness almost always resulted in a radical change in my career, location, and life. Once I reach the point that it feels like I am stuck, or even trapped, certainly a state of mind rather than circumstances, rather than challenging my attitude, I find it much easier—and fun—to try another makeover, another reinvention, another life change. By and large, my family has been somewhat tolerant of the disruptions, or at least good sports who recognize that restless spirit within me that craves—no demands—new stimulation and adventures.

I am sure that getting back into therapy as a client might "fix" this tendency, but, truthfully, I thrive on this wild ride.

Perhaps like many others there tends to be two very different and opposite forces that are most bothersome to me. The first, of course, is boredom and sameness, when it feels like I am not doing anything new and interesting, just repeating the same things out of habit. These are the times it feels like I am dying inside, when I need to shake things up. I just love the unexpected.

Except when I don't. The other major cause of stress and burnout in my work and life is exactly the opposite—the times when I am overwhelmed with too much to do, and when I am *way* beyond what I can handle comfortably. This, of course, is what I have been asking for, but once I enter the realm of chaos and uncertainty, I yearn for the good 'ole days when things were so easy and predictable. It would appear, then, that either end of the continuum is a potential source of compassion fatigue, burnout, and anxiety. It is just so challenging to find that perfect sweet spot, often referred to as "flow" that sits comfortably between boredom and anxiety (Csikszentmihalyi, 1975, 1990).

Stress, More Stress, Still More Stress

There has never been a time when mental health professionals have been under more overwhelming pressure than this particular era—except perhaps during a world war. Even before the pandemic and political upheaval throughout the country and world, almost every practitioner reported some difficulties related to stress, compassion fatigue, burnout, or boredom. Not surprisingly, we can only sit still and listen to tragic stories for so long before the accumulative effects take their toll.

There are some fairly obvious reasons why we face so much strain and challenges in this weird job in which we sit alone and listen to people's worst problems and fears. We work almost completely in isolation, ensconced in a private space, our day partitioned into individual hours while walking wounded visit with us for consultations. We entertain no interruptions when the meter is running and are then allocated just a few minutes between each meeting to take care of basic needs, using the bathroom, grabbing a snack or beverage, returning messages or calls, just keeping oneself grounded after a series of emotional interactions, one right after the other.

We are required to exercise perfect restraint and self-control during these encounters, withholding all personal needs, and focusing concentration intensely. And speaking of intensity, our conversations tend toward highly emotional outbursts and dramatic, disturbing revelations. The interactions with clients are both complex and confusing, sometimes completely unpredictable. There is an inherent ambiguity in the whole enterprise that often leaves us feeling lost and uncertain. The topics under discussion are usually provocative, secretive, and disturbing, potentially triggering personal reactions that are, at best, distracting. Finally, the nature of the work means we often deal with lost causes, chronic problems, and long-standing pessimism, which are not usually associated with quick and lasting results. No wonder we feel a sense of futility and helplessness at times.

If mental health professionals have a singular talent, it is the ability to adopt others' perspectives and respond empathically. But this almost necessarily leads to potential difficulties regulating boundaries between self and others. In addition, our job is significantly at odds with how our bodies were designed to operate. Nowadays more people die of obesity than starvation because of our relative inactivity. This pervasive sedentary lifestyle is a primary reason why there has been such a spike in heart disease, high blood pressure, cancer, osteoporosis, diabetes, and obesity.

Whatever stressful challenges we already encountered have multiplied considerably during more recent times. Clients are now presenting far more serious and intractable problems than ever before. The increase in social conflict, contagious diseases, mass violence, addictions, parental neglect, or abuse, coupled with diminished resources, has only made things far worse.

In addition to these societal changes, our own attitudes and habits make things even more stressful. Many practitioners claim they are just too exhausted to practice regular self-care, which just feels like one more additional burden. And of course, by the time someone might wish to add a recovery plan to restore equanimity, it may already be too late once the symptoms are in evidence. For those who are regularly active on social media, there is often additional perceived social pressure to pretend that everything is lovely and perfect and that our lives are just as fulfilling and interesting as everyone else's seems to be on social media sites.

Although technology has improved the quality and efficiency of our lives in so many ways, not just with our smartwatches, phones, tablets, and laptops but also with all the amazing software suites that simplify our assessments and record keeping. This certainly makes things more efficient, but another consequence of these technological innovations, like the prevalence of messaging, is that we are now available every minute of the day and night to the requests and demands from others beseeching us for assistance. The average person touches their phone hundreds (or thousands!) of times each day, perfectly willing to respond to any message or call in the moment no matter what else is going on at the time including an intimate conversation, sleep, or even sex. All the while we are listening and talking to someone, or just thinking about stuff, we hear the constant beeps of communications rolling in, many of which require some attention.

Distinctions Between Various Professional Stress Reactions

When helping people with depression, we know that the condition comes in many different types and forms (situational, major, psychotic, seasonal affective disorder, postpartum, melancholia, dysthymia, bipolar, atypical), each diagnostic entity treated a bit differently, whether in therapy or with medications and possible hospitalization. Likewise, the stressors that lead to boredom and burnout also appear in a variety of different forms, somewhat similar in symptoms but with different identifying names.

We are perhaps most familiar with *primary psychological trauma* because it is among the most common complaints brought to us by clients. It represents a direct personal experience with some major crisis, incident, injury, or disaster that results in an inability to cope effectively. It is typically characterized by severe anxiety, depression, and perceived threat to security. As observers/participants during interactions with people suffering from trauma and emotional disorders, mental health professionals are also vulnerable to their own stress-induced conditions. *Secondary trauma*, for instance, results from close proximity to someone experiencing major trauma, especially as a result of an intimate relationship that was high in emotional valence. We can include that one on the list since that's *exactly* what we do throughout the day (and sometimes night).

Other variations of this theme encompass the contagious effects of being a witness to catastrophic situations (*vicarious trauma*) or when we are exposed to acute and prolonged roles assisting others who are suffering (*compassion fatigue*). In worst cases, we may unconsciously internalize negative feelings, blur the boundaries between ourselves and others, and absorb fears, anxieties, and hopelessness that never actually "belonged" to us in the first place.

Last on the list is the type of chronic, unremitting stress on the job that results from interpersonal, administrative, workload, or political difficulties. Not only are our efficiency and therapeutic effectiveness compromised, but we may also experience symptoms of depletion, physical and emotional exhaustion, cynicism, and loss of satisfaction. Obviously, this condition not only affects one's professional effectiveness but also personal well-being.

By the time professionals identify, diagnose, and admit to their deteriorating condition, symptoms are likely already florid and possibly severe, affecting every aspect of their being, including physical sensations (aches, pains, exhaustion), cognitive functioning (concentration, intrusive thoughts), emotional reactions (depression, anxiety, sadness), behavioral indicators (poor coping, acting out, addictions), interpersonal connections (isolation, loneliness, mistrust), spiritual beliefs (questioning faith and meaning), and of course professional competence (efficiency, ethical restraint, morale, ultimate effectiveness). All of these can lead to feelings of helplessness and futility to change the situation and make an impact

The conditions that most likely contribute to burnout, compassion fatigue, and poor morale are frequently connected to a perceived lack of control over job responsibilities. Expectations from administrators and supervisors may be confusing, contradictory, or imprecise. In some cases, those in charge may be incompetent or clueless about what is going on, or else try to micromanage everything according to policies that are obsolete, inefficient, unfair, or inappropriate. Other factors relate to the repetitive nature of the work with little opportunity for variability, advancement, promotion, or new challenges. In extreme cases, the organization itself can be highly toxic, leading to the abuse of power by those in control, as well as continuous conflicts and competition among the staff. Backstabbing and undermining become the norm, sometimes further encouraged by those who engage in verbal abuse, shaming, and bullying.

When discouraged and demoralized professionals are interviewed about how and why they ended up so dispirited, they often point to mundane factors that get on their nerves and wear them down over time. This includes things like excessive paperwork, unrealistic scheduling, inequitable distribution of resources and referrals, poor compensation, and an unreasonable workload. Then added to the picture are also all the disruptions that can occur from personal losses, deaths, health problems, financial difficulties, family problems, and life transitions.

In spite of all these impediments, obstacles, and annoyances, not everyone reacts the same way and takes them on board. Whereas it is true that many practitioners experience major distress, others find ways to adopt a "stress mindset," also known as *eustress*, the processing of feelings in such a way that they feel exciting and stimulating rather than just a burden. Such an attitude is far more optimistic, hopeful, and encouraging, resulting in growth and learning rather than increased tension (Crum et al., 2013; Huebschmann & Sheets, 2020). Ultimately, this is what increases one's sense of well-being and satisfaction with work and everything else in life.

Takeaways

It should be evident from this discussion that mental health professionals need to do a better job of taking care of themselves, not only to prevent boredom, burnout, and the chronic effects of continuous stress but also to better demonstrate to our clients what we want most for them by modeling such commitment in our own lives. There are several key points to keep in mind, or better yet, to act on.

Self-Care Requires Honest Acknowledgment of Difficulties

Just as we are sometimes not very accurate in our assessment of how well things are working in our helping relationships, we are inclined to shrug off annoying and unpleasant symptoms. We engage in wishful thinking that things will improve of their own accord if just given enough time.

Expect Instant Relief

Get a massage. Drink a green smoothie. Go for a walk. Schedule a manicure. There has been an overemphasis on specific techniques and strategies, not to mention self-care products, that are alleged to make all the difference. And of course, they do not matter very much—for very long—especially when we return to the same conditions and forces that continue outside of our control.

Emphasize Simplistic Techniques

As in every other aspect of life, it's rare that any quick fix, tool, or technique will make much of a significant difference, at least one that has an enduring impact. The evidence is also pretty compelling that broad, personally designed, and contextualized strategies are far more likely to work.

Self-Care Implies Something Is Broken

Let's face it: something probably *is* broken in the sense that the current situation isn't working. But we are supposed to be experts, high-functioning muses, who represent the ideal of personal effectiveness. Understandably, we may be reluctant to admit to others, much less ourselves, that things feel out of control.

Deeper Issues

There are often underlying issues at work that lead to, or exacerbate, stress reactions. Self-care strategies may get at the most obvious, annoying symptoms but do not address the chronic, entrenched patterns that are operating to make things so much more difficult. These could be unacknowledged problems from the past (trauma, abuse, neglect), chronic health difficulties, family problems, interpersonal conflicts, personality features, addictions or substance abuse, or more nebulous existential questions in which there is a loss of personal meaning in work and life.

Limits of Self-Help

There's only so much we can do for ourselves without assistance, support, and guidance from others, especially professionals. We might not have any compunction about taking our car for service or calling a plumber when the toilet needs repair, but there is reluctance and resistance at times to get the help we need when we can't do it ourselves.

Questions for Reflection or Discussion

1. What are some aspects of your lifestyle and daily choices that are most unhealthy and ill-advised?

2. How do you tend to "medicate" yourself when under tremendous stress?

3. Who gets to you most, and what is it about those interactions that trigger you in undesirable ways?

28

Learning Resilience and Persistence in the Face of Suffering

I began to understand that suffering and disappointments and melancholy are there not to vex us or cheapen us or deprive us of our dignity but to mature and transfigure us.

—Hermann Hesse

The Lessons of Suffering

I had been working as the clinical director at an outpatient psychiatric clinic, responsible for the supervision of 15 other psychologists, psychiatrists, social workers, and counselors who were also some of my closest friends. We would organize retreats together, plan elaborate lunches for our weekly staff meetings, and hang out socially in small groups. Little did I know that beneath the surface, all kinds of strange and nefarious activities were going on behind the scenes. It may very well sound like I am making this up, or at least exaggerating a bit, but I absolutely promise that all that I am about to reveal to you is true. When everything going on finally came to light, it struck me that a situation comedy series could not have been any more ridiculous than what many of the therapists in the clinic were doing in their spare time or when nobody was paying much attention.

Things started to fall apart, or perhaps better said as coming into focus, when Blue Cross scheduled an audit of our staff's insurance billing. It was standard practice for them to check the credentials of the clinicians, a somewhat routine check as part of their assessment process. In this case, however, the auditors immediately discovered that one therapist appeared to have a forged license from someone who died many years ago. It turned out that this colleague and friend never actually graduated from his program, which was especially surprising because he was such an extraordinary and beloved therapist. Once this initial fraud was identified, it invited much deeper inquiry into everyone else's behavior—and oh, did it get ugly! It was found that another therapist in the clinic was scheduling two, sometimes three sessions, within the same hour and then shuttling back and forth between the rooms so she could double or triple charge for the same time. She ended up in prison, as did another fellow who was actually charging his clients to have sex with them—*in the office on his couch*! This illegal and ethical conduct turned out to be pervasive among several others. One woman was conspiring with her clients to cut secret deals to get extra fees under the table but without having to pay her share of expenses: she was coercing her clients to commit fraud with her!

Needless to say, realizing how naive, trusting, and oblivious I was to the behavior of the staff created a crisis of epic proportions. I no longer trusted my own judgment since I originally hired all these folks, and as their supervisor, I was supposedly the one responsible for their conduct. How did I miss all the cues and evidence regarding what was going on right under my nose? The system within the clinic appeared to be so dysfunctional that I had to get out of there.

Within a few weeks, I abruptly left the facility, disillusioned and broken. I seriously wondered whether it was time to try something different, a completely new career. I decided to take some time off from the job to recover, make sense of what happened, and consider honestly what my role had been in this catastrophe. I no longer wanted to be in charge of anyone else, nor to feel responsible for anyone besides my own clients.

I decided to sign up for an Outward Bound trip, reasoning that this adventure would provide time to think about my life, where it had been, and where it was headed next. The structure of the trip was designed to foster that sort of reflection since it consisted of the grueling physical demand of cross-country skiing in the wilderness of the Rocky Mountains, along with uncomfortable daily challenges that involved building and sleeping in igloos at night. Worst of all for me was that we were required to stick together as a team and make all our navigating decisions collaboratively. I am an aggressive, fit, and expert skier who loves to go just as fast as I can, bombing down a mountain or climbing rough, vertical terrain. Within our group, however, there were a few others who had never skied before, so they proceeded very slowly and awkwardly. It drove me absolutely bonkers. I was there in the first place because I was so tired and burned out taking care of other people, and yet here I was once again required to stifle my own preferences, slow down my preferred pace, and wait endlessly for others to catch up. This was a different kind of suffering than I ever imagined subjecting myself to as my form of penance.

I have always been pretty good at tolerating physical discomforts. Every mountaineer or endurance athlete understands that the supposed suffering associated with prolonged exertions is simply annoying rather than actually painful. Over time, one learns to increase tolerance for these kinds of challenges, eventually building levels of resilience and hardiness that allow better conditioning and performance. But this business of having to deal with other people's frustrating pace had been driving me crazy—that is, until I recognized that this was the same problem I had with some of my clients (and family members) when they did not conform to my expectations.

It is just so curious how we can witness or listen to a story unfolding, one with poignant drama, usually some misfortune that required significant adaptation and recovery afterward, and find that the narrative sticks with us long after the sessions are over. We are trusted (and burdened) to hear some of the most tragic experiences one could possibly endure—the death of a child or partner, the diagnosis of a fatal disease, losing one's home and possessions in a fire or flood, surviving abuse or sexual assault. It is precisely our clients' willingness (or desperation) to talk about the terrors and disappointments of their lives, as well as their recovery from such events, that teaches us so much about our own capacity to deal with adversities we face.

Resilience via Proxy

It is difficult not to feel inspired by many of the clients we have seen who have survived the most hellacious suffering and trauma and yet still managed to rise above these challenges to achieve so much in their lives. The historical record is filled with tortured geniuses who overcame early childhood abuse, neglect, violence, and trauma. Novelist Franz Kafka was abused repeatedly by his father. Poet Maya Angelou had been sexually assaulted. Playwright Tennessee Williams dealt with his beloved sister's mental illness, as well as his own alcoholism to cope with chronic depression, and yet produced an extraordinary body of work from *A Streetcar Named Desire* to *The Glass Menagerie*. There are so many other creative innovators (Virginia Woolf, Sylvia Plath, Ernest Hemmingway, Marilyn Monroe, Lenny Bruce, Charles Mingus, Vaslav Nijinsky, Mark Rothko) who struggled with their own inner demons, for better or worse, perhaps faltering in terms of their own emotional stability that eventually resulted in them taking their own lives and yet still finding sufficient resilience to maintain their creative output (Kottler, 2006). The same could be said for famous sports figures like baseball players Jimmy Piersall or Dock Ellis, cyclists Graeme Obree or Marco Pantani, football player Lionel Aldridge, or surfer Michael Aldridge, all of whom faced crushing mental disabilities and emotional breakdowns and yet maintained the highest levels of athletic performance (Kottler, 2019). Their life stories are so popular and compelling, even when they end in tragedy, precisely because these mythical figures demonstrated so much courage in the face of their emotional disturbances as a result of early trauma.

I remember one client, Mika, who had already lost her mother to cancer a few years previously, and then her father was seriously disabled and confined to a wheelchair. Her family had no regular source of income, relying primarily on help from neighbors since the government didn't provide any support or assistance. As if this wasn't enough to lead to despair, Mika also developed a chronic disease that compromised her health and ability to function. But the truly amazing part of the story was how joyful, optimistic, and determined this girl was in spite of all the setbacks and tragedies she had already faced before the age of 12. Yet there were still more challenges to come.

During all the conversations we shared, I could not help comparing Mika's life to my own. I thought about the things that annoyed and disappointed me most, and they seemed so incredibly insignificant and meaningless. I have worked with thousands and thousands of clients, supervisees, and students in my life, and yet Mika stands out as one of the few whose courage and passion superseded all the anguish and disappointments she faced.

There are names for this type of perseverance that we sometimes witness in people who are undergoing dramatic post-traumatic growth. We witness so often how people subjected to excruciating pain and tragedy somehow use these experiences to improve their strength and abilities for the future. It explains for some of us why we entered this profession in the first place, as a way to use our own suffering as a kind of inner resource to assist others.

If there is such a thing as "vicarious" or "secondary" trauma, then there is also a corresponding version that could be called "vicarious resilience" when we somehow take on greater resistance to disappointment and pain as a result of our clients' own accounts that we are privy to. I remember one time when Mika told me she hadn't eaten yet that day, and I felt such incredible respect and caring for her that I decided to fast the rest of the day in sympathy, just to better feel her pain (and reduce my own sense of guilt over my privilege).

By the way, Mika eventually did plead, beg, and lobby to receive sufficient funding to complete her education. After graduating from secondary school at the top of her class, she began a campaign to solicit donations to fund her medical education. She is now a practicing physician, one of the few females in her country to ever attain that position.

When Clients Become our Supervisors

There are many different sources and influences on the training and development of a mental health professional. Of course, it all begins with the personal experiences that shape our behavior, personality, values, and choices. These include those events that bolstered and strengthened our resolve and fortitude, as well as those that weakened or wounded us in certain ways. Upon graduating from secondary school, there were another series of critical events and exposure to varied sources of knowledge during university studies. Some of these experiences were part of the standard curriculum but the most enduring and influential ones likely occurred during social and informal interactions, conversations with faculty and peers, and many unscripted discussions. Once enrolled in an advanced training program that featured assigned and elective coursework, along with field experiences, internships, and supervision sessions, most of the basic skills and knowledge base are first introduced and curated. It is usually presumed that it is in this context that a true clinician is grown and mentored—and that is certainly the case, at least to some extent.

Once released from formal education and mandated supervision, set free to explore the world on one's own, further development mostly takes place by learning from one's successes and failures on the job, refining clinical decisions, and advancing skills and knowledge. Of course, there are required continuing education credits in order to renew one's license but let's be honest about that sort of thing: hardly anyone really takes those often tedious programs seriously, especially the ones online where it is so easy to complete the multiple choice quiz at the end.

Often unacknowledged and left out of the mix are the greatest and most influential mentors and supervisors of all—the relationships with our clients that impact us in so many unexpected ways. I once interviewed 25 of the most well-known living theorists and therapeutic practitioners to ask them a rather challenging question (Kottler & Carlson, 2006): Who is the client that changed you the most, the one who has had the most enduring impact on your life and work? If you think about it, that is a rather complicated and provocative question that could be interpreted in so many different ways. Indeed, a few of the theorists preferred to think about this in the context of how a particular client helped them to advance their theoretical development while others immediately thought of someone who profoundly affected them emotionally, or else who pushed them to discover an idea altogether novel and unique. Still others thought about this question in terms of the level of profound intimacy and engagement that occurred in a client relationship. In each case, practitioners representing more than a dozen different theoretical orientations revealed what it was about their interactions with a particular client that shaped them significantly.

If we assume that indeed our own clients are the ones who actually teach us the most about the value of resilience and persistence when facing unimaginable suffering, then it is interesting to review what most likely has the most impact on our own professional development and personal growth. This is one of the overarching themes of this book, to explore what we've learned as therapeutic practitioners.

Empathic transcendence. There is "regular empathy," the usual, pedestrian variety when we catch the tail end of someone else's deep feelings, and then there is the sort of deep, transcendent variety when we are so totally immersed in another's internal world that we can actually feel their pain as if it is our own. This might resemble the type of collapsed boundaries that we usually seek to guard against, but it refers instead to those special deep connections that sometimes happen. This occurs during those rare times when there is such a profound joining with one another that it is almost as if we can read each other's hearts and minds. One therapist of my acquaintance attributed many of the positive choices she had made in her own later life were the result of witnessing the strength, dedication, and resilience of a client she had helped.

Intimacy. A case could be made that the relationships that occur in counseling are among the most close, honest encounters that exist in this world. Since we are explicitly paid to keep the conversations private and confidential, people are willing to talk about subjects they have never broached before. There are rare times when these relationships not only attain a degree of empathic transcendence just described but also a level of genuineness, authenticity, and transparency that exists nowhere else. When else would we ever schedule an hour every single week to talk only about the most personal concerns—all without entertaining interruptions, distractions, or personal needs? Sometimes we might spend many months, if not years, continuing these intimate conversations, forging a level of intimacy that is truly unique and memorable.

Emotional arousal. When we study those experiences in life that most often produce enduring memories, they are usually those that triggered strong feelings, whether joy and satisfaction, or else guilt, fear, shame, and anxiety. These powerful emotions may have been the result of some direct experience during the session, perhaps an emotionally charged conflict or expression of rage, but often they are the result of being fully present when listening to the powerful narratives of suffering and resilience. Some therapists reported particular client relationships that stood out because they were so conflicted, difficult, challenging, and evocative beyond what the clinicians could comfortably manage.

Witness to profound change. If there is one extraordinarily lovely benefit of our work it is that we are privileged not only to be witnesses but also guides for those who are undergoing major life transitions. Sometimes we sit with someone and, right before our very eyes, we can see, hear, feel that something truly remarkable is taking place. We can hear people talk for the first time about doing things they have never done before, or accomplishing some task that seemed impossible, or simply reporting that as a result of our time together, their lives will never be the same. How can we ever forget such meaningful encounters?

Collapsed boundaries. We tend to remember the times we broke the rules or tried something that was not in the "instruction manual." These are sometimes risky experiments because they usually take place outside the usual parameters of how sessions are normally conceived. After the worldwide pandemic limited in-person access to mental health services, a whole new world of possibilities opened up for remote communications, but that is only the very beginning of what may soon be possible. Once we leave the confines of the office for some strategic reason, whether to go for a walk or field trip, supervise therapeutic activities, or conduct conversations in alternative settings, there may be new (better?) opportunities for growth but with the usual conventional boundaries put aside. It is precisely during these less formal times that many professionals say they have also been more powerfully affected by the interactions. I can testify that is certainly the case with those hundreds of "clients" (often students, colleagues, or individuals in the market for personal change) I have brought with me over the years to conduct service projects abroad. The debriefing sessions that are conducted each evening take place in remote regions of the world, often on a mountaintop, village hut, or disaster area. Hardly anyone returns from a journey like that the same person who left. And it is because the "training wheels" have been removed that these experiences tend to be far more impactful than conversations that take place in sanitized offices.

Validating cherished ideals. There is an interesting reason to explain why some clients might be more valued and remembered than others, and it may have little to do with that person and be far more related to a personal investment in an idea or approach. At least when interviewing famous therapists, those who make a living selling their books, marketing their workshops and products, and promoting their ideology, they are inclined to remember particular clients who were instrumental in developing their most favored theory. They love the idea that whatever happened in their sessions seemed to confirm that they had chosen the "correct" path. Thus Albert Ellis recalled vividly the one client who helped him to abandon psychoanalytic orthodoxy in favor of his own newly developed ideas on rational emotive therapy. Likewise, William Glasser, founder of choice theory and reality therapy, believed that his interactions with one client were profound and sacred, reinforcing the notion that he was following the best route. So many others also mentioned clients who stood out to them because they appeared to confirm their favored research findings.

Beyond challenged. It seems that the only thing more influential and potent than confirming one's favorite ideas, cherished ideals, and sacred values is having them challenged vigorously. Indeed, when asked to name a client who is most memorable, it is not surprising that experts would recall the one who was *most* uncooperative and frustrating. There could be many reasons for this, the first of which is that it triggered the therapist's own fear of inadequacy and incompetence but just as likely is that such behavior forced the professional to invent something altogether new. This may have also been responsible for them discovering their own unique viewpoint instead of merely following in the footsteps of their mentors.

Takeaways

There's altogether too much attention on what we learn in formal course offerings, mandated continuing education, and required supervision with someone who usually has a dual responsibility to also evaluate our worthiness. But it's really our clients who become our most important teachers. It is not only that they are the consumers of our service, but they are also experts in their own experience. During those times when we have been able to negotiate an open, honest, and *mutually* trusting relationship with clients, we are offered amazingly useful feedback on what we do that is most and least helpful. It is worth mentioning again that there is often a radical difference between what therapists believe they do that is most important (their interventions, preferred theory, favored strategies, creative technique) and what clients say was most helpful to them. Rarely do clients point to some fancy metaphor, brilliant interpretation, or well-timed reflection that made all the difference. Instead, they often reply quite simply that they felt heard and understood.

Questions for Reflection or Discussion

1. Who is someone in your life who has demonstrated extraordinary coping ability with suffering that seems unimaginable to you? Their resilience, persistence, and hardiness in the face of adversity inspired you in ways for which you are eternally grateful.

2. In addition to the themes mentioned in this chapter about how those we help also offer reciprocal gifts to us from what we learn, what are some other reasons you can think of for why and how mental health professionals are personally affected by their work?

3. Who comes to mind as someone you once helped during a difficult time in their life and yet it felt like you learned as much from the interaction as they did?

29

Setting Useful Goals—
That Are Achievable

A goal without a plan is just a wish.

—Antoine de Saint-Exupéry

When Clients Become Our Teachers
(Whether We Are Ready or Not)

"I'm sorry," Margot said with a shrug. "I just forgot."

"You forgot to complete the task you agreed was so important to you?" I repeated with more annoyance in my voice than I intended.

We had been over this so many times already. It seemed as if in every session, Margot would talk a good game, roll over, and do tricks like any well-trained pet, but it was all mostly for show. Of course, that is an exaggeration: You can surely recognize that I am *still* frustrated by this case after so many years.

Let me start over. Margot did not seem nearly as prepared and ready as I was for her to make needed changes in her life. I cared deeply for her and wanted desperately for her to regain some semblance of control over her life. But each time we would get close to translating her excessive talk into action, she would mention endless excuses for why she could not follow through to complete her commitments. Sometimes, as a way to censure her, I would lose patience and ask her directly, "Explain to me how you can possibly 'forget' to do something that every week you claim is absolutely essential in order for you to feel okay about yourself?"

Margot would just shrug and smile sheepishly.

Maybe it is just the scourge of my life but it has always annoyed me when I hear people say over and over and over and over and over again that they really need to do something important, yet they never seem to get around to it. This is not just a little procrastination; it is downright self-sabotage. In addition, it never seems to make much sense why someone would declare a cherished goal but then not seem to do anything to make it happen.

As our conversation progressed, Margot folded her arms and seemed to be pouting after I challenged her. I decided to try a more gentle approach, gritting my teeth to access greater patience. "Look, I know this is hard for you. I realize that you just might not be ready yet to take action on these things that you talk about each week." Oops. I scolded her again. I just could not seem to help it.

Margot looked up, stared at me for a moment, then resumed studying her feet. I examined them myself for a moment, wondering if there was truly something interesting about them. Nope. She was just punishing me with her silence and withdrawal whenever I called her on the resistance games she liked to play. But of course, they are not really "games" at all; they were clear signals that I was pushing her too fast and wanting her to take action at my preferred pace rather than her own. When I think about the case now, I realize why this was so challenging for me: because the two of us were on completely opposite ends of the spectrum when it came to setting goals and taking direct, decisive action to achieve them.

I am so obsessive-compulsive about staying on top of things that my email inbox is almost always empty at the end of the day. If someone writes me a letter (remember those handwritten or typed messages that arrived on paper, sometimes with stamps on the envelope?) I would always respond by the next day. I usually return messages within hours; I deliver book manuscripts months before the deadlines. I am *always* early for an appointment. I'm *hours* early to catch a flight. When I tell someone I'm going to do something it just gets done, and on time or early. My case files are always complete by the end of the day. I return student papers within one week of submission. Without exception. Ever. For over 30 years in a row, I never missed a day of exercise. Have I yet made my case that I am at the extreme end of the range when it comes to doing what I say I will do?

One reason I suspect I am so diligent about setting realistic goals for myself, the kind that I *know* I can complete within a specified period of time, is because I have sat with so many others who do not seem to get much of anything done at all, even after years of supposedly trying. There has thus been a consistent disconnect between my own fierceness to follow through on any commitment or task that I deem worthy, versus what I have observed among so many of the chronically helpless, disempowered, desperate people that have sought my help.

In previous disclosures, I already mentioned that I never believed I had much going for me. I did not believe I was particularly smart, attractive, athletic, well-connected, or charming. I figured about all I had to work with was a tendency to stick with reasonable but ambitious goals within my capability—and a determination to meet the objective without any possible excuses. I have always thought of that as my own superpower, the ideal strategy to compensate for all my many perceived limitations.

In my very first graduate class in counseling, I recall scanning the room and noticing that everyone seemed so much smarter and more capable than I could ever be. Some of them asked questions in class that I did not even understand, much less comprehend the answers. Everyone seemed to have more experience and a better educational background. It did not help that I was always the youngest person in the room since I graduated from college early. I tried to keep my mouth shut so others (and especially the instructor) did not discover that I was not nearly qualified to be in the program in the first place. I only applied to this particular school in the first place because they did not require GRE scores and had relatively low admission standards. Somehow I decided it was time for me to stand out in some way and maybe the way I could demonstrate that best was through my persistence to achieve whatever I said I would do—no matter what.

My first term paper was due to be submitted, and I decided this was going to be a turning point for me. I was tired of mediocre grades and feeling invisible. Although the assignment required us to write a 12-page paper (double-spaced) about the history of our behavior in group settings, I produced a 60-page, single-spaced tome covering every nuance of my behavior since birth. It was pretty impressive, I had to admit, resulting in my first A-plus grade. Finally, I received some validation that I might really have something to offer. Now I was off to the races because it was pretty clear to me that I did, in fact, have one thing that others seemed to be missing—and that was a desperate determination to wipe the slate clean and redefine myself as someone who always "gets things done."

This new self-image and bolstered personal identity was an absolute game changer, setting my achievements on fire with new-found productivity. It was all about following my new simple rules: (1) Declare what I am going to do. (2) Then do it. (3) Never offer excuses. Unfortunately, one of the consequences of developing this driven, compulsive nature is that I soon became intolerant of everyone else's tendency toward procrastination. When clients would complain to me, as Margot did, that nothing in her life ever seemed to change, I would shake my head and bite my tongue, bewildered why it always appeared so hard for others to reach their identified goals. Were the objectives unrealistic in the first place? Were there some feelings of ambivalence about what it would mean for others if they did follow through? Was someone else in their life actively sabotaging them? Or were they failing repeatedly to follow through just to drive me crazy?

What I learned from my clients, and a lifetime of observing others floundering in their efforts to put changes into action, is that I had discovered a secret that was born of my own impatience and frustration. Some of my clients had become my teachers not by highlighting behavior that I wished to emulate but rather because of choices they made that I vowed I would never repeat for myself. If there was anything that inspired me more to redouble my efforts at setting and achieving incremental goals it was observing so many of my clients who were unwilling or unable to do this themselves.

Counteracting Procrastination: The Secret to Achievement and Productivity

When you compare two people with the exact same job and identical responsibilities, one person rises to the occasion while the other falls way behind. There are strong opinions about what most contributes to one outcome or the other. One explanation would likely mention the importance of being realistic and practical about what can be accomplished. As obvious as that might seem, there are many reasons why that does not happen consistently for many people. And this is one of those lessons we learn frequently listening to our clients provide an assortment of excuses, reasons, distractions, impediments, complaints, annoyances, and disruptions as to why they do not, or cannot, fix whatever is wrong. It is impossible to listen to these endless reasons for inaction without asking oneself, "Okay, what have *I* been avoiding lately?"

Procrastination is the scourge of time management and a major source of stress in its own right, regardless of whether the intended objectives were ever reached. Surprisingly, this does not so much relate to a shortage of time as it does represent a reluctance to follow through on actions that one has already committed to. Among the vast majority of people who admit to this problem, it is not really a form of laziness or even inattention but a feeling of paralysis to motivate oneself sufficiently. Whatever desire one has to complete some goal, there are so many benefits to also putting it off as long as possible. Those who consistently postpone action often do so because it creates a degree of drama, urgency, and excitement, rushing around like a lunatic to get things done by a deadline that is either imminent or long past.

When people advertise themselves as prone to doing things at the last possible moment, they give themselves and others a compelling reason why the quality is less than desirable. After all, what do you expect from someone who dives into an assignment or project in a rush? As a side effect, it also invites others to jump in for a rescue when results are less than desired. Additionally, the habit tends to drive other people a bit crazy, which is kind of fun and empowering in a perverse way.

From our training, clinical experience, and research, most of us are quite familiar with the dynamics of declaring goals that are out of reach, thereby ensuring that efforts will fail. This is not just a single choice to postpone taking action with one situation but usually involves a habitual pattern of putting off today what could just as easily be done tomorrow. Or the day after that.

We know that certain strategies work best to overcome the persistent avoidance of tasks. Such an approach usually begins by helping someone become more aware of when, where, and how their behavior affects (and limits) their life. It is also important to understand that it takes considerable effort, energy, and commitment to change an entrenched habit of procrastination. Finally, reversing this trend takes place by making small, gradual, and consistent progress in manageable pieces. It also helps to challenge the excuses that are usually offered for why stuff wasn't completed as intended. Blaming the weather, traffic, economy, or fate are some of the common excuses.

We are experts at helping people counteract this tendency since this is an issue with so many of the clients we treat. There are dozens of techniques we might employ: recommending "to-do" lists and schedule planners, breaking tasks down into smaller, more attainable goals, challenging perfectionistic tendencies, reducing distractions, and committing oneself to diligent persistence. In the immortal words of Winston Churchill, "When you are going through hell, just keep going."

We discussed earlier how dysfunctional behavior (like procrastination) persists because it is somehow being rewarded or serves a "useful" purpose, even if those intentions are disguised. It is by making those motives far more explicit that the person is "ruined" and no longer able to get away with that behavior since it only works when you don't realize what's really going on. With respect to postponing action and completing tasks the sheer number of payoffs and "secondary gains" is pretty compelling.

- Perceived or anticipated failure can be held off as long as possible, postponing what you believe is going to be an inevitable disappointment.

- There is a great excuse for not performing well: "Of course, I could have done better if I'd really tried."

- There is an undeniable thrill, excitement, and drama of working under pressure, making things seem more exciting.

- You fail on your own terms, rather than on someone else's. Besides, with success comes additional responsibility so it is best to lower other people's expectations.

- You can slow down the pace of something that you feel ambivalent about completing. You can also negotiate more time to complete a task closer to your exacting, perfectionist standards.

- By defining yourself as a procrastinator, you can stay stuck and don't have to be responsible.

It is readily apparent from this review that there are many very advantageous reasons to engage in procrastination, not the least of which is that one can avoid doing the things that are most difficult or challenging, all while you attempt to let yourself off the hook. In other cases, it can represent a form of "acting out," sabotaging things on one's own terms—even if the side effects are often annoying.

Takeaways

Mental health professionals are researchers and scholars, as well as practitioners of our craft. As a routine part of our business, we are constantly updating our knowledge to improve our professional functioning and include the latest data and results from systematic inquiries. As just one example, we are well aware that well-being, life satisfaction, and so-called happiness are likely most improved with "intrinsic goals" that reflect one's deepest values, as opposed to mere "achievement goals" that relate to material possessions or accomplishments (Bradshaw, et al., 2022). While achievement-oriented goals certainly do provide a sense of pride and fulfillment, those feelings are usually somewhat fleeting and temporary. Intrinsic goals that are met tend to be far more long-lasting precisely because they are consistent with what is valued most in life.

We have so many conversations with clients in which they talk about their yearning for more power, greater income, career advancements, and other such goals. Although it is often important and useful to support greater productivity and improved performance, we also know, based on solid empirical evidence, that ultimately mental health and emotional functioning are best supported by the type of personally customized intrinsic goals that focus more on higher order needs that increase intimacy, connection, and a sense of empowerment.

It is virtually impossible to have conversations like this about reaching desired goals without applying the ideas to one's own life. There are therapists who actually specialize in behavioral goal attainment and yet are still always behind in keeping up on their own case files and follow-up protocols. What possible excuse could any of us have for avoiding action when we earn a living helping others to achieve their most cherished objectives? When we spend a good part of our time essentially advising, scolding, cajoling, and encouraging people to follow through on what they say is so important, it is difficult not to turn such questions toward ourselves.

Questions for Reflection or Discussion

1. Identify a task, assignment, job, or unfinished business that you have been avoiding for some time, creating unnecessary stress in your life. This is something that you really want to get done and out of your life, but for some reason you haven't been able to muster the time, motivation, or commitment to get it done. What could you do differently to get this done?

2. It was mentioned that procrastination can have certain benefits that make it difficult to change this behavior. Think of an example in your own life in which you "enjoyed" putting off a certain task because of the sense of drama it created, even though you might have paid a price for the neglect.

3. What are the ways that *you* most consistently waste time and avoid taking care of business?

30

Becoming a Better Parent, Partner, and Friend

To the world you may be just one person, but to one person you may be the world.

—Dr. Seuss

Changing Priorities Over the Life Span

I was a rather distracted new parent. I had just turned 30 and was battling for ascendence in my career. At the time I was stuck (trapped?) in a dead-end job with little opportunity for growth or advancement. I was spinning my wheels, but with few other options, it felt like I had no choice but to spin faster. I felt the crushing burden of responsibility to support my family since my wife had taken time off from her job while our son was young. My workload was intense, and often I did not return home until close to 9 p.m. after our son was already asleep.

I remember, with a certain amount of shame and definite regret, how often I was distracted by work during "family time." After an exhausting day, my little boy would approach me somewhat cautiously, "Dada, will you play with me now?"

"Sure," I would say, "just give me a few more minutes." Inevitably, I would be working on a manuscript, grading student papers, or reviewing my caseload for the following day.

Cary would slink away and occupy himself for a few minutes and then approach me once again. "Dada, you said you'd play with me."

"I will. I will," I promised. "I just need a few more minutes to finish this project, okay?"

Welcome to my life. That was just the way things would go and I hardly noticed. I was on a fast track to pursue my ambitious career. So much to do and so little time. Invariably, work seemed to take precedence over my roles as father and husband and friend. If pressed, I would say that it was not really about messed up priorities as much as the pressing urgency to meet deadlines. My family would wait but editors, students, and clients would not. Or so I justified my choices at the time.

With that confession, I am also aware that I was a pretty fabulous father in those days, attentive when I was around, and highly skilled at applying all that I know and understand about relationships to those in my family. I was a great listener—at least when I was not trying to meet work deadlines. My son grew up healthy, strong, moral, and kind, with a successful career that far exceeded my own achievements. Yet I still mourn the lost time that I could have spent with my family if I had not been so consumed by achievements and productivity. Maybe I am not being completely fair to myself since the reality was that I was just doing the best I could to balance and manage all my various responsibilities. In retrospect, I am pretty proud of how it all came together.

Fast-forward several decades, and I am still somewhat driven to accomplish as much as I can in the limited time I have left. The main difference between then and now is that I actually have much fewer demands on my time, leaving me with more opportunities to be responsive to those I love. I was reminded of this new reality when I was editing a manuscript recently that had a firm impending deadline. I had research materials strewn all over the table, my laptop and tablet open to different screens, a pile of notes to consult, and I was trying to compile all the material into some kind of coherent narrative. That is when I heard a little voice in the background, one that I realized I had been tuning out.

"Popi? Hi Popi! Whatcha doing?" It was my 3-year-old granddaughter, Caia, who was looking for some attention.

"Just working," I replied, somewhat distracted and focused on the task at hand.

"Can I ask a question?" she persisted.

I started to feel a little annoyed. I was on the cusp of finishing this chapter and I could finally see the pieces coming together. It was then that I had a flashback, or maybe a déjà vu experience, because I realized in that moment that this was all too familiar. I could remember my son pestering me with the same cry for attention, and I would usually hold him off for a bit. But I am a different person today than I was in my youth. As a grandfather, I have very, very different priorities than I did as a young father. I have learned a lot during those ensuing years, mostly from my workaholic clients who had so neglected their families in the pursuit of wealth, power, and fame. I had caught myself several times feeling contemptuous or critical of them, that is until I realized the extent to which I was refusing to acknowledge my own driven nature. Over time I eventually learned to slow down a bit. It also helped that I no longer cared very much about achieving anything beyond reaching my next birthday.

The pause that occurred after Caia interrupted me with her question was only a second or two, but it was sufficient for me to take a breath and remember what was really most important—and that was to be totally present for this curious (and bored) little girl who wanted some time with me. I immediately thought of what I would say to one of my clients if this occurred. That is actually not quite accurate: Instead, I recalled what a client had recently said to me in a session about his own changing values. He had been on a corporate fast track for a Fortune 500 company and was being groomed for the executive suite, even though it meant devoting even more hours to the office. He had been using our therapy sessions to explore a major career shift that would free him up to spend more time with his family, friends, and other interests. I never really learned the end of his story because, for reasons

I never discovered, our sessions abruptly ended. Maybe that was why the interactions with him still haunted me so much. I always wondered what happened to him.

This was also brought to mind because I had recently read a biography about Steve Jobs and his incredible single-minded devotion to his work, always at the expense of his family and health. There was one scene described in the book when Jobs was dying of cancer, tumors riddled throughout his body. As perhaps only he could pull this off, Jobs called together a meeting of all his various medical specialists—the internist, oncologist, neurologist, surgeon, endocrinologist, gastroenterologist, dietitian, and so on. At that point, Jobs wasn't willing to follow any medical advice, instead consuming magical smoothies to cure his ailment. During the meeting, the physician in charge launched a PowerPoint presentation to show the spread of tumors throughout his body and summarize the treatment options at this point (Job actually only survived 3 more weeks). In the middle of the recitation, Jobs interrupted to ask the good doctor why he was using PowerPoint instead of Apple's own Keynote software. He then proceeded to show the doctors how much better his technology was than theirs. It seemed that he still cared more about his products and legacy than his own life, much less his loved ones!

Personally, I found the book pretty inspiring and interesting, in spite of all the mean-spirited, neglectful, and strange behavior attributed to the Apple founder, disowning and neglecting his daughter among them. After I finished the book, I read a review that really had more impact on me than the biography itself. The reviewer was absolutely appalled by Jobs's choices and values. He concluded, "If you're going to fail at something, fail at building the fucking iPad. Don't fail at building children" (Austen, 2012).

This was to become my new mantra. So I closed my laptop and iPad and gazed down at this adorable little girl who said she wanted to ask me a question. I sat down next to her on the floor, and we started playing with her Barbie "dream house." I directed all my attention to her, just as I would be so willing to do with any client paying for my time. "You said you wanted to ask me a question, Caia?"

"Uh-huh." She nodded her had seriously. What did she want to know? The meaning of life? When is Barbie's actual birthday and last name? I waited for her to formulate her question. She seemed a bit hesitant. I was not feeling the least bit impatient or the need to resume my work.

"So, Popi," she finally asked after considerable thought, "do you make toots?"

"Toots? You mean farts?"

"Uh-huh."

"Of course I do! Everyone does!"

"Nah uh," she said, shaking her head. "Josie said she never toots. She's in my class at school. But I like toots. Do you?"

Of course I was giggling to myself all the while I realized this was actually an important conversation. *This* is what mattered most to me, and I could not believe it took half my life to catch on to that. How could I have ever imagined that whatever I had previously been doing was more important than that? It seems that the difference between my diluted level of attentiveness and responsiveness to my wife, son, friends, and colleagues earlier in life were considerably upgraded with age and experience. I credit what I learned from a few of my clients as the reason for that.

Counseling Skills in Daily Life

Let's acknowledge that there is nobody else on the planet more highly trained, experienced, and accomplished in relationship skills than a therapist or counselor. We are the consummate experts at building trust, exuding compassion and empathy, and listening to the subtle and disguised nuances of communication. We have within our repertoire a whole extensive catalog of optimal responses to almost any situation we might face—talking someone off a ledge or persuading them to do something they have been avoiding. Just take an inventory of all the amazing things that we know how to do to influence, guide, and respond to others.

In the first therapeutic skills classes, beginners are trained methodically to develop the best ways to actively engage others in meaningful conversations. We learn to clear our minds, resist distractions, focus concentration, and remain neutral. We practice proper "attending behaviors" that begin with proper posture and eye contact, followed by all the appropriate nonverbal cues (nodding head, smiling, frowning) and verbal encouragers ("Uh-huh, Really? Say more). We remind ourselves to access compassion, caring, and empathy while listening to clients tell their stories. We guard ourselves against excessive critical judgment or imposing our own agenda, preferring to allow the other person to work things out according to their own pace. Then we bring to the table all our well-rehearsed and favorite responses (reflecting, summarizing, questioning) to indicate our understanding and promote deeper scrutiny of the issues.

The knowledge skills, strategies, attitudes, beliefs, and values that are such an implicit part of our craft as relationship specialists are not something we just turn on and off when there is someone assigned to us for help. It is certainly the case that we attempt to maximize our attention, focus, and caring during professional encounters, but these are hardly just employed in all their glory—or not at all. Even our most casual interactions with others provide endless opportunities for us to become engaged in more intimate and responsive ways.

When reviewing the catalog of our training, abilities, and best practices, there is little doubt that so many of them become integrated into our core way of being. Over time, it often feels quite natural to slip into "listening mode," not necessarily because we intend to try to fix someone or offer our best therapeutic advice to a friend, colleague, or family member but rather because we have learned how satisfying it feels to truly hear and fully respond to someone who is sharing something important to them.

Aircraft pilots typically review a checklist of items prior to takeoff or landing, absolutely crucial things to review in order to maintain safety. Altimeter—set. Auxiliary fuel pump— off. Flaps—adjusted and set. Flight controls, fuel gauges, instruments, brakes, landing gear, all reviewed prior to taking off. We are inclined to do much the same based on our initial training. Just before a session begins, we usually proceed through our own checklist:

- ✓ Clear mind and resist distractions
- ✓ Remain neutral
- ✓ Focus concentration
- ✓ Take a deep breath
- ✓ Attending behavior (eye contact, lean forward, head nods)
- ✓ Practice "deep" listening
- ✓ Observe nonverbal behavior
- ✓ Being with (compassion, empathy, caring)

Other items might be added to the list, each of which acts as a reminder to remain fully present. These particular attitudes and skills that are such an integral part of therapeutic encounters are just as potent when interacting with *anyone* we meet in daily life, whether a casual encounter or a deep, intimate conversation with a friend or family member. Of course, just because we know these valuable skills does not necessarily mean we use them routinely—and there may be several good reasons why this is the case—often because we just do not feel like it. Exhaustion, stressors, frustrations, and usual routines do take a toll.

It is precisely because we know and can do so much that we are in the best possible position to apply these skills to the relationships we value the most. When we catch ourselves being lazy, disengaged, less than responsive to a loved one, that is not acceptable any more than it would be when we are with clients. All our abilities to heighten intimacy and trust, as well as to help people share their stories in such a way they feel honored and respected, work just as well with everyone else in our lives. It is almost a form of malpractice if a therapist is unwilling to treat loved ones with the same reverence and diligent attention that we demonstrate with those we are paid to help.

Takeaways

One of the things that eventually we learn to take on board for ourselves is a form of constant self-evaluation. Once formal supervision ends, or at least is limited or abbreviated, we are called upon to engage in our own form of self-supervision. This means that we are continuously monitoring our own behavior, as well as the ways we respond in the relationships that mean the most to us. In the context of counseling, that means we frequently solicit feedback from clients as to how well we are working together. We watch and listen to ourselves in action, always assessing the impact of the choices and actions we take. We notice when our attention is diverted, when our minds are wandering, and when we are off track and then immediately refocus and rededicate ourselves to the conversation. As much as possible, we attempt to identify any conflicts, breaches, or difficulties as they are occurring in the moment since that is the best opportunity to correct them. We have high standards for these relationships with our clients, recognizing we will never be as good as we'd like, and we can never settle for what we might already do well. How can we possibly be satisfied with treating our friends, colleagues, parents, siblings, children, partner, lover, or spouse with any less devotion than we would with those we are paid to serve?

Questions for Reflection or Discussion

1. Think of a recent time in which you were engaged in some helping effort and were especially pleased that you remained calm, attentive, focused, and completely responsive to the other person throughout your interactions. Then later that same day, someone in your personal life requested (or demanded) some attention or assistance, and you brushed them off or replied in a less than caring way.

2. What are some specific, definite ways that you would like to apply your therapeutic skills more actively to personal relationships outside of work?

3. If you are really honest with yourself, who are some of the loved ones in your life with whom you have been impatient, frustrated, or disengaged? How would you like to change the fabric of those relationships, and what are you going to do to make that happen?

31

Demonstrating Leadership

If your actions inspire others to dream more, learn more, do more, and become more, you are a leader.

—John Quincy Adams

Leading From Behind

We had already traveled 900 miles by boat down the Amazon River and had just transferred to a small, wooden canoe powered by a little outboard motor. We had reached a place where a small tributary branched off into the jungle, the water turning a deep coffee color. I was escorting a group of students to a small village at the end of this waterway where we were to spend a week helping to rebuild their school as part of their assignment in a class I was teaching called Advocacy and Social Justice. We were spending 4 months on a ship circumnavigating the world, visiting more than a dozen countries where we would stop in ports to participate in various projects—teaching English in Ghana and Namibia, visiting hospitals in Vietnam, interviewing survivors of the Khmer Rouge genocide in Cambodia, doing play therapy with kids on the Island of Mauritius in the Indian Ocean. Our most ambitious mission of all, however, was this journey to one of the most remote regions of Brazil where villagers still hunted with bows and poison arrows.

This may sound like an exciting and fun adventure, but it was packed with a number of inconvenient and uncomfortable challenges. For one, we lived in a tree house, far above the potential predator threats below—hungry caimans, anacondas, and other slimy creatures. We were confined to hammocks at night and told never to leave the confines of our elevated structure.

There were other physical discomforts, of course, but the main challenge for me was leading this group of college students around, most of whom were away from home for the first time in their lives and eager to test their adventurous legs. There had already been a number of discipline problems on board the ship after the young people consumed excessive alcohol in ports or tried to smuggle it on board. A few of them had already ended up in the hospital with alcohol poisoning. Within my group of students, it felt increasingly like I was losing control; the more I tried to clamp down on their behavior, the more resentment it seemed to spread. The previous day, while we were working in the village, a monkey climbed into our tree house exploring what we had left behind and managed to open one girl's backpack. Somehow this clever creature reached into the pockets and discovered a vial of pills which she managed to somehow twist off the childproof cap with her teeth. Then she proceeded to swallow about 20 Ambien sleeping tablets. When the girl returned to find the monkey guzzling her pills, she was so freaked out that she grabbed the struggling animal and actually reached into her mouth to rescue her pills. Apparently, the girl couldn't care less that the monkey consumed a lethal dose; all she cared about was that this was the end of her supply, and she could not fall asleep without them. This was just one example of the sort of behavior I was trying to manage effectively—and failing miserably.

I liked to think of myself as an expert on leadership since I had been researching and writing a book a book on the subject, applying the skills to everyday life. (Kottler, 2018). At various times previously, I had served in a variety of leadership positions as an academic department chair, administrator of a mental health clinic, and founder of a charitable organization. I had figured that taking a bunch of college students to build a school would be a walk in the park, which it kind of was—if that park consisted of piranha-invested rivers.

After a long day working in the heat and humidity, we climbed back into our canoe to return to our tree house for dinner. Because of my advanced age, the conditions seemed to take a huge toll on my energy. I was exhausted, hungry, and a bit out of sorts because I was so concerned about the continued safety of my group. I had already caught two guys who had smuggled a bottle of Cachaça, a local spirit made from fermented sugarcane. After I confiscated their contraband, they reacted with defiance rather than contrition.

Among all the leadership mistakes and miscalculations that I had already made, the worst was yet to come—and it still boggles my mind that this is how I finally lost the respect and cooperation of my team. The bell had rung signaling it was time to line up for the buffet evening meal, likely consisting of some sort of white meat, which I could never quite determine if it was sloth, alligator, tapir, or ocelot. Everyone was kind of milling around aimlessly, so I immediately got in line to grab a plate (actually banana leaves) and proceed to select my dinner choices. Eventually, the rest of the group followed my lead.

It was only the next day that I accidentally discovered what a terrible mistake I had apparently made, at least in the eyes of my crew. Some of the students gave me annoyed looks every time I was in the vicinity; for the life of me, I could not figure out what I had done this time to annoy them. Finally, I took one guy aside to ask him why he seemed so angry at me. At first, he just shook his head and started to walk away. I touched his arm and he visibly reacted with rage. "It was last night," he said, as if that explained it.

"Last night? What about last night?" I racked my brain, and it so happened that the previous evening was one of the few in which I avoided having to discipline anyone for breaking rules.

"You were first in line at the dinner," he said, again shaking his head.

"Yeah? So what?

"Well, you're the leader of our group. You're supposed to let us go first."

I was gobsmacked! These kids were 20 years old, and I was in my 60s. So I was supposed to defer to these young people even though sleeping in a hammock and enduring our discomforts was so much harder for me? This blew my mind! I lost the respect of the team I was leading because I got in line first instead of last?

I've learned a lot of things about leadership over the years, but this one took the prize. Surely, there had been other accumulative events and reasons why my team members did not much like or respect me. I am certain some of their resentment did indeed have to do with some mistakes I made along the way, but it seemed that most of the problem was their raging hormones and adolescent rebelliousness. I do not mean to let myself off the hook, but I can tell you that I was pretty angry myself for being unappreciated after working so hard on everyone's behalf.

This naturally bothered me for some time, and I made up all kinds of reasons and excuses for why things happened the way they did and why my leadership efforts were so misunderstood. It was sometime later that I was doing a research project on leadership, interviewing those from diverse settings who were involved in major social, political, and organizational projects. One of the most fascinating conversations was with the former head of the United States War College, a two-star general who had spent most of his life in charge of combat units or preparing future leaders. He was now the head of a leadership institute housed in a research university.

One of my first questions was to ask the general who among all the officers he had ever known or trained over the years was the single most impressive leader.

The general thought for a minute and then began to grin. "Well, he wasn't actually an officer at all."

"What do you mean?" I pressed.

The general then mentioned that during the Vietnam War, there had been close to 1,000 attempts by enlisted soldiers and marines to either assault or murder their officers, usually by "fragging" them (tossing a grenade into their tent while they were sleeping). He mentioned this statistic as the preface to his story about the greatest leader he had ever met because it illustrated how people will not follow leaders they do not respect or who put their own needs ahead of those they serve. Of course, we have all become quite familiar with this situation since so many corporate and political leaders seem to be more interested in lining their own pockets with privileges and rewards that are way beyond the reach of their followers. In addition, although military generals used to lead the charge into battle ahead of the troops, nowadays they are positioned at their safe headquarters far behind the battle lines.

The general recalled a marine unit that had been operating far behind enemy lines during the Gulf War in Iraq. All the officers had been killed, leaving a corporal as the highest ranking person in charge. They had been completely cut off from their supply lines and were running out of food and ammunition. When the corporal took inventory of their supplies, he discovered they had only a limited supply of MREs (meals ready to eat) left, perhaps sufficient to feed one person for a week. But the problem was that the dozen marines somehow had to survive for at least seven more days before rescue was possible.

Each morning, the corporal would ritually conduct a ceremony of opening one meal packet and carefully distributing items to each person in his unit—the apple sauce, soup packet, meat, vegetable, dessert, and so on. Once the items were distributed, he would take the little coffee creamer container for himself: that is what he lived on each day while he made certain that his marines received the most nutritious foods.

Once they were eventually rescued, the corporal was asked what he wanted most considering he would be recommended for a medal for his courage and leadership. The marine declined the offer and said the only thing he really needed was clean socks for his men. The general just shook his head as he told the story of "Corporal Creamer," believing that this marine represented the greatest leadership he had ever heard of because it demonstrated so clearly how extraordinary leaders always serve themselves last.

This story shared by the general finally provided a much more persuasive explanation for my own frustrating experience with the students in which they felt let down by me. Although I still insist that there were many other factors operating in that situation besides my own choice to be "first in line," I learned an important lesson that it does not necessarily matter whether those being led misperceive or overreact to a situation based on their own needs and perceptions. Leadership is not just about the actions we intend, or those we choose, but also how they are interpreted by those under our care.

Leadership in Everyday Life

We might not ordinarily associate the background of counselors and therapists with the ideal abilities for leadership positions in the wider world, but that is only because the corporate world has completely co-opted the discipline for the purpose of making companies and organizations more efficient and profitable. There is a pretty good reason for this considering that three quarters of all employees say that the greatest source of misery, stress, and dissatisfaction in their jobs is the result of an incompetent or unsupportive supervisor or boss. In addition, 80% of workers report they are disengaged from their jobs and feel unappreciated—and that was long before the pandemic (Kottler, 2018). Given that only 10% of new innovations are ever successful within organizations, it is apparent why books, blogs, and programs on leadership are the single most popular genre, almost all of them focused on corporate settings that promise instant results. Typical of these resources: *10 Seconds to Take Your Leadership From Good to Great.*

Of course, most of these sources focus almost exclusively on skills to increase productivity, efficiency, and marketing products while our own focus and priority have always been about improving well-being and life satisfaction. There has been precious little discussed about how those within psychological helping professions might adapt what we know and can do (relational engagement, trust building, listening skills, interpersonal sensitivity) to provide leadership on a much larger scale beyond a single client or family. After all, what we do for a living is influence and persuade people to take constructive action to improve their positions in life. We are also relational experts who are quite skilled at managing group behavior.

Let's take scheduled meetings as an example, the greatest scourge of time-wasting ever invented. The average person spends the equivalent of 2 years of life sitting in meetings. Employees complain about tedious meetings as the single greatest source of frustration in their lives—except for their clueless supervisors. Imagine, for example, if a highly skilled mental health professional was leading a meeting instead of a corporate manager who is mainly concerned about expenses, profit, and hitting sales or productivity targets. There would be attention directed not only toward getting through the agenda but also intensive focus on the interactive process, group dynamics, subgroup alliances, characteristic roles, and the other factors, all of which better ensure that everyone present feels heard, valued, and respected.

The main reason why meetings are such a colossal waste of time, besides their excessive frequency, is that they are so incredibly boring. People are allowed to ramble or dominate discussions, silencing and interrupting many others. What if, for example, someone with our background were to apply what we know and understand about the group process to facilitate meetings in a very different way? We have learned so much from our clients, as well as our less-than-exemplary colleagues, about what *not* to do if the goal is to make certain that *everyone* has a voice.

When group or team members are surveyed about what makes for a "great" meeting, one that is not only productive but also satisfying and maybe even enjoyable, their responses are quite different from the ones mentioned by those in charge. It was mentioned earlier that a similar dynamic of disconnection exists between the difference of opinion between therapists and their clients about what matters most. You might recall from an earlier chapter that whereas clinicians typically mention their theory and techniques as most important, or their interpretations as most valuable, clients almost never cite those things but instead say how important it was to them to feel understood. That is not to say that these other things are unimportant, just that clients say they do not value them as much. Something comparable also applies to attending meetings in that the members rarely mention the importance of getting through the agenda and instead say that a great meeting is one when they got to talk! I will say that again because it is so incredibly important: people just want to feel like they have a chance to express their opinions about things—and they do not even care that much if their ideas are acted on as long as they just had a chance to share their thoughts.

There are other norms and practices that most lead to optimal meeting outcomes, at least as conceived by those who are required to attend. First among them, as already mentioned, is that each voice is heard, acknowledged, and respected. Based on what we already know and do in therapeutic or support groups, we are also aware that it is important to act decisively in certain circumstances, such as

- when someone is apparently upset or confused and requires support or reassurance,

- when a member keeps interrupting others or talking incessantly,

- during times when it is apparent that people are bored or disengaged, and

- during tension, disagreements, or conflicts that must be acknowledged and worked through.

Each of us could create a list of those times when we believe a meeting or group has devolved into dysfunctional as opposed to highly optimal behavior, requiring some intervention or change in focus. Some of the most common examples of functional versus obstructive behavior about which we are most familiar are summarized in Table 31.1.

TABLE 31.1 **Functional and Dysfunctional Behavior in Meetings**

FUNCTIONAL BEHAVIOR	DYSFUNCTIONAL BEHAVIOR
Courteousness	Shaming, criticizing, complaining
Generating ideas and problem-solving	Interrupting and stonewalling
Exploring lessons from mistakes and prior failures	Being defensive and making excuses
Transparency and authenticity in communications	Manipulating and undermining
Suggesting constructive steps of action	Rambling and digressing
Clarifying and reflecting on the group process	Following self-serving agenda
Attentiveness and hovering focus	Withdrawing and disengaging
Speaking incisively and selectively	Monopolizing and domineering

Based on our unique training and experience, there are many secrets we know and understand to adapt our skills to provide leadership in everyday life. First and foremost, of course, it is all about the *quality* of relationships, collaboration, and mutual respect we can foster in a group. It is not just about getting through a list of objectives to call a meeting productive but also when the process was conducive to interesting, useful discussions that included everyone present. We also understand how important it is to start with a "check-in," just as we would do in a therapeutic group, making certain that each person has the chance to simply report their current status. We are experienced and creative enough to pose interesting, revealing, provocative prompts for members before we get down to business: "What's the most interesting thing you've discovered since we met last?" "What are you struggling with most right now?" What is some unfinished business that you hope we can return to?" What's something important to you that most of us don't know?"

It only takes a few extra minutes to quickly go around the group and make sure each person gets the chance to check in with whatever is most present. We are also well prepared to cut off digressions and rambling, making certain that the time is used efficiently and that every voice is heard. We are also highly skilled at redirecting complaints and negativity in favor of more constructive verbalizations. There is nothing that can destroy a meeting faster than a "pity party" when everyone sits around whining and complaining about things they cannot control or other burdens they carry. Probably the single most important principle of all is either to end meetings early or, better yet, just cancel them when there is really nothing urgent that must be decided.

By contrast, those who are most likely to be the absolute worst leaders are those who need to constantly exert their power and dominance over others. This style can actually work well during crisis situations but otherwise leads to disloyalty and a culture of fear, threat, and manipulation. Lousy leaders talk *way* more than they ever listen. They also never, ever admit they are wrong or make mistakes. Whenever possible, they blame others, luck, fate, the economy, weather, or other external factors. If they are ever caught lying, manipulating, or failing, they try to distract the issue, change the subject, or go on the attack. They take credit for successes and progress rather than acknowledging the contributions of others.

Takeaway: Practicing Leadership in Everyday Life

Leadership is not just about what we do (or not do); it is about the way we operate in daily life, the ways we treat people when we are in positions of power and authority, the ways we empower those with whom we are responsible for their actions. Throughout history, there have been some fairly consistent leadership attributes associated with those who are most expert and accomplished in their roles. Of course, they exude confidence (grounded in reality) and a proactive spirit (optimistic, inspirational), but that is also tempered by remarkable relational capacity (sensitivity, responsiveness), plus conscientiousness (dependable, reassuring, efficient). These are in marked contrast to the worst leaders who come across as arrogant, self-serving, volatile, unpredictable, and inflexible. They tend to believe in their own infallibility, dominance, and narcissism (think George Armstrong Custer, Napoleon, Alexander, Donald Trump). The worst among them are prone to rage, shaming, manipulation, bullying, lying, and impulsivity.

Hopefully, when mental health professionals are in charge of managing, facilitating, or guiding others, the leadership style is consistent with our strengths and unique abilities. Ideally, we practice leadership in any aspect of life in which we can make a useful contribution. We would also wish to model and practice the same behaviors that we expect of others. Instead of an exclusive focus on outcomes, we are also concerned and attentive to the process, making sure that when the group completes their work or leaves a meeting that they are feeling good about what was accomplished.

Questions for Reflection or Discussion

1. Who is your visionary leader, the one who embodies all you would wish to become?

2. Think of a time recently when you were stuck in the most boring, useless meeting in which it seemed like nothing was really being accomplished, and it felt like a complete waste of time. If you had been in charge, what would you have done differently to create a far more productive and satisfying experience?

3. What are some ways that you someday hope to attain a leadership position in some capacity?

32

Exploring Cultural Variations

Human beings seem to hold on more tenaciously to a cultural identity that is learned through suffering than to one that has been acquired through pleasure and delight.

—Margaret Mead

When Intention Is Not Enough

I could not figure out why every time I waved at people, especially children along the side of the trail, they would drop whatever they were doing and approach me. I was never asking for company; I was just saying hello, "Namaste," to them as we passed by. But for some peculiar reason, every time I moved my fingers up and down in a greeting rather than waving back, the children would come over to me. This went on for some time, and it was pretty confusing and annoying.

It was sometime later that I discovered the key to the mystery, or rather I asked our guide what was happening. At first, he did not want to tell me, clearly embarrassed on my behalf. "Come on!" I begged him. "You have to tell me why everyone keeps approaching me instead of waving back."

"Well, Jeffrey sir, you are not waving."

"I'm not? Then what is this?" Once again, I wiggled my fingers back and forth.

We were walking along a trail approaching a small Himalayan village where we would be visiting some children in a local school. We were climbing a steep path that required complete concentration so that I did not accidentally trip and fall to my death far below. I looked up for a moment and noticed some more children watching us. Not wanting them to realize how much I was struggling, I stood straight up, smiled, and waved to the kids in greeting. After all, it was the polite thing to do.

For some peculiar reason, the kids once again did not wave back but just stared at me and whispered to one another. My Nepali friend and guide tried to keep a straight face, but he could not help himself, "Oh, Jeffrey sir, that is not waving. You are not doing it right."

Doing it right? What was he talking about? Waving to someone is just about the simplest thing for anyone to do. Even babies know how to wave as one of their first social skills after smiling. "So," I pressed him, "are you telling me that I am not waving correctly?"

The guide waggled his head in that characteristic Nepali way, signaling "yes," "no," or "maybe." "Jeffrey sir, waving is when you move your hand back and forth like this. When you move your fingers up and down like you were doing, it just tells these people to come closer to you. I do not think they want to do that, and they are probably wondering why you are asking them to come closer. They think that maybe you have some candy to give them or something else."

I have so many stories like this, hundreds of them, probably thousands, in which I do something spectacularly stupid, rude, or misguided while visiting a new and different culture. The irony, of course, is that all the while I feel so proud of myself about how enlightened and knowledgeable I am about cultural diversity, I am acting like a perfect idiot. The extent of my arrogance is absolutely hilarious.

I have mentioned previously that I have lived and worked in dozens of different cultures, from the ivory towers of notable academic institutions in the United States to teaching and fieldwork assignments in Peru, Iceland, Greenland, Faroe Islands, Turkey, Venezuela, Nepal, India, Singapore, China, Vietnam, Thailand, Australia, New Zealand, Hong Kong, just to mention a few. I have also branched out far beyond the usual settings where mental health professionals might typically work and spend time on military bases or in corporate settings, charitable foundations, disaster relief locales, and medical schools.

Let's just say that I really enjoy immersing myself in new worlds. Actually, that is not quite true: I like the *idea* of working in new environments, but once I am there, I am often so overwhelmed and anxious trying to figure out what is going on that most of the time it does not feel much like fun at all—just a lot of confusion and mistakes. As much as I have traveled and been exposed to so many cultural settings, I still find myself in trouble when my arrogance and naivete take over. I make assumptions that are not necessarily valid, but even worse than that, after noting some difficulty, I still stubbornly persist in that behavior. This is all based on the misconception that my extensive experience in the past will not steer me wrong in new situations and novel environments.

Here's a clear example of what I mean. One of my favorite specialties is leading, teaching, and supervising group therapy. During the course of my career, I have led thousands of different groups and taught beginning and advanced courses on the subject hundreds of times. The variety and diversity of these groups have been astonishing. I have led different groups in which the members *only* spoke Cantonese, Nepali, Spanish, Icelandic, or Turkish, and I *still* felt like things went fairly well (perhaps in my delusion). It is such overconfidence that resulted in an amazing learning experience with one client, although it did not feel so amazing and wonderful at the time.

I was leading a group in a small town on the North Island of New Zealand. There were about a dozen young people in the group, all of whom aspired someday to become mental health professionals. I organized them in a circle and launched the group in the typical way by asking each person to introduce themselves very briefly by sharing their names and something significant about themselves. Things then proceeded in a predictable way as we went around the circle, that is until one guy launched into a rather lengthy, rambling disclosure that started to go *way* beyond the usual few minutes allocated for the task. Because he appeared to be the only Māori (Indigenous) person in the room, I decided to allow him a little bit of extra time, although I wondered if that was really fair to the others to do so.

Before I could figure out a way to redirect him so that others might have their turn before time ran out, the Māori young man launched into a longwinded speech about the history of his ancestors who had first traveled across the ocean to settle this country, after which he mentioned the name of his ancestral "canoe" or vessel. I was about to break in to interrupt him when he held up his hand to indicate he was not finished. He then proceeded to talk about the geographic landmarks near his community, mentioning the name of the nearby mountains and river. It was at this point my frustration got the best of me since he had already taken up far more time than he—or anyone—should be allotted. And he still had not even mentioned his name.

"Excuse me," I finally said, determined to get this back on track. "I notice that you've taken far more time than anyone else for this introduction, and yet you still have not told us your name."

I heard a gasp in the room and looked around to find everyone present was extremely embarrassed about something. I also noticed that the Māori guy had pulled his chair back and was crossing his arms. He looked furious.

But what was I supposed to do? I could not let him use up all the time we had to just drone on and on about all these details about rivers and mountains, without ever once mentioning anything personal. I was obviously missing something important. I knew enough to acknowledge that I was a visitor, a stupid foreigner mostly unfamiliar with the rituals and norms of this place. I understood that the Māoris, like Indigenous people elsewhere, had been exploited and oppressed in the past, and that entitled them to certain considerations to make up for past abuse. New Zealand considered itself a bicultural, bilingual nation. But did that also mean that this student was entitled to take over the group and not allow others a voice?

After the session ended, badly, I was indignant and angry myself. Why should anyone, regardless of their status or culture, be permitted to monopolize all the time and attention to the detriment of others? I immediately sought to commiserate with a colleague, complaining to him, "Can you believe what happened?"

I was expecting support and validation, but what I received instead was a good scolding. "What did you expect would happen when you ask a Māori to introduce himself? In our country, in this region, that is how they identify themselves. They would never consent to just saying their individual name, their personal identity, which is a Western convention. A first name would be provided only *after* he has told you the name of the historical boat that brought his ancestors to these shores, after which he has described the mountain and the river near his home. For most people that would be enough to identify his family. Only then would he volunteer his personal name.

"So, what are you saying exactly, that he is entitled to more attention and time because ..."

Before I could finish, my friend interrupted. "I am saying that I would never introduce such an exercise in class the way you did since it is fairly obvious to me that this would be highly offensive."

Well, I blew that one! Again! This happens to me all the time, or at least far more often than I would ever imagine. I could write a whole other book about all my cultural mistakes, gaffes, and my embarrassing moments that usually result from my belief that I really understand what is going on. I suppose what I have learned from all these errors and mishaps is that it is best to always operate in a foreign culture embracing an attitude of "not knowing" and "not understanding," a default position of modesty and humility. But sometimes I just cannot seem to help myself.

Thinking Like an Anthropologist

Each time we see a new client, we are also afforded the opportunity to learn about the multiple cultural identities that are considered to be most important to that person. We have learned over time that it is rare that anyone holds onto a singular racial, religious, or cultural affiliation, as opposed to a collection of such personal attachments. Each of us has been shaped by a number of biological, social, cultural, environmental, family, geographic, and personal forces. Certainly, there are dominant cultural identities that take precedence, usually related to one's ethnicity, religion, race, gender, or sexual orientation, to mention just a few of the possibilities. But there are also so many other identities that are less often recognized such as hobbies, sports teams, university alumni, social organizations, and club affiliations, among others. We understand all too well the extent to which people are complicated and cannot easily be reduced to a simple descriptor of being "Hindu," or "Mexican American," or a "New Yorker," or "gay."

We become students of cultural identity in much the same way that anthropologists study the norms, rituals, and customs of various groups. Among the first questions we might ask a client after hearing the litany of symptom complaints is to reveal one's cultural affiliations and identities (plural) that provide a context for the person's experiences. In each case we learn so much about what it means to be a refugee, Tagalog (Philippines) speaker, Latter-day Saint (Mormon), Republican, (Michigan) Wolverine (college football fan), vegan, Marine, or "hog" (Harley Davidson motorcycle) owner. Each of these "cultures," and so many others, may also form a small (or large) part of the person's self-perceived identity.

Every client teaches us about the values, norms, and heritage that they value most, whether a function of their family or personal choice. In each case, we are educated about the unique history and traditions, as well as the "rules" for conduct, within each of these cultural groups. We become experts delving into the nuances of these backgrounds, learning how to probe sensitively, and communicating an overriding interest and curiosity without being unnecessarily intrusive. We frame our questions in ways that allow clients the space to share with us what they consider most sacred and precious. We listen with careful focus and attention, all the while blocking internal whispers of critical judgment. We try to treat everything we hear with an open mind and heart.

The accumulative effect of our culturally curious perspective is that we walk through the world continually fascinated by the distinct habits and unique practices of people everywhere. Every city or location, no matter how large or small, has likely developed its own special ways of conducting business and daily affairs. Accents, cuisine, and wardrobes vary. The rules for traffic flow, communication, or courteous behavior may all have their own evolved norms. Consider neighboring adjoining countries such as Japan and Russia, India and China, Australia, and Papua New Guinea that occupy the same geographic region and yet have developed completely different cultural norms, languages, and political systems. And speaking of New Guinea, a relatively small Island country, they have over 850 different languages spoken, each representing a distinct cultural group. Large metropolitan cities like Los Angeles may have dozens of different insulated cultural pockets living right next to one another—Koreatown, Cambodia Town, Little Tokyo, Thai Town, Pico-Robertson (Jewish), Leimert Park (African American), Chinatown, Little Bangladesh, Little Armenia, Little Ethiopia, Filipinotown.

In multicultural nations within North America and Europe, perhaps one of the most important social skills of all is the ability to navigate varied cultural groups. It so happens that this is one of our own exemplary skills since we are so often required to relate to people from widely diverse backgrounds. It also makes us highly accomplished travelers if that is a life priority because of our supposed enhanced sensitivity to cultural differences.

If the "tourist" touches only the most superficial aspects of a culture, and the "traveler" digs much deeper to really experience aspects of the new place firsthand, then the "anthropologist" delves deeper still into what a culture and its people are all about. Ethnographic methods have been developed in which, as a visitor, we are able to enter a culture as a "participant-observer." This means attempting to "join" the host culture and become part of daily rituals and activities as a native, all the while observations are made about what *appears* to be happening. This perspective makes one more of an "insider" as far as manner and dress, yet still remaining an "outsider" when making clear observations about behavior and experiences. Of course, this is also what we do in our therapist roles.

Thinking like an anthropologist and field researcher, we are able to observe ways that conflict is managed, the way status is acquired and maintained, or the way problems are solved. We can examine several dimensions of space (how do people use their land and dwellings?), objects (what things do people value most?), activities (what do people do at various times?), goals (what is most important for people to achieve, and how do they do that?), and feelings (how do people describe and express their emotions?).

Taking on the role of a social scientist, we pursue two paradoxical goals, each of which makes the other more challenging. On one side, we attempt full and complete engagement with all people and opportunities that are available. We "go native," so to speak—eat the foods, speak the language, practice the customs, and even try to think as locals do. Yet pulling at us from the other side is the goal to be an objective, analytic observer of events in which the job is to see as accurately as possible what appears to be happening. Then the hard part is to figure out the underlying meaning of the events that were witnessed.

It is a magical experience indeed to consider alternative ways of viewing a single incident. When you seek to understand how local people see the same events in ways that are radically different, it forces you to consider other options that are possible, not just with that one situation but with anything else in the future. Once you get outside of your own parochial, self-centered attitudes, other possibilities emerge.

What is the value of such perceptual shifts? They're like stretching exercises for the mind. In other situations when you find yourself stuck, you can make similar changes in the way you view your predicament, alterations that can provide options that you might never otherwise consider.

Takeaways

As a function of our daily immersion in people's life experiences, we are consummate experts at exploring cultural diversity in so many of its unique manifestations. Over time, there is little that surprises us, although it's always astounding to realize the sheer variety of customs and norms that rule others' behavior. This not only better equips us in our helping roles and responsibilities but also prepares us to make the most of our own personal travels from one place to another.

It is through exposure to various cultures and travels to new and exotic locales that we learn all kinds of wonderful things that only complement what our clients have taught us about their own favored identities. Whether questioning a client about their cultural background or journeying through our own life adventures, we significantly broaden and expand our knowledge in so many ways. There are obvious gains in interpersonal sensitivity and cultural knowledge, as well as language proficiency, cognitive flexibility, and greater tolerance for ambiguity, complexity, and feeling or actually being lost.

Anyone drawn to adventures and new experiences is going to become lost at one time or another. It may very well be that becoming lost is not only inevitable but also desirable; this is when true adventures really begin. In spite of all the preparation and planning, and all the resources at one's disposal (maps, GPS, guides, internet, mobile phone, satellite phone), there is still no guarantee that you will not end up in places that were not on the itinerary, nor even on the map. Many people tend to remember those unforeseen events, unplanned detours, and unanticipated experiences as being the highlights of the visit in spite of the discomforts and inconveniences along the way. Maybe it is *because* of those mishaps and miscalculations that the experience was so memorable.

When traveling to new cultures or novel environments, it is useful to accept the premise that becoming lost is not altogether an unfortunate circumstance. Unlike at home, when getting lost means you will be late arriving somewhere that you need to be, during travel the only place you are supposed to be is where you already are. Also, whereas being lost on your own turf is a sign of ignorance, incompetence, or perhaps neglect, there is an honor associated with being lost as a traveler. After all, this is the first time you have ever explored this territory.

It is not that we should deliberately try to get lost more (although that is probably not a bad idea), merely that it is when we do lose our way, we potentially see the situation as an opportunity as much as a disaster. This is what separates the timid tourist from the adventurous traveler: The former makes every effort to ensure that nothing ever goes wrong; the latter recognizes that it is only unfamiliar situations that force them to adapt rather quickly to new behavioral patterns.

Questions for Reflection or Discussion

1. What are some ways that *your* development and growth have been shaped and influenced by culture?

2. Make a list of all the different personal and cultural identities that are an important part of who you are and what you value most. In addition to the "standard" candidates that might include race, religion, and sexual orientation, among others, what are several other "cultures" that you have adopted as your own?

3. What are some of the interesting and unique norms within your own family culture that have affected your development?

4. What are some examples of prohibitions and taboos in your culture whose persistence and existence in the first place don't make any logical sense to you?

33

Reinventing Yourself—
Over and Over Again

Traditionally, life has been divided into two main parts: a period of learning followed by a period of working. Very soon, this traditional model will become utterly obsolete, and the only way for humans to stay in the game will be to keep learning throughout their lives and to reinvent themselves repeatedly.

—Yuval Noah Harari

Cascade of Disappointments

I was sitting on the steps of the library watching students walk by. I was playing a game with myself, trying to guess which of the passersby were really smart based only on their appearance. This was during the days when engineering majors had pocket protectors stuffed with all their measuring and recording implements so they were easy to spot. But how could you tell if someone was really, really intelligent, like genius level, based on the way they look? Anyway, that was my research project for the morning, and I was excited about a breakthrough: I noticed a definite pattern that some people were walking out of the library carrying an armload of books, some of the volumes pretty hefty. I decided these were the people who looked pretty smart to me, or so I reasoned. I was so tired of being dumb, or at least average in everything I tried. I wanted to stand out in something, *anything* worthy of admiration.

I had been told for as long as I could remember that I was a "nice guy," which was essentially a code for "no other worthy talents." I basically agreed with this assessment since I could not really settle on *any* task or ability that was all that special. I was basically a "C student" in life, relegated to the middle of the pack. I just accepted this was my station in life so I had better adapt to the situation as best that I could. But while sitting in front of the library, separating everyone into two groups, "smart" or "average," I decided in that moment that I wanted to be smart too! I asked myself, What would it take for me to make that transition, for me to reinvent myself from someone who was thoroughly unremarkable to another person altogether who might be respected for the depth of his intellect? Could this even be possible? Could someone with mediocre grades and an unexceptional track record somehow change this pattern with a simple decision to do so?

So far, I had observed that people who appeared most obviously intelligent to me walked around carrying books, an obvious sign of intellectual curiosity. Well heck, I could do that! I know this sounds like a fairy tale, but I really did settle on that strategy as an opening move. I stood up from the step where I had been hanging out and strolled through the portal into the library itself, a place where I had previously never spent much time. I picked out an assortment of different books that, if not interesting, looked like impressive tomes. Remember, initially this was all about changing my image into someone who really did have something going for him. Sure enough, after carrying around books with me wherever I went, even going so far as to begin reading a few of them in my spare time, I noticed that classmates, and those in my residence hall, started asking me for help with their assignments. Over time, I started to believe that maybe I did have some talent that had yet to be fully mined.

This was a turning point, perhaps the single most important breakthrough in my life thus far, maybe ever, because it resulted in a complete rediscovery of who I was, or at least who I could become. I remember actually deciding that I desperately wanted to be smart, the kind of person that others would go to for help or to ask questions. It seemed remarkable to me that everything in my life could change if I actually followed through on this choice. It meant working harder than I ever had before. It meant challenging myself in new ways. Most of all, it meant teaching others, especially my parents, that I was not the person they always imagined me to be.

This realization that anyone, at any time, could choose to be a different person (within certain realistic limits) was astounding to me and has since inspired me several other times to initiate additional reinventions. We explored in a previous chapter how certain kinds of travel experiences can become transformative in this way once one is outside of the usual environment and influences and can experiment with new and different choices for one's behavior and core identity. Time and time again, ever since this experience in college, I have found myself struggling to explain to family, friends, or colleagues after I returned from a transformative adventure that I was no longer the same person I used to be. This meant I had to retrain others to alter their expectations of my capabilities. At various times, I have reinvented myself to adapt to new and different interests, but more often, it is because I yearn for new challenges and to test myself in novel ways.

Although it is so much easier to talk about dramatic examples from the past, I sense an inkling that this identity recalibration is happening again for me right now, even if the ultimate outcome is still shrouded and uncertain. These last few years I have endured a series of painful disappointments, perhaps inevitable after retiring from full-time teaching after a half-century. My last semester of teaching felt like a disaster. Although it seemed like I was working as hard as ever to be engaging, exciting, and interesting in the classroom, for the first time, students seemed far more concerned with the grades on their assignments than the content in the class. To make matters worse, instead of blaming them, I had to assume that something must have changed within *me*. Regardless of what was actually going on,

I felt my passion for continuing in this role evaporate rather quickly. If they do not appreciate me any longer, I reasoned while pouting, then maybe it is time to go somewhere else where my talents are more valued. But then again, I was always looking for an excuse to try something new and different.

Adding to the disappointments, after spending almost two decades at the same institution, I never heard from my colleagues again after I left. The pandemic killed in-person speaking engagements and workshops, my specialty. This retirement thing just took me by surprise. And then I was involuntarily "retired" as well from the charitable foundation that I created 20 years earlier. I felt discarded and useless, which reminded me of a previous research project interviewing elder therapists for a book about aging and therapeutic practice (Kottler & Carlson, 2016). During the interviews for the project, I had spoken with one recently retired counseling professor. She told me a story of attending a social event when someone there learned she was recently retired. "Who did you *used* to be?" the person asked her, completely unaware of how offensive that question might be. She remarked that as an aging woman, she now felt discarded and invisible. This was starting to seem familiar.

I am in my seventh decade of life, and I don't know how much time I have left. But then, I have mentioned previously that I have *always* felt that way. This time it is different because I really am approaching the end of my allotted time in this existence. Yet I still wonder if I have the chance, or if I can make the opportunity, to reinvent myself one more time. What could I do, or who could I become, if I moved in a completely new direction for my career and life? Questions like that make me dizzy with all the limitless possibilities.

When Fate Intervenes

Thus far we have mostly been exploring the process of reinvention as a voluntary action, a considered choice made after lengthy reflection. However, much of the time, we find ourselves in circumstances that were hardly a personal choice but rather the situation or predicament was thrust upon us as a result of things far beyond our control. I am writing this particular section of the chapter just a few days after a traumatic experience in which I had a freak skiing accident that resulted in a fractured leg and damaged ACL. Since this might very well mean that I will never ski or hike or run or climb mountains again, it is just about the most devastating injury I can imagine short of a terminal diagnosis of cancer. So, what do I do now? If all my life one of my core identities has been as an endurance athlete, what do I do once that is no longer possible—and not just gradually over time but after the single exploding pop of my knee?

The answer, naturally, is that this could result in a crushing bout of despair, depression, and helplessness. After all, I just lost (possibly forever) one of the most important parts of my life. I never skipped a day working out in some fashion. So obviously, if I am to recover from this catastrophe, it will mean a major reinvention of who I am now compared to who I used to be. If I am forced to abandon these athletic endeavors, I will no longer recognize myself. It is far too early to say how this will all play out and to what extent I will be able to adapt to these radically changing circumstances. But I will say that, once again, I find inspiration from the courage, resilience, and persistence of so many of my clients who had to deal with far worse disappointments than a sports injury. I do not mean to minimize the challenges that may lie ahead but merely to remind myself that this is exactly the sort of thing I have gone through hundreds of times previously with others who approached me for help. This is a resource that I have been hoarding for decades, waiting for the time when I might access the strength, optimism, and determination to invest the hard work to redefine myself all over again—even if none of this was ever chosen.

When Therapists Reinvent Themselves

It is almost as if we have seen the same film over and over again a hundred different times. It is basically the same plot: a person does not much care for the way things are going in daily life. Things seem too repetitive, or limited, or tiresome, or boring, or frustrating, or stressful and unsatisfactory. And yet this person yearns for something new and different if only it was possible to become someone else or at least someone new and different. This of course is what we encounter time after time in our counseling sessions, similar stories of people feeling stuck in their current predicaments and wishing they could somehow approach their lives in a radically different way. We reassure clients in such circumstances that it is not too late, that it is indeed possible to change their identities and transform themselves into someone else quite different. And that is as much true for us as anyone else. In fact, it is even more likely that we, among all others, have the power of reinvention. In the immortal words of George Bernard Shaw, "Life isn't about finding yourself. Life is about creating yourself." We are indeed experts at refashioning new, improved versions of a person's essential being. And our consistent message to those we help is that it is never too late to make desired changes.

Many spectacularly successful people finally found their true (or alternative) calling during the second or third chapter of their lives. In many instances, some of the most well-known high achievers only found their breakthroughs as they approached middle age. Jeff Bezos left Wall Street to launch his vision of Amazon. Dwayne "The Rock" Johnson was a professional wrestler before he became one of the most beloved Hollywood actors. Bodybuilder Arnold Schwarzenegger reinvented himself as the governor of California. Many within our own profession have also crafted alternative professional identities as a novelist (Irvin Yalom), songwriter (Bill O'Hanlon), musician (Daniel Levitin), media personality (Mary Trump), or even President of a Latvia (Vaira Vike-Freiberga). It seems that the nature of our work is that it often leads to expanding interests in so many other areas of music, art, literature, politics, or social policy. It is also quite common that our clinical interests and specialties evolve over time, sometimes to the point that we operate very differently than we did earlier in our careers. This may be a function of greater experience, additional training, new mentors, evolving interests, compassion fatigue, or far more personal catalysts.

It is somewhat amusing when a student, client, or supervisee who has not been seen in a while returns for additional tutelage. They typically resume the same rituals and habits as the last time they visited, sitting in the exact same place (assuming we have the same furniture), starting the same way, and expecting the identical treatment that they had experienced previously. But of course, since so much time has passed, none of us are the same person, therapist, or teacher that we used to be. Each of us has learned a few new things, discarded practices that no longer seemed potent, and added a number of new and different facets to our therapeutic approach—and personal life. Every book you read, every show or film you watch, every conversation you have, every experience in life affects you in incremental and sometimes even profound ways. I acknowledge that I have likely reinvented myself as a therapist more times than I can remember in my career, having taken on board a dozen different theoretical approaches over the years. It is sometimes bewildering for a returning client to discover that I just do not follow the practices that I used to favor.

Contagious Effects

Listening to tales of reinvention can become infectious, triggering a desire for change in one's own life. All day long we hear stories of people who are sick and tired of the way things are and decide they wish to do something about that. When such determined and courageous people walk out of the office, they sometimes leave us wondering, "Hey, why can't I do that as well?"

Of course, it is entirely possible for any of us to refashion our signature style, whether in appearance, values, choices, or therapeutic approach. The biggest challenge is that it usually requires a degree of misery, if not desperation, with the status quo to invest the time and hard work into unlearning what we already know and doing something else instead. Whereas others might very well stroll along at their usual stumbling pace, oblivious to any other options available, we spend a significant chunk of our lives in the company of people who are constantly stirring things up for the sake of new possibilities.

When reading the biographies of influential theorists and thinkers in the field, the trajectory of their lives follows a somewhat predictable template. They were typically going about their business operating within the traditional and acceptable parameters of the times. For the majority of such figures from the previous century, that meant they were likely practicing orthodox psychoanalysis or behavior therapy. Although during interviews, they may have claimed that their ongoing evolution to develop their own approach resulted from some diligent research, or some epiphany that resulted from a breakthrough, it is just as likely that they were influenced by clients who brought to their attention some facets of the change process that had previously been ignored. More often than not, they discovered such new developments when they applied novel ideas to themselves after witnessing something interesting that occurred in sessions.

Sigmund Freud actually "invented" psychoanalysis by first applying the analytic method to himself with rigorous discipline. Albert Ellis abandoned his psychodynamic training and switched to his own rational-emotive method after enjoying the benefits of disputing his own irrational beliefs. This leads to an interesting reciprocal flow of influence between client and therapist in which each partner in the process says and does things that have considerable effects on the other.

Takeaways

Not everyone wants or needs to reinvent themselves or change the direction their lives have taken. Sometimes committing to the hard work of sticking with a tough job or challenge is the more courageous and optimal preference. Reinvention does not only take place by making huge, sweeping transformations in one's behavior, job, or circumstances but also by continuously questioning one's choices followed by incremental adjustments that provide even greater satisfaction.

The reality is that it is just really difficult to remain immobile in a chair all day while we listen to such inspiring stories of struggle, adversity, and adventure. One clear lesson that we learn from our clients is that settling for contentment leads to a kind of inertia and stunting of future growth and learning. Benjamin Mays, the original founder of the American civil rights movement, observed that "the tragedy of life is often not in our failure, but rather in our complacency; not in our doing too much, but rather in our doing too little; not in our living above our ability, but rather in our living below our capacities."

The process of personal transformation and reinvention is often romanticized as an ideal for which we should all strive at various times in our lives. It is an effort that is universally championed and applauded, yet hidden and disguised are all the ways that significant others attempt to undermine or sabotage such attempts because of all the annoying adjustments it would mean for *them*. We have witnessed time and again how our clients make concerted efforts to change some aspect of themselves, or to reconceptualize who they are and what might be possible, only to find friends and family members working actively to undermine any progress so that *they* can remain more comfortable and maintain control.

The takeaway that we have witnessed so often with those we help is that reinventing oneself is really, really difficult. There are just so many obstacles and forces at work that undercut intentions to make significant changes. Excuses abound: a shortage of time, too much effort involved, lack of coping skills, difficulty remembering, and so on. Ultimately, however, one of our greatest gifts has been to witness this process of reinvention unfold in all its various permutations, revealing not only the mistakes that others make but also eliciting envy and wonder toward what determined individuals can do when it is the main priority of their lives.

An Update

It is now several months after my catastrophic injury, which I imagined would require a major reinvention of my life. I was prepared to give up some of the activities that give me the greatest pleasure and satisfaction. Well, that's not really true: I was *not* willing to surrender quite yet. It was clear I would need to make some significant adjustments in my expectations in terms of what might be possible, but I decided to reinvent myself once again in such a way that I could function quite well during physical adventures, just not at the previous pace and intensity. After working my butt off in physical therapy, devoting several hours each day to rehabilitation, I found that I could indeed walk normally, even run at a slower pace. And with certain adjustments (a brace) I could even hike and ski again.

Each of us undergoes similar accidents, traumas, or catastrophes that can often lead to subsequent personal reinventions—*if* we process the experience in such a way as to counteract despair and disappointment. That is another one of the lessons we have learned from our clients about the critical importance of accepting those things (the past, fate, bad luck, accidents, other people's behavior) that we cannot control or change and instead focusing on new opportunities to become something different (better?) than we ever anticipated or imagined.

Questions for Reflection or Discussion

1. Think of a time in which you were dissatisfied with some aspect of yourself and simply decided to change that. How did making one small adjustment lead to other changes that occurred afterward?

2. Who comes to mind when you remember someone close to you who was undergoing major life changes that had a contagious effect on you as well?

3. Why do you suppose people resist change or reinvention when it's so obvious that the current state of things is never going to prove fruitful?

34

Feeling Useful

We reward people a lot for being rich, for being famous, for being cute, for being thin... one of the values I think we need to instill in our country, in our children, is a sense of "usefulness," in other words, are we useful, are we making other peoples' lives a little bit better?

—Barack Obama

An Angel on the Curb

I was walking along the street, not far from my home, when a blur of movement caught my attention. Then I heard sounds—loud cries, actually.

"Baby, Baby...Baby."

It was some kind of chant. A girl's high-pitched voice. I lost the part in the middle, but she seemed to be saying "baby" in that familiar, teasing tone common to children who sense they have gotten under someone else's skin.

Sure enough, I looked down the block to see a tall girl standing over a smaller boy who was sitting on the curb crying. The boy's head was tucked between his knees and his hands covered the back of his neck, as if he was protecting himself from a further assault. The girl just stood over him, repeating her chant: "Baby. Baby." With no response from him, except for a few pitiful sobs, she kicked his foot in disgust and walked a few feet away.

As I hurried closer to the scene, I noticed there were papers scattered all over the sidewalk and street like huge snowflakes. There was a backpack lying open in the street; it had been run over a few times by some passing cars.

Just as I reached the boy, a bus pulled up to what I now realized was a school bus stop. The girl climbed on the bus, without even a glance backward, and the vehicle pulled away. The boy still sat on the curb, his head buried in his lap. He was crying even louder now that his nemesis was no longer around.

"Hey, there," I said to the boy, sitting down on the curb next to him. He jerked in a startle response, looked up at me from underneath his arm, and then continued crying.

"You had a bit of trouble, huh?" I said.

The little head nodded.

"That girl looked pretty tough," I ventured." Big, too. I guess she was giving you a hard time."

Nod of the head more pronounced this time.

"Come on," I said in a cheerful voice, as if I came upon scenes like this all the time. "Let's pick up your papers before they blow away."

The boy looked up at me and presented the most beautiful smile I had ever seen and perhaps will ever see again. It felt like I was an angel who had been sent to right this wrong.

We spent a few minutes retrieving his schoolwork and stuffing it back into his bag. The boy got a special kick out of our joint effort when I went out into the street and stopped traffic so he could collect the papers that were lying in harm's way.

"So, when's the next bus?" I asked him as we resettled ourselves on the curb.

"I don't know," he shrugged. "Maybe a few minutes."

"Mind if I wait with you until it comes? Just to keep you company?"

The boy looked at me shyly and smiled. So we sat on the curb together and chatted. He told me that the girl was a bully who was constantly bothering the little kids. Usually, she picked on someone else, but that person must have gotten a ride to school that day because *he* was the only victim available.

I never learned the boy's name, never saw him again. But I will never forget watching the bus pull away and seeing his face through the window. He was still looking at me with awe—uncertain if I was real, or an angel who had swooped down out of the clouds.

This encounter not only made my day, but it felt like one of those deeply spiritual moments that nurtures one's soul. One of the most defining features of my life has not just been the desire to feel useful but the absolute *need* to do so. Perhaps because I felt so inadequate early in life, I still constantly evaluate my worth and value as measured by what I do to make a small difference in the world. Each night before I fall asleep and review the day, I keep score of who I helped. I do not mean in my role as a professional but rather the informal chances throughout the day to be useful to others in some way. These could be mostly small efforts of kindness or consideration but, on occasion, fate places me in opportunities where I can really be useful to someone in need. These feel like gifts to me that help redeem the suffering of my own life.

Fixing a Hand

I recall another such opportunity to feel (and be) useful when I was walking through a rather isolated region of the world. Given the difficulty of the terrain above 14,000 feet, I had been concentrating only on my breathing and my next steps, occasionally glancing up at the snowy Himalayan peaks reaching up into the clouds. Suddenly, I caught a glimpse of movement along the side of a rocky slope—it was an elderly man stumbling down the path grimacing in pain. He was holding his arm, bent at the elbow, with his hand upright as if in a perpetual greeting. In spite of his advanced age, he seemed far more nimble on his feet than

I could ever hope to achieve. I had spent the past 5 hours laboring up and down a yak trail on the way to some villages where I was organizing educational programs in local schools.

The guide who was escorting me spoke to the old man for a few moments and then turned toward me. "Sir," he said to me, "you help man." This was not a question but rather a direct order. It was all the more remarkable because the guide was usually so deferential, if not obsequious.

I approached the old man cautiously, not exactly sure what was expected of me, nor how I was supposed to help him. Once I approached him, I could see more closely that his swollen hand was so covered with blisters that it looked like a balloon about to burst. There were dozens of white, pus-filled sores running along his fingers and palm, almost as if they were caterpillars crawling underneath his skin.

The old man was a dignified gentleman, dressed in a white shirt, vest, and tights, a long knife at his side. He had a thin, perfectly groomed mustache on his upper lip and the characteristic *Gurung* hat on his head. He was an impressive figure, all the more so because although his hand was grossly disfigured, he was obviously under great control of the crippling pain.

"You help him," the guide said to me again, pointing to the old man's hand.

Help him? I'm a therapist, not a surgeon. What was I supposed to do? I never felt more useless.

The old man looked at me and managed a smile between his tight lips. He held out his hand as if it was a foreign object that belonged to someone else. He turned it one way, then the other, displaying the network of bloated blisters that covered both sides.

"What happened?" I asked him, with the guide interpreting, partially out of curiosity but also to stall for time until I could figure out what I was supposed to do. I was no doctor, at least not a real one. The last thing in the world this guy needed right now was a psychologist.

The old man and the guide spoke for several minutes before it was announced with simple clarity: "boiling water."

"He spilled boiling water on himself?" I asked. "Is that what happened?"

Both men nodded.

Because I was a foreigner, it was common for locals to believe that I possessed medical supplies and expertise that far exceeded their own meager resources. They were not far wrong considering that the nearest medical facility was a 2-day walk down the mountain. If this man did not receive help from me, he would most likely have to deal with this on his own. It seemed I had no choice except to treat his condition or he might have very well died of infection.

I looked into my supplies and found some gauze and antiseptic cream, which I proceeded to apply to the blistered hand. No matter how delicately I spread the lotion, I could hear the man's involuntary gasp. Adopting the manner of a doctor that I was now pretending to be, I handed him aspirin to take for the pain. "Take two of these now, another two before you go to bed tonight." I felt myself stifling a nervous giggle once I realized I was reciting the line from some doctor show on television. If truth be told, I have rarely felt as useful as I did just then, acknowledging the envy I felt toward medical colleagues who can actually fix things with sutures, surgeries, and medications.

The old man looked at me with genuine gratitude, as if I had just saved his life, or at least his hand. He brought his hands up to his chin, forming the steeple gesture of respect in this part of the world. "*Namaste*," he said and then turned and headed back up the slope with his hand still held aloft.

I walked on for the rest of the day, up and down more mountains, through rice paddies and mustard fields, passing herds of water buffalo, troops of monkeys, mule trains, and porters on this Himalayan highway. All the major Annapurna peaks were visible throughout the day, draped in clouds. There was more scenery and stimulation than anyone could ever hope to encounter in a lifetime. Yet I could not get that old man and his hand out of my mind. I was haunted by that encounter, and I couldn't figure out why it had such a huge impact on me.

Then it came to me: I fixed something! At least, I think I did. Surely I had not done any harm in my brief foray as an emergency physician. Even if the aspirin and antiseptic didn't make much of a difference, I know—I am *certain*—that my words of reassurance soothed the man's pain.

I am someone who has no mechanical aptitude whatsoever. I can barely change the batteries in the television's remote control. I often break light bulbs while changing them. Unfortunately, I seemed to have chosen a profession in which I am rarely sure that I ever really helped anyone. Even when I do think I made a difference, I am never quite certain whether the effects will really last, or even if my clients are just reporting imaginary progress. Most of the work I do, as a teacher or supervisor or clinician, often takes many weeks, months, or even years to see substantial, visible changes.

Yet in about 15 minutes, I dressed the wound of someone in need and helped him to feel better. I have no idea, of course, what happened to the man after our paths diverged. Maybe he lost the use of his hand or even died of infection. But I would like to think that, regardless of my rather simplistic attempt at practicing medicine without a license, I eased his suffering in ways that I long for every day with my clients or in opportunities that come along during daily life.

Spinning Wheels

We have discussed in earlier chapters how there are many different personal reasons why someone would choose to become a mental health professional. For some people, it might have just been a school or job opportunity that opened up, providing a convenient and easy choice to make. For most of us, however, it was a chance to feel useful in some way, to make a difference in the world, at least in some small, measurable way.

As much as therapists and counselors are encouraged, pressured, scolded, mandated, and required to engage in "do-good" activities beyond their normal work responsibilities, much of the time these are just token efforts that involve a lot of talk and precious little sustained action. It is really about feeling good about ourselves rather than actually doing anything meaningful and significant for others that will endure over time. That's why so-called slacktivism has taken over social media, instances when individuals broadcast the sort of minimal efforts they have invested in some cause—wearing a ribbon or wristband, "liking" a post, signing a petition, boycotting a company, contributing a modest donation, sending out a message alert. These can certainly be useful in rather minimal ways, but they are mostly easy, convenient, relatively effortless ways to feel like one is somehow being useful. But of course, there is a distinction between concerted, dedicated, consistent, and sustained actions versus those that are just essentially symbolic gestures.

People do things all the time because it makes them feel good about themselves, bolsters their status and self-image, or earns them future reciprocal favors or rewards. People are also inclined to extend themselves toward others when it is most convenient and easy rather than because there was actually some compelling need for their contribution. Of course, there is nothing wrong with enjoying some benefit as a result of helping others, especially if it is a feeling of goodwill. On the other hand, some people thrive on being needed, having others indebted and grateful to them. It can become a demonstration of their sense of control and power over others. It is sort of like accumulating debt markers from people who might owe favors at some time in the future. Every helping effort is viewed as transactional with the full expectation that the obligation will someday be repaid on demand.

If the goal is truly to do more than just spin one's wheels in a tiny effort, there are certainly alternative ways to maximize contributions and influence. Most of these efforts have already been field-tested in sessions and can easily be adapted or expanded to other ways to be useful in daily life. This begins with the intention to look for opportunities that others have not noticed or addressed, instead of simply following the latest trends to advocate on behalf of global warming, economic disparities, or the dismantling of democratic institutions (all of which are extremely important). Such issues are easy to get on board with because of existing organizational structures and the company of like-minded folks who share similar values. Nevertheless, there are still so many neglected problems that could use considerable help even if they do not receive nearly as much attention and publicity.

Takeaways

Mental health professionals are ideally suited to become useful instruments for change in the outside world beyond the office. We are already well aware of those efforts and strategies that are most and least likely to be effective, knowing for example that criticizing, shaming, and critically judging others are usually less than helpful. In addition, it is important to remind ourselves about the lessons we've learned about being accessible, supportive, and helpful to others:

- **Give to others willingly and generously—without the need for gratitude.** This is actually the best indicator that actions are meant selflessly, without some expectations of reward.

- **It's not about you, it's about me (unless it's not about me, it's about you).** In clearer language, this acknowledges when there is a tendency to either overpersonalize or project onto others distorted reactions.

- **Look for opportunities to help people who have no other resources.** All too often certain programs that are already well staffed still attract more volunteers than they need, while other issues, problems, and crises are virtually ignored. Rather than taking the easy road, we've learned from our clients that anything really worth doing is *hard.*

- **Persist in efforts that might seem hopeless.** We know about lost causes. We are well versed in those life predicaments that seem to have no possible resolution. We spend half our lives with people who have surrendered their faith and hope. And yet we have also learned that if we stick with them, if they believe they just have someone in their corner, sometimes that is enough.

- **Avoid excuses and blame.** When some people find themselves in situations or opportunities to extend themselves they immediately say to themselves or others, "Hey, that's not my job!" I don't have time," or "It's just not convenient right now." We recognize those as perhaps legitimate reasons but they also represent the choice to avoid reaching out to be useful—*even when it is not their job to do so.*

- **Just listen, really, really listen.** That is our magic antidote for any malady. It is our superpower. Whether in the supermarket, pharmacy, or standing in line, sometimes the kindest, most generous thing we can ever do to make the world a more civil place is to just lend our ear(s). It sounds so easy but, heck, that is already what we do for a living, so it is sometimes the *last* thing we would want to do when off the clock. Still, more than anything else, it is what almost everyone craves the most in their life: someone who does more than just pretend to listen.

- **Realize it is sometimes enough to just be fully present.** And even when we cannot find the patience to listen without interruption, the very least we can do is remain present and continuously engaged.

- **Ask difficult questions.** This is another of our fortes. We are excellent at asking really good, probing questions, the sort that uncovers secrets and reveals critical information. We are among the few who know about "open" versus "closed" prompts, those that encourage elaboration instead of eliciting one-word responses.

- **Just ask how you can be of help.** People don't always need what it is that we are offering. That could be said even stronger: People do not usually need what we *prefer* to offer. It makes sense that anyone offering assistance would rather do what is most convenient and effortless—offer a donation or pat on the back. But most of the time, those in need have something different in mind. It may not be realistic or possible to deliver what is desired, but people still really appreciate it if we take the time to ask what they want most.

- **Sometimes it is better to do less rather than more.** One of the first things that therapists learn from their clients is that they desperately want us to give them advice and tell them what to do. It is even what they imagine as our essential job—and when we dutifully inform them that our role is actually to help them figure things out for themselves they often become frustrated and disappointed. We learn over time that often the *worst* thing we could ever do is give them advice since we will either get blamed if things do not work out or else we end up building greater dependency. So we have learned to back off when we can and allow those we help to do the bulk of the work. But this is the challenge: Since we are not really supposed to tell our clients what to do with their lives, it feels so freeing to be able to dispense advice at will to anyone else who asks.

- **Be dependable and utterly reliable.** It is difficult to overestimate how important it is to just show up on time and deliver what was promised. Again, this is something that is such an integral part of our professional responsibilities, it is hard to imagine otherwise. We are all about enforcing clear and consistent boundaries, beginning and ending on time. If we do nothing else, our clients come to depend on our consistency and the same could be said for anyone else we hope to help.

- **Do not just identify and explain but show and model.** The best teachers, mentors, and supervisors are not just those who understand and can explain matters but those who can demonstrate in their own behavior what they offer to others. If it is fortitude that is required in the face of adversity, or equanimity when dealing with crises, then that is *exactly* what we exude in our own presence. This also means demonstrating courtesy, sensitivity, and kindness toward everyone we encounter.

- **Assess progress and keep track of outcomes.** It may be the scourge of our professional lives, but we are constantly and relentlessly expected to justify our existence, document carefully our sessions, codify our diagnostic impressions, keep track of our hours logged for recertification, monitor client progress, and measure current indices compared to treatment goals. Supposedly this is to support continued funding, apply for new sources of income, or provide data for research and administrative purposes. In spite of the annoyances, it does help to know more about the specific impact of our efforts, what works best and worst, allowing us to be more effective and efficient in the future. The same holds true with any other attempts to be helpful: It is essential that we collect accurate, honest feedback from those we are assisting, or we may be just wasting our time.

- **Measure success in life not by personal achievements but rather by the good we have done for others.** Last and most important of all is the way we assess and measure our own sense of happiness, well-being, and life satisfaction. In addition to the usual indices related to the size of one's practice, annual income, social standing, job position, quantity of friends, "likes," referrals, or social invitations, one additional standard can be evaluated each day by the extent to which you helped others.

Questions for Reflection or Discussion

1. Identify several somewhat neglected social issues or problems that concern you most. What do you believe are the reasons they have been ignored and what might be done to bring greater attention to them?

2. What are the ways you feel most and least "useful" in your daily life?

3. If you were going to tackle some widespread issue, problem, or difficulty that is dear to your heart, how might you recruit others to join you in an effort to address them?

35

Improving Well-Being (and So-Called) Happiness

When one door of happiness closes, another opens, but often we look so long at the closed door that we do not see the one that has been opened for us.

—Helen Keller

Happiness Is Always Temporary

It is an interesting question to ponder: When were you most happy or satisfied with your life? What immediately jumps to the surface of your mind? There is likely an assortment of remembrances rattling around, competing for primary attention. The first thing that hit me was standing in the delivery room holding my son for the first time. Of course, I was mostly anxious and terrified, absolutely flooded and overwhelmed, but if I had to pick only one word to describe that fateful moment, it would have been "happiness."

As an adult, it seems like almost all of my so-called happy moments involved achievements of some kind, getting accepted into programs, being offered jobs, winning awards, receiving an unexpected but well-deserved bonus. As we will discuss, these may not really qualify as moments of "happiness" since they are such fleeting celebrations of joy, often quickly replaced by anxiety over the likely responsibility and consequences.

It feels like every rung on the ladder of success that I have ever managed to climb never came very easy. I remember receiving word that I was finally admitted into a graduate program after so many rejections or a book proposal was finally accepted by a publisher after a dozen others declined. Yet whatever happiness I experienced was soon clouded over with the realization that now I would have to deliver what was expected, a prospect that honestly felt quite uncertain. In addition, driving ambition and compulsive achievement have been, in some ways, the scourge of my life because anything I ever attain is quickly followed with the question, "Okay. Now, what's next?"

Each of these celebratory moments that appeared to lead to my happiness was eventually truncated. Lost during the sprint for recognition and accolades were some of the precious moments that I missed along the way while I was so distracted or overwhelmed with getting stuff done that I believed was so important at the time.

If, however, we disqualify experiences that produce only temporary joy, what then would be a more enduring, relatively permanent state of satisfaction? It must be a time when all the senses are fully engaged, when we are learning and growing as much as ever before, when we are doing something that not only feels productive but also meaningful and important beyond our own needs and interests. That is one reason why researchers prefer not to talk about "happiness" any longer because it is just so fleeting rather than any kind of permanent state of contentment (Diener, 2012; Diener & Seligman, 2004).

Moods fluctuate constantly, not only as a result of things that happen in our lives, triumphs, disappointments, failures, and surprises but also because of the ways we choose to think about these events. As such, whatever we imagined might be happiness is so often altered and influenced by life circumstances, environmental and social influences, and even one's stage of life. We have witnessed with our clients how often they become obsessed and driven to pursue goals that only make them more miserable. Time and time again, we are reminded of important lessons to consider what really matters most in our lives, not just the outcomes we achieve but also the process along the way.

If you think about it, the relentless pursuit of happiness is actually what makes people so miserable since it can never be maintained indefinitely. In addition, such a persistent pursuit often ends up distorting our sense of time, leading to feelings of even greater urgency to get things done (Kim & Maglio, 2018; Schooler et al., 2003). Disappointment and relapses are virtually inevitable, perhaps best captured by comedian Mitch Hedberg who once confessed, "I'm sick of following my dreams, man. I'm just going to ask where they're going and hook up with 'em later."

Ups and Downs

The times in my life when I have felt most consistently satisfied, and perhaps attained a state of well-being, occurred when I have felt most productive. I am not saying that I actually *was* productive, just that it *seemed* that way at the time. I tend to be most content when I am busy doing something that is so interesting and engaging that I absolutely lose myself in the activity, the condition Csikszentmihalyi (1990) described as "flow states." So when I recall those periods when I have felt happiest, they most often took place when I have been joined by others in some kind of shared, collective, meaningful activity. I do not just mean a single event but rather an ongoing commitment that brought us all closer together over time and accomplished something meaningful.

I so vividly recall a time I was interviewing at-risk children to determine if they were eligible for scholarships and support to remain in school. This was in a very isolated region where not all children could afford to attend school because of demands at home. I visited one family in the village that seemed to be in particularly dire straits. Apparently, the father had recently died of AIDS but not before infecting the mother with the disease that he contracted from a brothel. The mother was now so sick that most days she could not get out of bed to care for her 5-year-old twin girls. They were pretty much left to fend for themselves. There had been one stretch of 10 days when the little girls had nothing to eat at all except what they could beg from neighbors.

The mother had already sacrificed so much in her life, and given up so much, that she was unwilling to surrender to this final humiliation. She was now left alone to support her children. She had no job, no marketable skills, no education, no family support, no land, and no resources.

"I know that I will die soon," the mother confessed to me. "But who will look after my children? What will happen to them after I'm gone?" she was so despondent she had no tears left to shed. All she could do was rock back and forth and think about her babies, her children, her wasted life.

I took the mother's hands in mine and just waited for her to make eye contact. I then promised her that her children would be taken care of after she was gone. I would make certain that they would have a home and be able to continue school. I have never been so committed to a vow than I was in that moment.

The mother paused for a moment and looked at me intensely, trying to decide if I was truly serious about this promise. Then she nodded her head and gripped my hands even harder. The smile on this woman's face was something I have so deeply etched in my memory, I wonder if it will still be with me when I take my own last breath. The mother said that she was now calm and happy. The prospect of her own death no longer frightened her. She was almost ready. But now she could die in peace.

I was so moved by this encounter, so fulfilled and satisfied, that I scuttled off to find a private space where I could cry without drawing attention to myself. I do not think I ever felt greater well-being (even happiness) in my life. It felt like fate or the forces of the universe guided me into this particular time and place just so I could be present for this remarkable experience that has stuck with me after more than 20 years. But here is the thing about the surge of joy and satisfaction I felt in those moments—naturally, they did not last very long. I always promised myself after I returned from one of these annual service trips that I would refrain from my relentless pursuit of more achievements, more possessions, more, more, more of whatever else I crave that I believed would make me happier. Although I vowed I would rededicate myself to serving others rather than continuing to accumulate things, the effects never lasted very long.

Once I returned home, I noticed a pair of shoes I wanted and wondered if I should upgrade my laptop or phone. It was as if in spite of my best intentions, I was still allowing myself to relapse back to my default position of always striving for more of something, regardless of what I have already attained. Nevertheless, although the burst of joy and happiness may have dissipated over time, the feelings of well-being have stayed with me ever since. This is a state of being that not only holds feelings of goodwill, satisfaction, and even euphoria at times but also includes those times of suffering, discomfort, and difficult challenges. Our moments of happiness may sometimes become lost in these discomforting times, but what remains on solid footing, regardless of the ups and downs, is the belief that what we are doing is indeed worthwhile.

Predictors of Happiness and Well-Being

This appears to be the "golden age" of research these days on life satisfaction, happiness, well-being, self-care, and related subjects. Popular publications, journals, books, websites, apps, and programs all proclaim they have discovered the hidden secrets to inner peace. They are not exaggerating in the sense that most of the recent findings have challenged most of the usual things that people do that they believe will provide them ultimate happiness—more money, more friends, a bigger house, a better car, a job promotion, and so on. This is not exactly a new breakthrough considering that theologians and philosophers have been exploring these issues for thousands of years and reached the same consensus.

As a brief review of these findings, mental health professionals are already quite familiar with many of the misconceptions that people have about what makes them most happy and satisfied. We are also aware of those things that people value or attempt to do that actually make little difference in the ultimate quality and satisfaction of their lives. We know, for instance, that physical attractiveness may garner attention and admiration, but it does not mean that such individuals are happier with their position in life. People often complain about the climate and weather, yet that also does not predict increased happiness: those who live in California with 300 days of sunshine are not any happier than those who reside in Michigan with half that amount. Similarly, as much as people believe that their gender, age, income, education, or intelligence might be significant factors in predicting happiness, these variables are far less important than imagined.

So much of the work we do with clients involves helping them to have far more accurate expectations and realistic goals regarding their choices and actions. People spend way too much time spinning their wheels, focusing on things that do not really matter very much while ignoring the core variables that make the most difference. This is a case in which what we learn from our clients is often what *not* to do to improve our own lives.

If I might be so bold and ambitious as to summarize the vast body of research, these appear to be some of the main themes that might better guide our interventions with clients, as well as better target our own choices and behaviors.

Personality traits. There are particular characteristics that are most associated with life satisfaction, the most obvious of which is a certain optimistic, hopeful temperament. People who display resilience in the face of disappointments and setbacks are more likely to enjoy a stable mood platform regardless of the challenges they face.

Relational intimacy. Whether with family members, a partner, or friends, love makes anyone's world go around. Those who report strong trusting relationships, have a supportive social network, and feel close and understood by loved ones are among the happiest and most satisfied individuals, regardless of their position and location in life.

A sense of purpose. This comes in many different forms, whether meaningful work, productive activities, parenting, mentoring, or a feeling of accomplishment in some other life task. It also helps when those efforts, sacrifices, and commitments actually result in better outcomes for oneself and others.

Managing emotions. This is our bread and butter. Almost everything we do in our sessions is teaching people how to better control and make sense of their feelings.

Avoiding social comparisons. So much dissatisfaction and unhappiness result from comparing what other people have in contrast to one's own situation. The research is consistent on the subject: Once you are "comfortable," meaning you have enough to live reasonably well, to meet basic needs plus some desired luxuries, having more money does not appreciably lead to greater happiness or contentment.

State of mind. Most people describe themselves as "moderately happy," a subjective assessment of their life. Yet some individuals we know are rather moody and volatile, overreacting to whatever occurs. Attitude, of course, is almost everything. It is not what we have that matters—or what we don't have—but rather how we choose to view this situation. This especially involves a capacity for self-forgiveness and self-compassion after mistakes, failures, and lapses.

It is perhaps this last factor that we invest so much of our focus, time, and attention when assisting people who are considerably less than content with the ways their life is going. It sometimes seems futile trying to persuade clients that they would be far better off if they stopped engaging in behavior that is not providing them with a more stable sense of well-being that they crave rather than simply a jolt of temporary pride or joy. We witness so often the ways that people's lives are out of control, overfocused on work, possessions, material success, and external validation instead of what we know makes the most difference, especially state of mind, attitude, and social support.

Takeaway

We learn from our clients how misinformed and misguided they are with respect to which behaviors, habits, and practices will ultimately lead to greater life satisfaction and well-being. As mentioned, people tend to invest their money and time pursuing relatively short-term surges in joy that may result from consumer purchases, drug-induced thrills, or other temporary appeasements. It does not even matter how happiness or well-being are evaluated since consistently devoting time and money to "purchase" moment-to-moment experiences (especially travel, entertainment, social events, nature, outdoor experiences, meals) produces greater happiness than any material consumption (Kumar et al., 2020).

With regard to our own lifestyle and personal situations, this is another one of those chapter takeaways where we are reminded to practice in our own lives what we advocate for others. All too often, practitioners can become sidetracked by the pursuit of accolades (publications, promotions, possessions, awards) at the expense of true contentment. Perhaps most important of all is our ability and willingness to better recognize increases in stress or discomfort as they are occurring before they become a problem. When this is combined with an acceptance of those things that are beyond our control, efforts can be more effectively targeted toward actions that produce the best outcomes. It also helps to minimize unrealistic expectations so disappointments are reduced. Finally, it's important to feel and express gratitude for life's gifts and let go of things that are beyond one's control.

Questions for Reflection or Discussion

1. What are the greatest mistakes that you observe others making in their pursuit of goals they say are important but seem to you to be relatively meaningless?

2. How would you define what it means to be or feel "happy" in your life? What are the features of this condition that are most important to you?

3. What are some of the obstacles that you expect will likely sabotage or undermine your attempts to pursue a meaningful life of contentment?

36

Living 100 Lives

We live vicariously through stories, because our own lives provide so few opportunities for high-stakes adventure and noble sacrifice.

—Sarah Cross

Aladdin's Lamp

I once overheard a colleague complaining about me mention to his friends, "I don't know about that guy—he sure moves around a lot." Left unstated was the judgment that perhaps I was either looking for something I could not find or else fleeing from something that was getting closer. In either case, the message was that I was somehow suspect, unstable, or unsavory because I did not stay in one place for very long. After completing a review of my checkered employment history, I realized that I have spent time in a *lot* of different places. Prior to going to graduate school, I had worked as a salesman, purchasing agent, and travel courier, among other jobs. After my therapist training, I worked in crisis intervention, school counseling, mental health services, outpatient psychiatric services, medical education, private practice, social services, corporate consulting, and social justice advocacy, plus 18 different universities. It might seem like I am boasting but I am actually defensive and embarrassed about my short attention span. Eventually, I settled down to spend almost 2 decades living in the same city, but that did not curtail my wanderlust to continue traveling the globe in search of new adventures and ways to become more useful.

My reputation as an academic nomad has been well deserved. I become bored easily with routines. I feel restless and itchy when I have stayed too long in one spot. I am always curious about what life might be like somewhere else, somewhere I have never been before. I have wondered at times what kind of role model I have been for my clients, students, and readers, leading the life of a gypsy, packing up and moving my family every few years. What is wrong with me that I cannot sink roots and establish myself as a permanent part of one place or another?

When I was a child and first learned about a creature called a genie, someone who granted wishes after rubbing a lamp, I spent a lot of time thinking about what I might wish for. I considered several popular options—unlimited wealth, improved appearance, another few inches of height, straight hair, or a better-functioning brain. But after long consideration, I settled on one wish above all others—that I could experience 100 different lives. Since I could not quite make the leap of faith that allows one to believe in reincarnation (besides, who would want to come back as a slug?), the next best thing would be to strike a bargain for an infinite number of lifetimes (at that time, the number 100 seemed infinite enough).

Well, obviously (I hope), I have grown up a bit since then. I no longer believe in genies or the tooth fairy. I have not, however, given up the aspiration that I could live a hundred lifetimes, even if I have to squeeze them into just a handful of decades. I still go about living my life with urgency, almost desperation to see, do, and experience everything and anything that I can before the clock runs out. During this brief ride that I have been granted, I want to do as much as I can before the old roller coaster comes to an abrupt halt, launching me out into space, nothingness, or the land of worms.

It so happens that I (and perhaps you) selected the perfect career and lifestyle to pursue the journey of a hundred (or a thousand) lives. Every client I see in counseling offers me a glimpse into another existence that is beyond my reach. Most people wonder what it might be like to be homeless or wealthy, to be a professional athlete or a prostitute, to have been born on a reservation, in a refugee camp, or in the lap of luxury. There are films and shows produced every week that reveal what it is like to be a rock star, corporate raider, drug dealer, private detective, or astronaut, yet we have access to these same kinds of personal stories every week.

Not only is a therapist privileged and honored to learn the most intimate secrets of others' lives during a time when they are most in upheaval, but we also get to ask lots of personal, intrusive questions! "So what is it like exactly for you to work in a job as a professional cuddler and then in your spare time as a professional bridesmaid?" We would hope that these inquiries are remotely related to the client's presenting complaints, but they need not necessarily be so; most people like to answer personal questions when they have an attentive listener. While I do my best to censor nosy wonderings that are just for my own curiosity or entertainment, it is so easy to justify almost any line of inquiry under the guise of getting a feeling for the client's world. Presumably, I need a sense of the client's diverse experiences if I am ever to understand what is going on. Or so I tell myself.

A client walks in who is a Franciscan monk, Las Vegas dancer, water slide tester, or snake milker, and I think, "Wow! I've always wondered what that must be like." As I get to know clients over time in such an intimate way, I experience their lives vicariously. I learn from the monk what it is like to walk the streets of the inner city as a source of spiritual support, breaking up fights, providing comfort to lost souls without hope. Many months later, after the monk leaves my care, grateful for the help I have provided, I realize that I will miss him dearly. I liked living through him; no, I *loved* it. I learned what monks do to find reciprocal love. I learned about the inner politics of the Church. I learned my way around parts of my city that I am too fearful to visit in person.

I lived another life through a Vegas dancer as well. What is it like to do the same shows, day after day, for *years* without a break? What do you see out there when you are onstage? Are you propositioned often? How do you handle that? What do the women talk about backstage when they are getting ready to begin the performance? My questions are endless. I want to know what each life is like. This is more than just voyeurism, although I suspect that all therapists have a healthy dose of that. For me, the act of helping is predicated on my being able to enter fully into the client's life, not as an observer but as a kind of "participant." When the relationship ends, whether in weeks or years, I must move on to other lives, sometimes wistful that I can no longer be a dancer or a monk.

Clients are people on the move. They are in transition. They are questioning every aspect of their lives, making decisions to change forever the patterns they are living. They are taking tremendous risks, testing their own limits, reaching far beyond what they ever imagined possible. In most cases, they are oozing with excitement over what they are initiating and learning. They are in uncharted territory without a map, yet somehow they are stumbling around to find their way. They are reporting on the new vistas they have seen, the novel experiences they are creating. Am I jealous? You're darn right!

Here I sit in my same old chair. It is Wednesday, so that means I began the morning by following my usual daily rituals and habits, working out, commuting to the office, taking my usual seat in preparation for the assortment of lives that will file in and out during the day, telling their stories, reporting their progress. I will go to meetings in which colleagues will debate and argue about things that do not really matter very much. Not only will nobody remember what we did in this meeting a few weeks from now but also no one will much care. And I will wonder, for the 11,000th time, what the disputes had to do with helping people to grow and learn. Students in class will ask the same questions I have heard so many times before, and I will strive to answer them in different ways, as much as to entertain myself as to provide definitive responses. It is not that what I am currently doing is uninspiring or uninteresting. It is just so challenging for me to repeat the same activities, tasks, and daily routines day after day. It feels like the precious moments of my life may be squandered if I am just repeating myself. Honestly, I do not see how anyone can do *anything* for more than a few years without feeling like they are essentially living the same life over and over again. Not me. One hundred lives down, maybe another hundred to go.

Vicarious Learning and Change via Proxy

Homo sapiens, as a species, is hardly a finished product. Evolutionary forces have been operating at a glacial pace to refine our bodily systems in response to changes in the environment, advances in technology, and cultural influences. Some of these changes, like our upright stance, opposable thumbs, and oversized brain developed in response to geographical shifts once our ancestors relocated from the forests to the savannas hundreds of thousands of years ago. But other evolutionary changes have been far more recent (less than 10,000 years) such as the ability for adults to digest milk, mutated genes that created blue eyes, lighter skeletal system, immune protective genes against diseases, and a cooler body temperature.

The human brain has also evolved over time to its current structure, tripling in size during the last few million years in order to hold all the advanced functions we need to survive. Scientists have found it challenging to compare differences between ancient and contemporary brain compositions since there are no existing hominin brains to weigh, study, and measure—only their empty skulls. Nevertheless, it is clear that there have been many new structural developments and reorganizations of the organ as a means for making verbal language possible, improving long-term memory processes and movement sequences, as well as facilitating social cooperation and coordination. The cerebral cortex has considerably enlarged just as the shape, size, and structure of the cerebellum and parietal lobe have been reconfigured.

Most of these evolutionary changes occurred in response to the need for more and different cognitive and perceptual "tools" to function in very different environments from which our systems were originally designed. Humans are quite unique in our ability to adapt to so many different climates from Arctic regions to high altitudes, deserts, jungles, or plains. Perhaps one of the most remarkable adaptations of all relates to the ways the brain has been tweaked to help us better scan the environment to become aware of potential dangers or any novel stimulus. That is why the senses and brain tend to become most aroused when encountering any new experience or unknown feature, attempting to work out how this might be useful knowledge in some way. Almost all growth and learning are thus stimulated by exposure to something new and different.

Another major evolutionary change in brain development is singularly unique to our species in the form of storytelling (see Chapter 16). Our brains are specially equipped with the ability to learn vicariously via others' experiences. We discussed earlier how this capacity allows us to accumulate significant knowledge and intelligence without jeopardizing our safety. People tell us stories about their failures, triumphs, disasters, mistakes, adventures, tragedies, and struggles, and we pay close attention to the lessons that were learned so we do not fall into the same traps or miss valuable opportunities.

This whole volume is, in a sense, a collection of the significant lessons we have learned as a result of being privy to our clients' stories of tragedy, triumph, and struggles along the way. It is easy for any of us to rattle off an extensive list of all the fascinating obstacles and dangers we have been taught to avoid as a result of hearing so many tales of disaster and recovery. We have learned well over time that whining and complaining about things we cannot control is a complete waste of time and energy. We have heard so many stories from people who never seem to be satisfied because their identities are so defined by their achievements, financial success, and accolades. After each and every session is over, we are often left to wonder, "Okay, how does any of this apply to my own life?" Or, "Hmm. What can I use from this conversation that might be helpful to me?"

The stories we hear are often revelatory but also sometimes haunting and disturbing, offering warnings and important lessons to take to heart. Yes, these narratives can induce vicarious trauma, in addition to possible growth and insights, but even *that* is a kind of gift that teaches us something about our limitations.

Our unique knowledge, training, and capabilities make us especially amenable to being influenced and shaped by vicarious learning opportunities. It is not that unusual after a session is over that we realize the extent to which we have been affected by what we have heard. The parallel lives that we are permitted access to typically follow a finite number of narrative plots that form the basis for almost all stories that are told whether in films, novels, plays, operas, or therapy sessions. They are stories of "rags to riches" (*Cinderella, Ugly Duckling, Shrek*) in which clients eventually discover their true potential after battling some injustice or prejudice against them, or they involve a quest of some kind (*King Arthur, Lord of the Rings, Harry Potter*) in which clients are searching for enlightenment or authenticity. Then there are also the familiar tragedies (*Romeo and Juliet, Titanic, Bonnie and Clyde*) we hear about every day in which clients tell tales about their misadventures and devastating losses. Maybe the most impactful stories of all are those that signal a rebirth (*Beauty and the Beast, A Christmas Carol, The Frog Prince*) when clients demonstrate extraordinary courage to reinvent themselves in a dramatic way. There are the stories we hear that signal all the ways that personal transformation might be possible—not just for those we help but also for ourselves.

Takeaways

The most valuable lesson that arises from being observers, sometimes passengers, during the quests and journeys of our clients is to venture out to the edges of the world to create our own new adventures. While it is true that living vicariously through books, movies, shows, and our clients' stories is both entertaining and enlightening, it can also inspire us to launch our own new and different lives, whatever form that might take in our careers or personal lives.

Not everyone is suited, or even interested, in living one hundred lives; some people are pretty satisfied already with their station in life and view their current condition as acceptable enough that they are not interested in upsetting the applecart, so to speak. This is the same reason why some individuals yearn for adventure and excitement, while others prefer to remain comfortable in circumstances that are already quite safe, secure, and manageable. For most of us, however, even if there is no pressing desire to live one hundred lifetimes, it sure is entertaining and interesting to grab a glimpse into a few dozen alternative existences. Sometimes discovering what others are up to does not so much encourage us to follow their lead as to realize that what we already have is pretty darn good.

Questions for Reflection or Discussion

1. What do you think about the idea that mental health professionals are afforded the opportunity to live 100 or more lives through the vicarious joining of our clients' journeys?

2. How have you been most inspired, influenced, and motivated by someone else's story to initiate some significant change or transformation in your life?

3. As you look forward to the next decade of your life and career, what are at least three distinct "lives" you'd like to experience?

37

Writing Things Down

Fill your paper with the breathings of your heart.

—William Wordsworth

Journal Lost—and Found

I remember a friend and colleague of mine who had just returned from a trip abroad. When I asked him about the highlights of his travels, he rattled off an extensive list of all the wonderful experiences he had. Then he casually mentioned at the very end that the airline lost his luggage, so he had to get along with what he had been wearing on his back, plus a few things he purchased. I wondered how he had managed to shrug off such a potentially disruptive event so that it did not ruin his vacation. He just shrugged and said, "You know, we're therapists!"

What he meant is that we spend every working day of our lives talking to people about letting disappointments go and making the best of challenging situations. So, how can we possibly neglect to apply this to ourselves when things do not go our way?

In earlier chapters, there was a discussion about the lessons we learn from clients related to talking to ourselves in more constructive ways, how such internal conversations, whether aloud, or writing in a self-reflective journal, are among therapists' most valuable abilities that save us a lot of heartbreak. In addition, the more fluent we become in talking to ourselves constructively, the better we are able to do so with those we are helping. Many mental health professionals confess that after spending a long, hard day in sessions, they may often feel physically and mentally exhausted, but they also admit that they are the most mentally and emotionally grounded afterward. That is why we are encouraged by mentors and supervisors to spend considerable reflective time thinking and writing about our innermost thoughts and what they reveal.

For the past 60 years, since I first began a journal during adolescence described in the first chapter, I have been carefully documenting the events, experiences, and revelations of my life. Many of these musings ended up as the introductory personal stories that launched each of these chapters. Originally, I began this enterprise as a form of self-therapy, a way to work through my confusion and problems long before I imagined I would ever enter the profession as a practitioner. Over time, this became a seminal project in my life, a place where I jotted down new ideas and insights, rantings and complaints, future research projects, dialogues with myself, poetic descriptions of daily events—a repository of everything significant that I have lived and experienced. I imagined that someday I would conduct a life review, start from the beginning, and follow the chronological sequence of my struggles and triumphs, my disappointments, failures, and achievements. I also wondered if someday I might also use this voluminous material that filled a whole file cabinet to construct my own memoir.

I mentioned in the first chapter that over the course of my life, beginning in high school, I kept a detailed, ongoing narrative of my life and career. My notes, entries, and musings spanned thousands of pages jotted on paper, restaurant menus, and even a roll of toilet paper when that was the only option available. I also collected my most precious possessions in the form of correspondence with some of my mentors and heroes, archives that sparked particular memories that could be retriggered.

Although I have been so compulsively diligent in jotting down almost every day what I have learned, what puzzles me, what I am thinking and feeling, what I plan to do next, what I plan to do in the future, I have never actually gone back to review what I have written. Oh, I have tried a half dozen instances, but every time I start reading entries, it brings up memories that are still so tender, shameful, or painful. I kept postponing the time when I might review this life's work since I had devoted most of the days of my life to its creation and maintenance. Finally, however, I worked myself up to begin preparing for this arduous and overwhelming task. I went into my study to locate the files in the cabinet and was then reminded we had just redecorated and refurnished the room.

"Where's all the material from the file cabinet?" I asked my wife.

"What stuff?"

"You know, all my journals and correspondence that were in the drawers that I've been keeping all my life."

"You mean in that file cabinet that we donated to the Salvation Army, the one they picked up last week?"

"Yeah. Where did you put all the files?"

It turns out that although my wife emptied the top drawer of the cabinet that held *her* files, she assumed I would have done the same with the bottom half.

Yikes! The documentation of my life's work was now gone. Forever. *Adios. Arrivederci. Au revoir. Sayonara.*

So, how do I let this go? How could I possibly talk to myself in such a way that I could move on? This was one of the major catastrophes and disappointments of my life, and there was nothing I could do about it. I could mourn. I could cry. I could stamp my feet in rage and frustration. I could blame my wife, myself, or the truck driver for not checking the cabinet before taking it away. But it was still gone. And there was nothing I could do to change that. Well, there was one thing I could try to do, so I called the Salvation Army to check the file cabinet for me but they said all the drawers had been emptied. So that led to the next question about what happened to my most precious, sacred, and valuable possessions. Did I mention that my most secret thoughts and feelings were contained within? Now I wondered if an employee of the agency, or some homeless person, recovered my journal and was now reading the most private moments of my life. It was not just the loss that was driving me crazy but how negligent and stupid I was for not safeguarding my treasure.

I have never been that good at letting go of such self-castigations. I have been known to torture myself over and over again for perceived slights or humiliations. I frequently recite the same monologues to myself, imagining my impassioned defense, saying all the things I wish I had said to someone who hurt me. All the while, I recognize that this is self-inflicted suffering, something I am doing to myself as a form of masochism.

To stop the ruminating, let go of what I could not control or fix at this point, required some vigorous self-talk inside my head. I thought about jotting these reactions in another journal entry but that only retriggered my anger once again. Like so many of my clients, I can be brutally hard on myself, self-critical to a fault. I know that I am hardly alone in this endeavor since our species is not only gifted with the ability to think and reason but more remarkably, to spend a lot of time thinking about our own thoughts. This is both a gift and a plague.

Self-Monitoring, Self-Reflection, and Self-Analysis

We are called upon to meticulously record and keep track of almost everything that we do. There are time sheets to note the hours we are working, payment forms, billing forms to be sent to clients or their insurance companies. Then there are client intake forms, information and health history forms, consent for treatment, informed consent, authorization for release of information, agency policies related to social media or privacy, treatment plans, symptom screening forms, progress notes, quarterly summaries, discharge protocols, and therapeutic contracts. These are all the paperwork requirements that may be part of the agency or institution, but there are very good reasons why we might wish to write other things down, including more private, confidential thoughts about the nature of our work and its outcomes.

In a book about "how doctors think," Groopman (2008) describes a physician who was so consumed with improving his surgical successes that he systematically recorded in a journal every mistake he had ever made in his medical practice and dutifully acknowledged every failure with a patient. This sort of honest and open self-scrutiny, committed in writing, is what helped him to become one of the most extraordinary physicians the author had ever encountered. In a similar vein, perhaps the single most significant takeaway from all our explorations is that it is not enough to become exposed to important lessons and new ideas from our client interactions if they are not actually remembered, accessible, and personalized in our own lives.

As highlighted in several studies (Ericksson et al., 1993; Gladwell, 2008; Miller & Hubble, 2011) developing true exceptional expertise is not a matter of talent alone as much as it reflects extraordinary hard work and diligent focused practice. What this means is that in any domain, activity, or career, the best among us are those who work hardest at examining the effects of what they do, after which they make appropriate adjustments in light of feedback from their clients (Miller et al., 2020). Such exemplary practitioners are committed to their own self-monitoring and continued growth by systematically noting and recording the impact of their interventions.

There are several distinct steps to this process of learning from our mistakes, failures, and miscalculations, as well as what appears to work best in certain situations. This resumes a discussion about the value of honoring our imperfections that began in Chapter 7 on processing disappointments and failures.

Listen to feedback. The process begins with paying very, *very* close attention to the input that our clients offer. They sometimes do this directly ("I don't like that," "That's not helping"), as well as in more subtle and disguised ways ("That was very helpful; I just don't know why it didn't work"). These are the golden opportunities to record both the things we could do more frequently in the future, as well as other things we do not ever wish to do again.

Watching is even better. One of the most useful clinical teaching and supervision methods records sessions for later playback and review. While during training years, this option was an integral part of the curriculum, it is rare for most of us to continue this practice in some form after graduation. When that is not feasible or practical, the next best option is to write down personal summaries of what happened, separate from the standard progress notes that must follow certain templates. Keeping such private and personal session logs allows for much more detailed, free-flowing, and honest descriptions of conversations.

Admit when you are lost. As long as we persist in denying what we really do not understand about what is happening—which of course is most of the time—we do not have the opportunity to learn more about our lapses and how to upgrade our data. Some clinicians find it useful to keep a running record of instances when they've been confused or uncertain. Since that is my default condition most of the time, I have voluminous records that catalog my growth and learning trajectory.

Watch for internal "noise." This refers to all the distractions and personal reactions that occur during any session, including those biases and perceptual distortions that compromise the ability to see and hear clearly. It helps considerably to monitor carefully such responses so that they don't interfere with accurate assessments and optimal clinical choices. Even more revealing are the times when we feel most distracted by particular intrusive thoughts and lingering feelings from the recent and distant past that interfere with our ability to remain present and focused. An interesting question to consider: Why are you feeling bored or disengaged in a session? Where does your mind wander most consistently?

Challenge and confront biases. Once distortions, exaggerations, or misperceptions are identified and acknowledged, the next step involves committing them to memory so they are not repeated. There is no excuse for being aware of one's limitations and lapses and yet still continuing to indulge them because of neglect or laziness. Lesson number one that we frequently tell clients is that when you discover that an approach is not working, stop doing that and try something else instead.

Stop settling for complacency. The only way that we improve in any endeavor is by pushing ourselves to take things to the next level. This means practicing those skills, strategies, and interventions that feel awkward and uncomfortable until such time they become more natural. Whether playing a musical instrument or an athletic activity, most people tend to practice those pieces or skills that are already well within one's repertoire. What distinguishes exceptional performers in any domain is their persistent commitment to work diligently on those skills that are found to be lacking.

Recognize you will likely never be (or feel) good enough. In spite of how hard you work, how diligently you practice, how carefully you monitor your abilities and work to improve them, you will still never, ever be as good as you would like to be. You can practice for a lifetime, for multiple lifetimes, and still never come close to the level of expertise that is ultimately desired. Although this is a realistic limitation, it is also one of the intriguing rewards of the profession that we will always strive for a degree of excellence we can never reach.

The main idea that underlies reflective journaling in almost any form is that it becomes a type of self-care, if not self-therapy. There have been several studies indicating that keeping a systematic record of one's personal thoughts, feelings, ruminations, and ideas can lead to significant cognitive and emotional benefits, not the least of which is enhanced memories of the past. In addition, journaling has been found to be useful in reducing anxiety, promoting increased self-awareness, regulating negative emotions, disrupting obsessive thoughts, promoting a deeper understanding of oneself and others, facilitating enhanced psychological well-being, and even improving health conditions (Krentzman et al., 2022; Monk & Maisel, 2021).

Different Forms for Different Purposes

Journals can take so many different forms in a person's life, depending on one's interests, goals, and preferred communication style. Some people dutifully add entries every day, jotting down random thoughts, floating ideas, whatever comes to mind that seems worth jotting down for consideration in the future. Others may just write when the mood suits them, whether a few times each week or month. Still others, especially professionals, might use their journals as a systematic repository of clinical decision-making, keeping careful track of cases, outcomes, mistakes, and successes. Finally, some people prefer prompts or even a workbook to get them going, especially those who are attempting to make daily writing a signature habit (Kottler, 2012). The main idea is that the particular form, style, structure, and process that the journal follows is dictated by the author's intended goals and preferences. For instance, some people like to go "old school" with paper and pen to jot down their musings, while others favor journaling apps on their mobile devices that allow them to record 5-minute entries to describe ideas or thoughts they wish to hold onto. The particular structure and form hardly matter; it's all about self-expression, whether in the form of artistic scribblings, poetry, or long-form narratives.

Novelist and poet Jim Harrison discovered that his subconscious mind was frequently trying to help him at times, sending him warnings, glimpses of plans, plot structures, characters he might invent, or simply ponderings about things that interest him. "That's why I keep a journal," he explains, "not for chatter but for mostly the images that flow into the mind or little ideas. I keep a running journal, and I have all of my life, so it's like a gold mine when you start writing." Or in our case, when we begin helping people or ourselves.

Journal entries often begin with prompts that get the mind and spirit to reflect on recent or past events. Typical starters might home in on goals for the future ("Three things that I will accomplish during the next year..."), express gratitude toward someone or something for feelings of goodwill ("I am most appreciative of..."), or perhaps attempt to make sense of events from the past ("Lingering resentments I feel that I wish to banish..."). A more unstructured style might involve simply giving oneself permission to express thoughts and feelings about *anything* that seems interesting, provocative, confusing, or enlightening.

Initially, it does not matter very much *what* you choose to write about; rather, it is more about the commitment to the process, a decision to become more systematically reflective and analytic about one's own thoughts, feelings, and behaviors. The most important lesson of all from such efforts is to become more scrupulously honest with ourselves. When a lifetime "loser" and consistent failure, a self-described drunk, addict, and gambler, finally found some semblance of contentment and success, it was not by trying harder but, in one sense, giving up and accepting the realities of his situation. "It was his simple ability to be completely, unflinchingly honest with himself—especially the worst parts of himself—and to share his failings without hesitation or doubt" (Manson, 2016, p. 3) That, of course, is what we ask clients to do in therapy, a challenge that we are now turning back onto ourselves.

Not the End of the Story

I do not wish to leave anyone with the impression of a tragic ending to the story of the lost journal that began this chapter. Here is what eventually unfolded: Over the course of the following days after my journal disappeared, I tried talking to myself about the crushing disappointment and then decided to launch another journal entry to discuss my frustration and how I could possibly recreate so much of my past that had been lost. I actually found ways to use this personal example in a few of my sessions with clients, intending to demonstrate that there are tools available to help process disappointing experiences in more healthy, self-enhancing ways. Then I would tell them about my lost journal, almost with pride but also a glitch in my stomach. Like so many personal lessons I have learned over the years, this was a golden opportunity to use with my clients—and use it I did.

It was more than a week later that I awoke suddenly from a deep sleep, trying to hold onto a fragment of my dream. In the reverie, there had been an image of a small room, maybe a closet of some kind, although it was shaped in an odd size that seemed somehow familiar to me. This seemed important for some reason although I could not yet say why. So I just lay still in bed and tried to grab onto whatever pieces of the dreamy image that I could. It was dark inside the room in my dream, so my view was obscured, but I could see a single light bulb hanging from a tilted ceiling. Hmm, I *knew* I had seen that somewhere but I could not recall exactly where. I tried to peer deeper into the darkness, and all I could make out were several boxes lying on the floor. Once again, I knew I had seen these boxes somewhere, but before I could figure out where, I was now fully awake. For some reason, I kept returning to that dream throughout the rest of the day, each time trying to penetrate deeper into the darkness to determine what those boxes were all about. Then, suddenly, unexpectedly, the memory started to clear.

I rushed home from the office to check out a hunch that had occurred to me based on the recollection. Those boxes in the dream sure looked like the sort that would hold files in them. And that dark, closet-like room sure resembled the space underneath our stairway. I had to check this theory out, and sure enough, discovered that I (or someone) had indeed packed my journal into these boxes and stored them under the stairs prior to getting rid of the file cabinet. Did I somehow do this and not remember it? Did my wife do this on my behalf? Or was it some kind of helpful spirit creature that saved my journal? I honestly have no idea, but I have been grateful ever since. And I am still proud of how talking to myself helped me to let my disappointment and frustration go even before I recovered my prize. This I learned from my clients.

Questions for Reflection or Discussion

Since this is one of the closing chapters to our exploration, the current discussion poses a few penetrating questions to consider writing down your responses on paper, an app, or an electronic file. After all, that is what this book is really about—the lessons we learn from our study, practice, and client interactions that can be applied directly to our own lives. Here are a few queries designed to help you write (or talk) to yourself, and those you trust, about the ways you are growing and learning.

1. Bring to mind a client (or someone you've helped in the past) who had had a profound influence or effect on you, either in terms of your professional development or in some far more personal way. Write (or talk) about what happened with this individual that was so powerfully impactful.

2. Describe the most memorable or unusual case you have encountered, someone you helped or tried to help, that is likely to stick with you for a long time. In what ways was this particularly revealing to you, not just to better understand other people but also your own behavior?

3. Recall a memorable relationship with someone you helped in which you felt some
    kind of deep empathy that was beyond anything you had experienced before. There
    was some meaningful and intimate connection with this person such that the level
    of trust, caring, and alliance between you was special and unprecedented.

And One Last Question

Looking back on all the reflective questions that were previously introduced, let your mind
wander to review many of the people you have ever helped in your life. Record a list of some
of the most impactful characters and the meaningful lessons you learned from them.

38

Leaving a Mark, Creating a Legacy

If you're going to live, leave a legacy. Make a mark on the world that can't be erased.

—Maya Angelou

Wishing to Be Remembered

"I promise I'll never forget you! Please don't forget me!"

I turned back and waved to the girl calling out to me in the distance. I could still hear her yelling something as I turned toward the road, but the words were lost before they could reach me. I spent over 20 years of my life visiting this village or others nearby. I devoted so much of my time, energy, money, and resources to supporting this girl and hundreds of others quite like her, all of which required considerable sacrifices, devotion, and putting so many other things on hold. I spent the equivalent of years away from my family. I endured earthquakes, contagious diseases, threats of violence, strikes, corruption, and even a 10-year civil war, all in an attempt to make sure my life's work continued after I was gone.

Given the number of discomforts, physical challenges, emotional trauma, and interpersonal conflicts involved in this work, I somehow persisted not just for others' welfare but to solidify my own continued legacy. We all wish to be remembered for something, and *this* was how I wished to be recalled. They did not need to erect a statue in my honor, but I sure appreciated and thrived on the enthusiastic displays of gratitude. It somehow made all the sacrifices worth the considerable effort.

I am not sure why it feels so important to be remembered. I used to care about leaving behind a body of work that would be valued after I am long gone. I used to care about the critical reviews of my books after they were published. I used to care about the number of "friends" who "liked" what I posted on social media. I even recall when I used to read the participant evaluations of my workshops so I could do more of whatever they wanted and preferred, just so they would like me more. A few things, though, have never changed: I still care desperately that my readers, clients, and students are satisfied with my ability to help them and feel like they are making solid progress. But there's one more thing I care about more than everything else, and it has become a bit of an obsession.

I have mentioned previously that I pretend every day is my last one, so I had better make the most of it (which I rarely do). Like others of my advanced age, I cannot help but notice the ages of celebrities who have died recently, many of them younger than I am. I just cannot help but wonder how much time I have left. On some level, I would have no complaints if things ended for me sooner rather than later, especially considering that it feels like I have done almost everything I have ever wanted to do and been everywhere I have always wanted to visit. I do not mean that as a boast as much as a sincere acknowledgment and acceptance that I have been a busy guy most of my life. But there is still one major fear that terrifies me—that I will not live long enough for my granddaughters to remember much of me. The memories of my own mother, who died so long ago, or my father who vanished into his stroke-idled shell decades ago, have mostly faded.

As I have aged, my ambition has taken a back seat to other priorities that are more closely linked to a much more focused and limited goal. I have let go and moved on from the pursuit of prior achievements that no longer hold much meaning or satisfaction. I do not care much any longer about being remembered by anyone other than my closest family members, most of all my young granddaughters. I tried to explain this to my son not long ago, that I hoped I would live long enough that his daughters would remember me, but I started sobbing before I could fully explain what I meant. I think he understood anyway, feeling much the same way about his own life priorities.

It is one of the most astounding, yet burdensome, conditions of the human experience that we are likely the only living creatures that continuously (obsessively?) contemplate our own mortality and eventual annihilation, a perspective that has been explored by philosophers like Plato, Buddha, Nietzsche, Kierkegaard, Heidegger, Sartre, and Camus throughout he ages. It was Ernest Becker (1973) who explored deeply "death terror" and the ways we are inclined to deny the reality of our brief, temporary existence. Manson (2016) more clearly and profanely simply observed that "it scares the shit out of us," so much so that we do everything in our power to hide from this inevitability by creating a "conceptual self" that will survive beyond our physical demise. "This is why people try so hard to put their names on buildings, on statues, on spines of books," or why we devote so much time helping others so "that we will be remembered and revered and idolized long after our physical self ceases to exist" (Manson, 2016, p. 192). Certainly, this is a powerful force that operates within most helping professionals, the desire to become immortal as a result of our commitment to serving others who will continue to hold us in their memories.

I think that each of us, in our own unique ways, wishes to be remembered for something meaningful that we accomplished, something significant that we contributed to the welfare of others. We all wish to leave a legacy that makes the world a little better as a result of our presence. If we have had a relatively lasting influence that made a difference in people's lives, then we have also explored many of the ways the lingering effects in those relationships have been reciprocal, teaching us significant lessons and learnings that improved the quality of our own lives.

Catalog of What Mental Health Professionals Learn From Their Clients

Now that our review of lessons learned from client interactions is coming to a close, it may help to summarize the main themes that have been covered thus far. Given enough time and space, each of the following lessons could easily have qualified for its own chapter. These include not only the 38 subjects mentioned in the various chapters but also material that is revealed in surveys and studies conducted with practitioners (Casement, 1991; Guy, 1987; Goldfried, 2001; Hatcher et al., 2012; Hatcher, 2014; Kang & Yang, 2019; Katz, 2002; Kipper-Smith & Hatcher, 2014; Kottler, 2022a; Kottler & Carlson, 2006; Orlinsky & Ronnestad, 2005; Yalom, 1989).

One therapist (Tartakovsky, 2016), for example, reflects on many of the lessons she has learned from her clients that represent a comprehensive legacy of reciprocal teaching that took place in her helping relationships. These included some familiar themes that have been explored earlier: (1) people change only when they are ready to do so, not according or our preferences and schedules; (2) being authentic, genuine, and honest is the key to the most intimate, engaged connections; (3) our work often involves helping people to tell better and different stories about who they are and what they are capable of doing; (4) people have almost a limitless capacity for courage, love, and forgiveness if provided the space to access them. Mental health professionals might mention many of the significant takeaways that are listed below.

The stuff. This includes all the content, ideas, beliefs, experiences, stories, warnings, and instructions we glean from the intense conversations we have every day. We learn about the most arcane, unusual, and sometimes bizarre stuff that people do when they are alone, when nobody is watching, when they are with others, when they wish to hurt themselves or chase away those that they love most. Every client we see teaches us all kinds of interesting things about their way of life, how and why they think or act the ways they do, their culture, background, and history.

Helper's stance. The attitudes and values that we bring to therapy sessions do not just dissipate once there is nobody around for us to help. We are drilled in the critical importance of being reasonably (but not universally) accepting, (mostly) nonjudgmental, and (almost) always supportive and caring toward others. We know well the incredible power of just listening to someone without interruption, or even the need to explain or defend anything. There is something altogether magical about having someone hovering so closely and attentively.

Empathy and compassion. One of the accumulative effects of spending so much time with people during their most upsetting moments is that our own reservoirs for deep understanding and resonance are significantly strengthened. Our capacity for deep feelings and caring in other situations may also be correspondingly improved to the point where it sometimes seems like we can read people's minds—which in a sense we really can.

Realistic expectations. There is so much we learn from clients about how their anticipated plans and goals are often doomed because their expectations are not based in reality, or even what is likely possible. They demand that others live according to their rules, and then become surprised and disappointed when they do not comply. They describe the most ridiculous assumptions about how people should behave based on their own stated preferences. We attempt to caution them about the traps they set for themselves and the inevitable conflicts that will arise because of their rigidity, but often to no avail. Surely some of this sinks into our own consciousness, teaching us to be careful about making demands of others that they are either unwilling—or unable—to meet. Another facet of this lesson is that sometimes we expect too little from others, willing to settle for mediocrity in the level of intimacy we experience with a partner or friend. We see this all the time with clients who are willing to remain stuck in relationships that not only do not meet their needs but at times become abusive.

Complexity and confusion. The nature of our business is that we are almost always talking to people about things that are infinitely mysterious and unknowable. "Why don't I usually get what I want in life?" "Why do people act the way they do?" "What is the real cause of this problem?" "What should I do that will make me most satisfied?" "How does therapy work anyway?" No matter what the issue and problem that is ever brought to us, it is likely that it has been around for a while and has been relatively impervious to any attempt to change it. Most of the reasons why people are suffering are subject to multiple sources and influences, some of them ultimately unknowable. Over time, we develop a greater tolerance for ambiguity, uncertainty, and confusion since it is usually our default position.

Moral dilemmas. Clients not only bring to us their thorny moral choices but also trigger our own ethical conflicts. They are searching for answers to the question regarding what is "right" and what is "wrong," all the while we are trying to figure out what is acceptable conduct regarding our own behavior. Which boundaries are permeable? Which rules can be broken if for a greater good? What are some of the gray areas that permit flexible choices based on the circumstances? We are often called upon to help people decide for themselves which actions they could—or should—take, followed by an honest assessment of what it would be like to live with the consequences. There is nobody else, except perhaps a moral philosopher, who spends as much time as we do exploring the confounding questions regarding what ought one to do.

Self-deception. Sometimes we have to marvel at people's ability to lie so boldly to themselves and others. It is simply astounding how in the face of such overwhelming evidence and consistent feedback that one's attitudes and beliefs are completely at odds with some semblance of objective reality that this self-deception can still continue. We've learned how this can become both highly adaptive and self-protective, as well as extremely detrimental to one's health and well-being. We are also encouraged, if not forced, to reconsider all the ways we are lying to ourselves about things we'd rather avoid or ignore. This challenge to resist deceit, lies, fabrications, and distortions of reality is made that much more difficult in recent times because of the prevalence of such behavior among corporate and political figures, as well as so-called social influencers. Who could have ever imagined a time when a significant part of the population, as well as politicians, would accept and embrace the concept of "alternative facts," much less bald-faced lies that elections were stolen, vaccinations are a secret plot by the government to monitor (or poison) us, or just that it is perfectly okay to spout crazy theories that have no basis in reality, nor any legitimate evidence to support them?

What lies behind, what lies ahead. Throughout the developmental life stages, there are certain critical changes that take place related to the inevitable and predictable aging process. Since some of our clients tend to be both younger and older than we are, they are often struggling with challenges that we have already navigated earlier in life, or else those that await us in the future. It is a kind of unique education to be exposed to those adjustments from our older or elderly clients that we will someday encounter. It is a kind of vicarious rehearsal when we hear them talk about their memory issues, sleep disruption, or physical decline. It is also fascinating to hear about the new and different experiences that lie ahead once we reach elder or grandparent status. It is as if we are afforded an up-close and personal preview of coming life attractions and a complete overview of the human lifespan that was not just described in textbooks or lectures. From this closeup exposure we learn important lessons that may not have been introduced in the traditional sources: (1) life stages are not necessarily invariant and always predictable; (2) developmental stages are far more varied than we were led to believe, shaped by cultural, gender, personality, and life experiences; (3) chronological age does not necessarily match one's assigned life stage.

Mortality, death, and other existential crises. Irvin Yalom (2009, 2020, 2021) famously made this one major theme of his life's work, obsessed with the subjects himself and thus eager to explore them with his clients. He loved to include terminally ill cancer patients in his groups to shake everyone up. At one point, he justified that whereas death is ultimately what destroys us, it also *saves* us in the sense of forcing us to look into the void in order to create greater meaning in life. For anyone who has worked with terminally ill patients, or those struggling with chronic illnesses or major disabilities, we are forced to come to terms with our own fears of helplessness and eventual passing. The impending threat of eventual extinction is also what propels us forward to engage with life with greater passion and joy. After all, in the words of Mark Twain, "The fear of death follows from the fear of life. A man [or woman] who lives fully is prepared to die at any time."

Enduring suffering. Almost everyone complains at times about the annoyances, discomforts, disappointments losses, and setbacks of their lives but nothing quite compares to some of the stories we hear from our clients. It is sometimes almost too much to process, these tales of abuse, exploitation, and devastating tragedies. How do people survive such horrific experiences and still manage to keep going, still hold onto hope and faith? We witness levels of resilience and courage that are almost unimaginable. We see people get knocked down over and over again, and yet still persist in their efforts to recover and make the best of their predicaments. Like many of our subjects, this can have contagious effects on our own willingness and ability to put up with our own losses and disappointments.

Coping strategies. We are experts at what works best and what probably will not work at all when it comes to straightening out personal problems. We know, for instance, that it is far better to accept responsibility for one's difficulties rather than blaming others or external factors that can't be controlled. We also know that it is important to acknowledge struggles without feeling stuck in them or that it's a good idea to solicit support from others without allowing dependency to take over. We spend all day sitting with people helping them to figure out the best courses of action, and there's little doubt that such continual practice helps us turn these coping strategies inward when required. We may not always be inclined to exercise our superpower on demand, but we are highly skilled at pulling ourselves out of a funk as needed, all thanks to the rehearsals we've completed with clients.

Recovering from trauma. We help people put the pieces of their lives back together after tragedies and losses. We begin by recognizing the chaotic fragments of memory are the source of confusion, disorientation, and continuous wounding. As such, the first step usually involves reorganizing the intrusive images into some kind of coherent chronology after which we introduce an assortment of coping strategies that are designed to lower the emotional resonance of the recollections. These same methods are accessible to us during our own catastrophic losses, providing reassurance and internal support until such time that we regain a semblance of control. And if that is not entirely possible or practical because of the nature and severity of the difficulty (terminal illness, catastrophic trauma, death of loved one) then we are also well schooled in the importance of the times when we have no other choice except to embrace suffering as an inevitable consequence of life.

Past and present. It is one thing to learn in class or books about how early childhood experiences shape current behavior and quite another to see these dynamics unfold before our very eyes in such compelling and powerful ways. Over time, we develop a much greater appreciation for our own behavior, and even therapeutic interactions, especially those that are so influenced by our own family of origin issues, a few of which are still unresolved. We also learn from our clients that it is not necessary to become a prisoner of the past, and it is entirely possible to escape from those confining chains to become someone entirely new and different.

Letting go. Time and time again, we find ourselves listening to clients who remain stuck in the mire of their own stubbornness and rigidity, refusing to consider alternatives other than what they are already doing that is clearly not working. But it is hard to abandon patterns that are so familiar and comfortable regardless of their negative effects. This obstinacy gets in the way of any possibility for growth and future development, a lesson we have learned to take to heart when we find ourselves feeling trapped in situations that are untenable.

Gratitude. This might sound snarky, but one of the most compelling lessons we learn from our clients is the blessing that we are not them. There might be aspects of our lives that are frustrating and disappointing, but compared to what some of our clients have to deal with, we are on easy street. When we find ourselves complaining about how tough things feel, or how things aren't going our way, we thank a few of our clients for reminding us how good we have actually got it compared to how awful things could be. It is not unusual after a particularly grueling session is over that we think to ourselves immediately, "Wow, and I thought my situation was untenable!"

Arrogance. I'll never forget standing in line at a movie theater, waiting for the doors to open, when I noticed a guy I recognized walking by. Well, this dude never really walked as much as strutted. He was a well-known psychiatrist in the community with a reputation for self-importance that just oozed from every pore. There was another, shorter line off to the side where a half dozen or so people were waiting patiently to use the pay phone (remember those?). This was prior to the widespread use of mobile devices, so you can tell right away this was decades ago. Nevertheless, this incident still had a huge impact on me because of how I recognized myself in a small piece of this jerk's behavior. Instead of waiting his turn, the psychiatrist walked up to the very front of a line where a woman was already engaged in a spirited phone conversation.

"Excuse me," the psychiatrist said to her.

The woman looked annoyed at the interruption, raised an eyebrow, and then turned her back on him to continue her conversation.

"I said excuse me!" he repeated in a much louder voice that now captured everyone's attention who was standing in line.

The woman looked at him with something like amusement mixed with scorn, shook her head, and resumed the conversation.

"Hey lady!" he announced even more stridently, attempting to once again attract her attention. "Look, I'm a doctor," he explained to her, as if that explained why he was entitled to interrupt her and cut the line.

The woman placed her hand to cover the speaker on the phone, turned around to face him fully, and said, "Well, your mother must be very proud." Then she turned her back once again to finish her conversation.

There was a whole crowd of people observing this interaction, and we all spontaneously broke out in applause as this arrogant doctor slinked away in shame. As much as I despised everything that the psychiatrist stood for in terms of his narcissism and self-importance, I could not help but also see myself (and a few other colleagues) in his behavior.

For Better and Worse

There's no question that the conversations that we have with clients impact us in an assortment of ways, providing tremendous gifts as well as burdens. Most typically, there has been extensive research and discussion in the literature on the negative effects that result from countertransference, projective identification, and collapsed boundaries. The literature is also chock full of studies that examine the ways that practitioners suffer compassion fatigue, burnout, and vicarious trauma as a consequence of getting so close to others' suffering. There are also other contagious effects that often lead to exhaustion, mental fatigue, feeling like a martyr, and a tendency to pathologize one's own behavior.

In spite of such challenges that are so often mentioned, we have also explored some of the personal benefits and rewards that result from our work, especially how we become more patient, compassionate, and wise over time. We are constantly finding new insights and understandings, making new discoveries as a result of digging deeply into others' lives. We also enjoy deeper affiliation and caring with others as a direct consequence of heightened interpersonal skills. In addition, clinicians often report increased humility, greater resilience, renewed faith, and a sense of wonder at the human capacity for courage and persistence in the face of so many obstacles.

Clients' experiences and stories become the impetus for recognizing our own humility, for teaching us that we may know a few things and can do a few special things, but that does not make us godlings. Our ultimate legacy is not only knowing that we have helped people and made the world a better place in some small way but also that we have better equipped ourselves with the power to improve the quality of our own lives—thanks to the lessons we have learned from our clients.

Questions for Reflection or Discussion

1. Create an extensive, exhaustive list of all the lessons that you've learned from those you've helped. Brainstorm as many different items as you possibly can, after which you should organize them into four or five categories that capture their main themes. Give those categories names that hold the essence of their primary effects.

2. What was missing for you in the discussion throughout the book? Which items or issues were not mentioned that you think are especially important to consider?

3. When all is said and done as our journey together comes to a close, what is likely to most stick with you?

References and Sources

Aguilera, L., Reed, K., & Goulding, J. (2020). Experiences of engaging in therapeutic storytelling. *Mental Health Review Journal, 25*(1), 47–61.

Appel, M. (2008). Fictional narratives cultivate just-world beliefs. *Journal of Communication, 58*, 62–83.

Austen, B. (2012, July 23). The story of Steve Jobs: An inspiration or a cautionary tale? *Wired.* Retrieved April 2014, from http://www.wired.com/business/2012/07/ff_stevejobs/all/.

Bailey, R. J., & Ogles, B. M. (2023). *Common factors therapy: A principle-based treatment framework.* American Psychological Association.

Baumsteiger, R. (2019). What the world needs now: An intervention for promoting prosocial behavior. *Basic and Applied Social Psychology, 41,* 215–229.

Becker, E. (1973). *The denial of death.* The Free Press.

Beckmann, C. (2017, January 31). *Research reveals adventure travelers primarily motivated by transformation. Adventure Travel Trade Association.* https://www.adventuretravelnews.com/research-reveals-adventure-travelers-primarily-motivated-by-transformation

Botwin, S. (2020). *Thriving after trauma: Stories of living and healing.* Rowman and Littlefield.

Boudreau, P., Mackenzie, S. H., & Hodge, K. (2022). Adventure-based mindsets helped maintain psychological well-being during COVID-19. *Psychological Sport Exercise, 62,* 102245. https://doi.org/10.1016/j.psychsport.2022.102245

Bourdain, A. (2007). *No reservations: Around the world on an empty stomach.* Bloomsbury.

Bradshaw, E. L., Conigrave, J. H., Steward, B. A., Ferber, K. A., Parker, P. D., & Ryan, R. M. (2022). A meta-analysis of the dark side of the American dream: Evidence for the universal wellness costs of prioritizing extrinsic over intrinsic goals. *Journal of Personality and Social Psychology, 124(4), 873–899.* https://doi.org/10.1037/pspp0000431

Branson, D. C. (2019). Vicarious trauma, themes in research, and terminology: A review of literature. *Traumatology, 25*(1), 2–10.

Bressi, S. K., & Valden, E. R. (2017). Reconsidering self-care. *Clinical Social Work Journal, 45,* 33–38.

Casement, P. J. (1991). *Learning from the patient.* Guilford.

Cozolino, L. (2006). *The neuroscience of psychotherapy.* W. W. Norton.

Croft, D. P., Johnstone, R. A., Elliss, S., Nattrass, S., Franks, D. W., Brent, L.J.N., Mazzi, S., Balcomb, K. C., Ford, J.K.B., & Cant, M. A. (2017). Reproductive conflict and the evolution of menopause in killer whales. *Current Biology, 27*(2), P298–P304.

Crum, A. J., Salovey, P., & Achor, S. (2013). Rethinking stress: The role of mindsets in determining the stress response. *Journal of Personality and Social Psychology, 104*(4), 716–733.

Csikszentmihalyi, M. (1975). *Beyond boredom and anxiety.* Jossey-Bass.

Csikszentmihalyi, M. (1990). *Flow: The psychology of optimal experience.* Harper & Row.

Cuijpers, P., Reijnders, M., & Huibers, M. J. H. (2019). The role of common factors in psychotherapy outcome. *Annual Review of Clinical Psychology, 15*, 207–231.

Deaton, J. D., Ohrt, J. H., Linich, K., McCartney, E., & Glascoe, G. (2022). Vicarious posttraumatic growth: A systematic review and thematic synthesis across helping professionals. *Traumatology.* https://doi.org/10.1037/trm0000375

Desautels, L. L. (2023). *Intentional neuroplasticity: Moving our nervous systems and educational system toward post-traumatic growth.* Wyatt-MacKenzie Publishing

Diener E. (2012) New findings and future directions for subjective well-being research. *American Psychologist, 67*(8), 590–597.

Diener E., & Seligman M. E. (2004). Beyond money toward an economy of well-being. *Psychol Science in the Public Interest, 5*(1), 1–31.

Docan-Morgan, T. (Ed.). (2019). *The Palgrave handbook of deceptive communication.* Palgrave Macmillan.

Dolev-Amit, T., Rubin, A. & Zilcha-Mano, S. (2021). Is awareness of strengths intervention sufficient to cultivate wellbeing and other positive outcomes? *Journal of Happiness Studies, 22*, 645–666.

Dossey, L. (2018). The helper's high. *Explore, 14*(6), 393–399.

Driscoll, C. (2009). Grandmothers, hunters, and human life history. *Biology and Philosophy, 24,* 665–686.

Elkins, D. N. (2019). Common factors: What are they and what do they mean for humanistic psychology? *Journal of Humanistic Psychology, 62*(1). https://doi.org/10.1177/0022167819858533

Elliott, R., Bohart, A. C., Watson, J. C., & Greenberg, L. S. (2011). Empathy. In J. C. Norcross (Ed.), *Psychotherapy relationships that work* (pp. 132–152). Oxford University Press.

Ericksson, K. A., Krampe, R. T., & Tesch-Romer, C. (1993). The role of deliberate practice in the acquisition of expert performance. *Psychological Review, 100*(3), 363–406.

Freud, S. (1992). To C. G. Jung. In E. L. Freud (Ed.), *Letters of Sigmund Freud* (p. 257). Dover.

Friskie, S. (2020). The healing power of storytelling. *The Airbutus Review, 11*(1), 19–27.

Gaines A. N., Goldfried, M. R., & Constantino M. J. (2021). Revived call for consensus in the future of psychotherapy. *Evidence-Based Mental Health, 24,* 2–4.

Gelitz, C. (2021, February 9). Humans are pretty lousy lie detectors. *Scientific American.* https://www.scientificamerican.com/article/humans-are-pretty-lousy-lie-detectors/

Gladwell, M. (2008). *Outliers: The story of success.* Little, Brown, and Company.

Goldfried, M. (Ed.). (2001). *How therapists change: Personal and professional reflections.* American Psychological Association.

Gottschall, J. (2012). *The storytelling animal: How stories make us human.* New York: Houghton Mifflin.

Grencavage L. M., Norcross J. C. (1990). Where are the commonalities among the therapeutic common factors? *Professional Psychology: Research and Practice, 21*, 372–378.

Groopman, J. (2008). *How doctors think.* Houghton Mifflin.

Gurven, M., & Kaplan, H. (2020). Beyond the grandmother hypothesis: Evolutionary models of human longevity. In J. Sokolovsky (Ed.), *The cultural context of aging: Worldwide perspectives* (4th ed., pp. 53–66). Praeger.

Guy, J. D. (1987) *The personal life of the psychotherapist.* Wiley.

Haller, E., Lubenko, J., Presti, G., Squatrito, V., Constantinou, M., Nicolaou, C., Papacostas, S., Aydın, G., Chong, Y. Y., Chien, W. T., Cheng, H. Y., Ruiz, F. J., García-Martín, M. B., Obando-Posada, D. P., Segura-Vargas, M. A., Vasiliou, V. S., McHugh, L., Höfer, S., Baban, A., Dias Neto, D., da Silva, A. N., Monestès, J.-L., Alvarez-Galvez, J., Paez-Blarrina, M., … Gloster, A. T. (2022). To help or not to help? Prosocial behavior, its association with well-being, and predictors of prosocial behavior during the coronavirus disease pandemic. *Frontiers of Psychology, 12.* https://doi.org/10.3389/fpsyg.2021.775032

Hames, J. L., Ribeiro, J. D., Smith, A. R., & Joiner, T. E. (2012). The urge to jump affirms the urge to live: An empirical examination of the high place phenomenon. *Journal of Affective Disorders, 136*(3), 1114–1120.

Hammel, S. (2018). *Handbook of therapeutic storytelling.* Routledge.

Hart, C. L. (2019, October 10). Some lie a lot. *Psychology Today.* https://www.psychologytoday.com/us/blog/the-nature-deception/201910/some-lie-lot

Hatcher, S. L. (2014). *What psychotherapists learn from their clients.* Xlibris.

Hatcher, S. L., Kipper-Smith, A., Waddell, M., Uhe, M., West, J. S., Boothe, J. H., Frye, J. M., Tighe, K., Usselman, K. L., & Gingras, P. (2012). What therapists learn from psychotherapy clients: Effects on personal and professional lives. *The Qualitative Report, 17*(48), 1–21.

Havlin, L. (2019, June 4). Is your self-care practice fueling your burnout? *Dazed Digital.* https://www.dazeddigital.com/beauty/soul/article/44713/1/self-care-practice-fuelling-burnout-capitalism

Hawkes, K. (2004). The grandmother effect. *Nature, 428,* 128–129.

Hawkes, K. (2021). The centrality of grandmothering in human evolution. *Integrative and Comparative Biology, 3,* 765–781.

Henyon, H. (2021). *Storytelling as a therapy tool: Using story to heal trauma and abuse.* Lifestyle Entrepreneurs Press.

Hogan, J., Hogan, R., & Kaiser, R. B. (2010). Management derailment. *American Psychological Association Handbook of Industrial and Psychology, 3,* 555–575.

Hoorens, V. (1993). Self-enhancement and superiority biases in social comparison. *European Review of Social Psychology, 4*(1), 113–139.

Howe, D. (2013). *Empathy: What it is and why it matters.* Palgrave.

Huber, A., Strecker, C., Hausler, M., Kachel, T., Höge, T., & Höfer, S. (2020). Possession and applicability of signature character strengths: What is essential for well-being, work engagement, and burnout? *Applied Research in Quality of Life, 15*(2), 415–436.

Huebschmann, N. A., & Sheets, E. S. (2020). The right mindset: Stress mindset moderates the association between perceived stress and depressive symptoms. *Anxiety, Stress, and Coping, 33*(3), 248–255.

Hyatt-Burkhart, D. (2014). The experience of vicarious posttraumatic growth in mental health workers. *Journal of Loss and Trauma, 19*(5), 452–461.

Kang, J. H., & Yang, S. (2019). A therapist's vicarious posttraumatic growth and transformation of self. *Journal of Humanistic Psychology, 62(1).* https://doi.org/10.1177/0022167819889490

Katz, P. (2002). Lessons my patients taught me. In L. T. Flaherty (Ed.), *Adolescent psychiatry* (pp. 3–23). The Analytic Press.

Kelly, J. (2019). Influence of outdoor and adventure activities on subjective measures of resilience in university students. *Journal of Experiential Education, 42*(3), 264–279.

Kim, A., & Maglio, S. J. (2018). Vanishing time in the pursuit of happiness. *Psychonomic Bulletin and Review, 25,* 1337–1342.

Kipper-Smith, A., & Hatcher, S. L. (2014). Learners about life and art. In S. L. Hatcher (Ed.), *What Psychotherapists Learn From Their Clients* (pp. 29–53). Xlibris.

Kirschenbaum, H. (2008). *The life and work of Carl Rogers.* American Counseling Association.

Kohut, H. (1977). *The restoration of the self.* International Universities Press.

Kooperman, D. (2018). When the therapist is in crisis: Personal and professional implications for small community psychotherapy practices. *The American Journal of Psychotherapy, 67*(4), 309–411.

Kottler, J. (1992). *Compassionate therapy: Working with difficult clients.* Jossey-Bass.

Kottler, J., & Blau, D. (1989). *The imperfect therapist: Learning from failure in therapeutic practice.* Jossey-Bass.

Kottler, J. A. (1987). *On being a therapist.* Jossey-Bass.

Kottler, J.A. (1997). *Travel that can change your life.* Jossey-Bass.

Kottler, J. A. (2006). *Divine madness: Ten stories of creative struggle.* Jossey-Bass.

Kottler, J. A. (2012). *The therapist's workbook: Self-assessment, self-care, and self-improvement exercises for mental health professionals* (2nd ed.). Wiley.

Kottler, J. A. (2014). *Change: What leads to personal transformation?* Oxford University Press.

Kottler, J. A. (2015). *Stories we've heard, stories we've told: Life-changing narratives in therapy and everyday life.* Oxford University Press.

Kottler, J. A. (2018). *What you don't know about leadership but probably should: Applications to daily life.* Oxford University Press.

Kottler, J. A. (2019). *Fallen heroes: Tragedy, madness, resilience, and inspiration among famous athletes.* Cognella.

Kottler, J. A. (2021). *Practicing what you preach: Self-care for helping professionals.* Cognella.

Kottler, J. A. (2022a). *On being a therapist* (6th ed.). Oxford University Press.

Kottler, J. A. (2022b). *Unexplained mysteries of everyday human behavior.* Cognella.

Kottler, J. A. (2023). *Healthy aging in action: Roles, functions, and the wisdom of elders.* Cognella.

Kottler, J. A., & Balkin, R. (2020). *Myths, misconceptions, and invalid assumptions of counseling and psychotherapy.* Oxford University Press.

Kottler, J. A., & Balkin, R. (2017). *Relationships in counseling and the counselor's life.* American Counseling Association.

Kottler, J. A., & Carlson, J. (2002). *Bad therapy: Master therapists share their worst failures.* Routledge.

Kottler, J. A., & Carlson, J. (2006). *The client who changed me: Stories of therapist personal transformation.* Routledge.

Kottler, J. A., & Carlson, J. (2009). *Creative breakthroughs in therapy: Tales of transformation and astonishment.* Wiley.

Kottler, J. A., & Carlson, J. (2011). *Duped: Lies and deception in psychotherapy.* Routledge.

Kottler, J. A., & Carlson, J. (2016). *Therapy over 50: Aging issues in psychotherapy and the therapist's life.* Oxford University Press.

Kottler, J. A., & Englar-Carlson, M. (2019). *Learning group leadership: An experiential approach* (4th ed.). Cognella.

Kottler, J. A., & Parr, G. (2000). The family therapist's own family. *The Family Journal, 8*(2), 143–148.

Kottler, J. A., & Safari, S. (2019). *Making a difference: A journey of adventure, disaster, and redemption inspired by the plight of at-risk girls.* Cognella.

Krentzman, A. R., Hoeppner, B. B., Hoeppner, S. S., & Barnett, N. P. (2022). Development, feasibility, acceptability, and impact of a positive psychology journaling intervention to support addiction recovery. *The Journal of Positive Psychology,* 1–19.

Kruger, J. (1999). Lake Wobegon be gone! The below-average effect and the egocentric nature of comparative ability judgments. *Journal of Personality and Social* Psychology, *77*(2), 221–232.

Kumar, A., Killingsworth, M. A., & Gilovich, T. (2020). Spending on doing promotes more moment-to-moment happiness than spending on having. *Journal of Experimental Social Psychology, 88.* https://doi.org/10.1016/j.jesp.2020.103971

Lakshmin, P. (2018, October 5). We don't need self-care; we need boundaries. *Op-Med.* https://opmed.doximity.com/articles/we-dont-need-self-care-we-need-boundaries-79042584b318?_csrf_attempted=yes

Lazar, L., & Eisenberger, N. (2021). The benefits of giving: Effects of prosocial behavior on recovery from stress. *Psychophysiology, 59*(2). https://onlinelibrary.wiley.com/doi/10.1111/psyp.13954

Mafessoni, F., & Lachmann, M. (2019). The complexity of understanding others as the evolutionary origin of empathy and emotional contagion. *Scientific Reports, 9,* 5794.

Manning-Jones, S., de Terte, I., & Stephens, C. (2017). The relationship between vicarious posttraumatic growth and secondary traumatic stress among health professionals. *Journal of Loss and Trauma, 22*(3), 256–270.

Manson, M. (2016). *The subtle art of not giving a fuck.* HarperCollins.

McBeath, A. (2019). The motivations of psychotherapists: An in-depth survey. *Counselling and Psychotherapy Research, 19,* 377–387.

Miller, S., & Hubble, M. (2011). The road to mastery. *Psychotherapy Networker, 35*(3), 22–30.

Miller, S. D., Hubble, M., & Chow, D. (2020). *Better results: Using deliberate practice to improve therapeutic effectiveness.* American Psychological Association.

Miller, W. R. & C'de Baca, J. (2001). *Quantum change.* Guilford.

Monk, L., & Maisel, E. (Eds.). (2021). *Tranformational journaling for coaches, therapists, and clients.* Routledge.

Morris, Z. S., Wooding, S., & Grant, J. (2011). The answer is 17 years, what is the question: Understanding time lags in translational research. *Journal of the Royal Society of Medicine, 104*(12), 510–520.

Neimeyer, R. (Ed.). (2016). *Techniques of grief therapy: Assessment and intervention.* Routledge.

Neimeyer, R. (2022). *New techniques of grief therapy: Bereavement and beyond.* Routledge.

Norcross, J. C., & VandenBos, G. R. (2018). *Leaving it at the office: A guide to psychotherapist self-care.* Guilford.

Orlinsky, D. E., & Ronnestad M. H. (2005). *How psychotherapists develop: A study of therapeutic work and professional growth.* American Psychological Association.

Peterson, C. & Seligman, M. E. P. (Eds.). (2004). *Character strengths and virtues: A handbook and classification.* Oxford University Press.

Posluns, K., & Gall, T. L. (2020). Dear mental health practitioners, take care of yourselves: A literature review on self-care. *International Journal of Advanced Counseling, 42*(1), 1–20.

Ren, Z., Gao, M., Wang, M., & Qu, W. (2018). Personal transformation process of mental health relief workers in Sichuan earthquake. *Journal of Religion and Health, 57,* 2313–2324.

Rogers, C. (1957). The necessary and sufficient conditions of therapeutic personality change. *Journal of Consulting Psychology, 21,* 95–103.

Rogers, C. R. (1995). *On becoming a person.* Houghton Mifflin.

Schooler, J. W., Ariely, D., & Loewenstein, G. (2003). The pursuit and assessment of happiness can be self-defeating. In J. Carrillo & I. Brocas (Eds.), *Psychology and economics* (pp. 41–70). Oxford University Press.

Schulz, A. W. (2017). The evolution of empathy. In H. L. Maibom (Ed.), *The Routledge handbook of philosophy of empathy (pp.* 64–73). Routledge.

Schutte, N. S., & Malouff, J. M. (2019). The impact of signature character strengths interventions: A meta-analysis. *Journal of Happiness Studies, 20*, 1179–1196.

Seligman, M., & Csikszentmihalyi, M. (2000). Positive psychology: An introduction. *American Psychologist, 55*, 5–14.

Seligman, M. (2011). *Flourish: A visionary new understanding of happiness and well-being.* Atria.

Serota, K. B., Levine, T. R., & Docan-Morgan, T. (2022). Unpacking variation in lie prevalence: Prolific liars, bad lie days, or both? *Communication Monographs, 89*(3), 307–331.

Shackleford, K. E., & Vinney, C. (2020). *Finding truth in fiction.* Oxford University Press.

Skovholt, T. M., & Trotter-Mathison, M. (2010). *The resilient practitioner: Burnout prevention and self-care strategies for counselors* (2nd ed.). Guilford.

Spaulding, A. E. (2011). *The art of storytelling: Telling truths through telling stories.* Scarecrow Press.

Spense, D. P. (1982). Narrative truth and historical truth: Meaning and interpretation in psychoanalysis. W. W. Norton.

Tartakovsky, M. (2016, May 17). *Therapists spill: The biggest lessons I've learned from my clients.* https://psychcentral.com/lib/therapists-spill-the-biggest-lessons-ive-learned-from-my-clients#1

Tay, S., Alcock, K., & Scior, K. (2018). Mental health problems among clinical psychologists: Stigma and its impact on disclosure and help-seeking. *Journal of Clinical Psychology, 74*(9), 1545–1555.

Tedeschi, R. G., Shakespeare-Finch, J., Taku, K., & Calhoun, L. G. (2018). *Posttraumatic growth: Theory, research, and applications.* Routledge.

Thomas, L. (1978). *Lives of a cell.* Penguin.

van Agteren, J., Iasiello, M., Lo, L., Bartholomaeus, J., Kopsaftis, Z., Carey, M., & Kyrios, M. (2021). A systematic review and meta-analysis of psychological interventions to improve mental wellbeing. *Natural Human Behavior, 5*(5), 631–652.

Verigin B. L., Meijer E. H., Bogaard, G., & Vrij, A. (2019). Lie prevalence, lie characteristics and strategies of self-reported good liars. *PLoS ONE, 14*(12), e0225566.

Victor, S. E., Devendorf, A., Lewis, S., Rottenberg, J., Muehlenkamp, J. J., Stage, D. L., & Miller, R. (2021). Only human: Mental-health difficulties among clinical, counseling, and school psychology faculty and trainees. *Perspectives of Psychological Science, 17*(6), 1576–1590.

Victor S. E., Schleider, J. L., Ammerman, B. A., Bradford, D. E., Devendorf, A. R., Gruber, J., Gunaydin, L. A., Hallion, L .S., Kaufman, E. A., Lewis, S. P., & Stage, D. L. (2022). Leveraging the strengths of psychologists with lived experience of psychopathology. *Perspectives of Psychological Science, 17*(6), 1624–1632.

Wampold, B. (2015). How important are the common factors in psychotherapy? An update. *World Psychiatry, 14*(3), 270–277.

Yalom, I. (1989). *Love's executioner and other tales of psychotherapy.* Basic Books.

Yalom, I. (2009). *Staring at the sun: Overcoming the terror of death.* Jossey-Bass.

Yalom, I. (2020). *Becoming myself: A psychiatrist's memoir.* Basic Books.

Yalom, I. (2021). *A matter of death and life.* Stanford University Press.

Yasgur, B. S. (2018, January 11). Challenging stigma: Should psychiatrists disclose their own mental illness? *Psychiatry Advisor.* https://www.psychiatryadvisor.com/home/topics/mood-disorders/depressive-disorder/challenging-stigma-should-psychiatrists-disclose-their-own-mental-illness/

Index

A

Achievement goals, 190
Adams, John Quincy, 198
Adler, Alfred, 57, 62, 105, 154
Adventures, 129–135. *See also* Travel
Advocacy. *See* Social justice and advocacy
Affective empathy, 93. *See also* Empathy and compassion
Alternative identities, 216
Amatt, John, 135
American Psychiatric Association, 67
Andretti, Mario, 122
Angelou, Maya, 181, 248
Anxiety. *See* Stress
Apple, 194
Arrogance, 254
Assessment, 64–69. *See also* Diagnostic assessments

B

Bad leadership, 26–27
Becker, Ernest, 249
Behavioral model, 67
Bezos, Jeff, 216
Biases, 30–36, 243
Boredom, 171–178. *See also* Stress
Bourdain, Anthony, 135
Brain, 2
Bruner, Jerome, 2
Burnout, 107, 171–178. *See also* Stress

C

Cash, Johnny, 37
Chronological age, 252
Churchill, Winston, 189
Clients, 250–254
    as greatest teachers, 182–185
    impact, 254–255
    lessons learned from, 250–254
Closed questions, 68
Cognitive-based approaches, 4
Cognitive behavior therapy (CBT), 2
Cognitive empathy, 93. *See also* Empathy and compassion
Cognitive errors, 33–34. *See also* Biases; Prejudices
Compassion. *See* Empathy and compassion
Complacency, 244
Composure. *See* Patience and composure
Conceptual self, 249
Conscientiousness, 108
Coping strategies, 253
Counseling skills, 195–196
Countertransference reactions, 5, 153, 155

Creative breakthroughs, 161–166
Cross, Sarah, 234
Csikszentmihalyi, M., 229
Cultural variations, 206–212

D

Dealing with difficult people, 51–56
Death, 252
Death terror, 249
Descartes, Rene, 2
Developmental life stages, 252
Developmental model, 67
Diagnostic and Statistical Manual of Mental Disorders (DSM-5), 67
Diagnostic assessments, 66–68. *See also* Assessment
Diagnostic decision trees, 65
Diagnostic models, 67
Dichotomous thinking, 34
Disempowerment, 33
Disney, Walt, 96, 158
Dostoyevsky, Fyodor, 2
Dumas, Alexandre, 16

E

Earthquake in Nepal, 57–58
Einstein, Albert, 7, 77, 153, 165
Elizabeth II, Queen, 151
Ellis, Albert, 4, 105, 161, 218
Emotional arousal, 183–184
Emotions, 232
Empathic affirmations, 93
Empathic explorations, 93
Empathic transcendence, 183
Empathic understanding responses, 93
Empathy and compassion, 89–94, 250
Erickson, Milton, 154, 161
Erikson, Erik, 2
Eustress, 108, 176
Evolutionary changes, 236–237
Existential crises, 252

F

Failures, 37–43
    avoiding acknowledgement of, 40–41
    perception of, 37–40
    protocol for processing, 42
Families, 151–156
    difficult members, challenges of, 154–156
Fatigue. *See* Stress
Feedback, listening to, 243
Feeling useful, 220–226
Finding Nemo, 101
France, Anatole, 70
Frankl, Victor, 154

Freud, Sigmund, 2, 49, 62, 82, 83, 84, 105, 118, 123, 154, 162, 218
Frontal cortex region, 2

G

Galilei, Galileo, 123
Gallup, Gordon, 162
Gates, Bill, 43
Gibson, William, 64
Glasser, William, 161, 184
Goals, 186–191
Gratitude, 253–254
Greenson, Ralph, 161
Grief and loss, 45–50
Groopman, J., 242
Group dynamics and leadership, 23–29

H

Happiness and well-being, 228–233
    predictors, 231–233
    ups and downs, 229–231
Harari, Yuval Noah, 213
Hardiness, 108
Harrison, Jim, 245
Hedberg, Mitch, 229
Heidegger, Martin, 2
Hendrix, Jimi, 43
Hesse, Hermann, 179
Historical truth, 71
Huie, Jonathan Lockwood, 89
Humanistic model, 67
Hurricane Harvey, 58–59, 90

I

Icelandic Winter, 130
Illusory-superiority phenomenon, 72
Immediacy, 141
Internal noise, 243
Internal talks/voice, 1–2
International Classification of Disease (ICD-11), 67
Interpretation, 4
Intimacy, 183
Intrinsic goals, 190–191

J

James, Henry, 62
James, William, 2, 62, 105, 154
Jamison, Kay Redfield, 153
Jobs, Steve, 43, 194
Johnson, Dwayne "The Rock", 216
Johnson, Susan, 55
Journal/journaling, 2, 240–246
    different forms, 244–245
    reflective, 244
Jung, Carl, 2, 49, 51

About the Author

Jeffrey A. Kottler is one of the most prominent authors and presenters in the fields of counseling, psychotherapy, health, education, and advocacy. He has written over 100 books about a wide range of subjects, including *Practicing What You Preach: Self-Care for Helping Professionals; On Being a Therapist; The Secrets of Exceptional Counselors;* and *Unexplained Mysteries of Everyday Human Behavior.*

Jeffrey has been a counselor, therapist, supervisor, researcher, and educator in a variety of settings including preschools, middle schools, mental health centers, crisis centers, hospitals, medical schools, refugee resettlement agencies, nongovernmental organizations (NGOs), universities, community colleges, private practices, and disaster relief settings. He is also the founder of Empower Nepali Girls, a charitable organization that supports and mentors at-risk children. He has served as a Fulbright scholar and senior lecturer in Peru and Iceland, as well as worked as a visiting professor in New Zealand, Australia, Hong Kong, Singapore, and Nepal. Jeffrey is Professor Emeritus of Counseling at California State University, Fullerton. He currently lives in Houston, where he works on projects related to refugee trauma with the Alliance for Multicultural Services.

Milton Keynes UK
Ingram Content Group UK Ltd.
UKHW050813150124
436053UK00003B/9